Dual Imminence
of the Rapture and the Day of the Lord

Derek Walker

Contents

Introduction

The Bible speaks of certain dramatic events that must shortly come to pass (Revelation 1:1). This refers to (1) the Tribulation, a coming time of Divine Judgment upon the whole world (otherwise known as the Day of the Lord), and (2) Christ's Coming in the Rapture for His Bride (John 14:1-3, 1Thessalonians 4:13-18). In order to have an accurate grasp of Bible Prophecy, it is necessary to understand the relationship of the Rapture to the Tribulation, and especially the timing of the Rapture in relation to the Tribulation. Even among believers in the Pre-Tribulation Rapture there is a lack of clarity on this issue. The purpose of this book is to shed light on this, by presenting and proving the vital doctrine of Dual Imminence (a term coined by Robert. L. Thomas). Dual Imminence simply states that the scriptures speak of BOTH (1) Christ's Coming in the Rapture and (2) the Start of the Day of the Lord as being IMMINENT events (that is, they could both happen suddenly, at any time, without warning), and the reason they are both imminent is that they are simultaneous. That is, when Christ comes to remove His Church from the earth, He will then immediately initiate the Day of the Lord on the earth. Thus, the Day of the Lord will begin on the same day as the Rapture. Thus, if Dual Imminence can be proved, then the doctrine of the Pre-Tribulation Rapture immediately follows.

In this book, I expound all the main prophetic passages in the New Testament, systematically covering the teachings of Jesus, Paul, James, Peter and John, and I demonstrate that Dual Imminence is consistently taught in all of these scriptures. In fact, it is the golden thread, which runs throughout all the New Testament prophetic scriptures, connecting and harmonising them all together. Thus, it is the main common theme of New Testament Prophecy, and therefore must be a great importance. Once your eyes are open to see this truth, you will find these prophetic scriptures opening up to you in a new way, and you will have a clearer, deeper and more accurate understanding of them. Dual Imminence is like a missing key, hidden in plain sight, which unlock the full meaning of these scriptures, enabling us to see how the whole prophetic teaching of the New Testament comes together into a perfect unity. In particular, I show how all the apostles built their prophetic doctrine on the foundation of the prophetic teaching of Jesus, especially in the area of Dual Imminence.

Sadly, Dual Imminence is a relatively unknown subject, even among students of Bible Prophecy. Many have not heard of it, and if they have, they just see it as an interesting side-issue, but not having any great importance. The only articles I have seen on this subject are by Robert. L Thomas, which I have found very helpful in developing my own thoughts. So, as far as I know, this is the first book on Dual Imminence, and as such breaks new ground in presenting this doctrine in a systematic way, by surveying the whole New Testament. It has been exciting for me, to discover this truth everywhere from Matthew to Revelation, and I hope that you will share in this same excitement. It is not just another prophetic truth, but it is a central truth, known by Christ and all His apostles, which is embedded in all their prophetic teachings, so if one tries to read New Testament Prophecy without this revelation, one's understanding of it will be significantly lacking. In other words, embracing the truth of Dual Imminence will impact the whole way you understand the prophecies of Jesus and His apostles, making them come alive in a fresh way and bringing them into sharper focus, so that you can feel the full force of what they were saying.

Belief in the imminent Return of Christ is life-changing, for if we believe that at any moment, we could find ourselves in the Presence of the Lord Jesus Christ, and stand before His Judgment Seat to give an account for our life, that would motivate us to greater holiness, evangelism and zeal in serving Him now. This urgency is intensified by Dual Imminence, which adds to that the truth that at any moment the Day of the Lord will start on earth, when the whole world will come under Divine Judgment. The early Church lived in the light of imminence, which is one reason it was on fire for God, but since then the Church as a whole has lost its belief in imminence, even to the point of not seeing the relevance of Bible Prophecy to our everyday life. As a result, the Church has lost much of its zeal. My prayer is that through reading this book, your heart will come alive with the hope of the Lord's imminent Return to receive His Bride, when He will also initiate the Day of the Lord on earth. Then you will surely make sure that you are ready for what is coming next.

In order to have an accurate understanding of the sequence of end-time events, it is also necessary to have a precise grasp of where Daniel's 70th Week fits into the picture (the last 7 years leading up to Christ's Coming in power and glory to establish His Kingdom on earth). One reason why Pre-Tribulation believers have shied away from embracing Dual Imminence is that they assume the Tribulation to be identical with the 70th Week. If this were true, it would mean Dual Imminence is impossible, because the 70th Week starts when the antichrist makes a covenant with Israel for 7 years (Daniel 9:27). This event is clearly not imminent, and so the Start of the Tribulation could not be imminent, if the Tribulation is identical to the 70th Week. Those who make this assumption either say the Rapture takes place at the Start of the 70th Week (not realising the contradiction with the clear Biblical teaching that the Rapture is imminent), or they say that the Rapture can happen at any time, and then there will follow an unknown period of time before the Tribulation begins with the antichrist-covenant (contradicting Dual Imminence). There is a simple solution to this problem, and that is to realise that there is no scriptural basis for saying the 70th Week is identical to the Tribulation. It is true to say that the whole of these 7 years are part of the Tribulation, but they do not necessarily form the whole of it. They are the last 7 years of the Tribulation, which might last months or years longer than 7 years. Once this is understood, then we can see that the 70th Week does not create a barrier to accepting Dual Imminence. The Rapture will initiate the Tribulation, which is when the antichrist will start his rise to power (Revelation 6:1-2), and then sometime later he will make a covenant with Israel, which will initiate the 70th Week (the final 7 years of the Tribulation). This is explained in more detail in the final chapter of this book, where I also demonstrate that the antichrist covenant happens at the 7th Seal in the sequence of events described in Revelation.

The first 3 chapters of this book provide a detailed overview of what the Bible teaches about the Tribulation, in both the Old and New Testaments. An in-depth knowledge of the nature and events of the Tribulation is necessary to have an accurate understanding of Bible Prophecy. Although you could skip these chapters, if you want to get straight into the study of Dual Imminence, they do provide a foundation for fully understanding the later chapters, by providing their Biblical context. In particular, they show how the New Testament teaching on the Day of the Lord builds upon and develops the revelation of the Old Testament. Then the later chapters show how the New Testament reveals the imminent Rapture of the Church, which is part of the Mystery, hidden in God during the Old Testament times. Finally, when all this revelation of the Rapture and the Tribulation is crowned by the truth of Dual Imminence, we see how the whole body of Bible Prophecy comes together in perfect clarity and unity.

In conclusion, this book is designed to bring you into a deeper and more accurate revelation of Bible Prophecy, and I believe that even seasoned students of the Bible will receive an increased understanding of God's prophetic Word through reading it, and then be inspired to live a higher life as a result.

"Maranatha!" (1Corinthians 16:22), which means: 'Come, Lord!' or 'Our Lord comes!'

.

Chapter 1: The Tribulation

The aim of the first 3 chapters is to give an overview of the Bible's teaching on the Tribulation, describing its main features, giving a foundation and framework to understand its more detailed features, which we will explore later. This special period of time plays a vital part in Bible Prophecy, but sadly the Church generally has a weak understanding of it. The Tribulation will last at least 7 years (Daniel 9:27). It commences after the Church Age and ends with Christ's Return in power and glory: **"Immediately after the TRIBULATION of those days the sun will be darkened, and the moon will not give its light... and they will see the SON of MAN COMING on the clouds of heaven with power and great glory"** (Matthew 24:29-30).

The Sufferings and the Glory of the Messiah

The Old Testament prophets had 2 kinds of visions of the Messiah, called (1) the SUFFERINGS and (2) the GLORY, which are fulfilled in the 2 Comings of Christ. These were completely different in nature, corresponding to the 2 main Purposes that God is accomplishing in history through the Messiah: (1) SALVATION and (2) KINGDOM. Thus, there are 2 Programs of Christ: (1) His Salvation Program, and (2) His Kingdom Program, and as history unfolds, He is moving both of these Programs forward together to their completion. He will defeat all His enemies who rebel against Him and establish His KINGDOM on earth, but will do so in such a way as to SAVE as many people as possible. This duality is seen in that He is both Saviour and Lord (King). The prophets saw Him coming first as the suffering Saviour – first, as a Prophet proclaiming God's Word, and then as a Priest offering Himself up to God as the final Sacrifice to purchase our SALVATION, and the rising from the dead. Then they also saw Him returning to the earth in power and glory as the Judge and King, to establish His KINGDOM. Jesus Christ fulfilled the first in His first Coming as the Saviour, and He will fulfil the second in His 2nd Coming as the Lord and King.

However, it was not revealed to the prophets how much time would elapse in-between. Like looking as 2 mountains in the distance, they could not see the valley or distance in-between, whether the 2nd peak comes immediately after the first one or whether there is a big gap between them. This was kept as a MYSTERY hidden in God, because it depended on Israel's decision to accept or reject Christ in His first Coming, because according to God's covenants with Israel through Abraham, Moses and David the Kingdom had to be established through Israel. Had God revealed in advance that there would be a 2000-year gap, due to Israel's rejection of Christ as her rightful King, then that would have violated Israel's free-will. When Israel rejected Christ, then God started to reveal the

Mystery, which describes the kind of time and the length of time between the 2 Comings of Christ (1Peter 1:10-11), which we now know as the Church Age.

Although the Old Testament prophets did not see the Church Age, they saw the time immediately before and leading up to Christ's Return to establish His Kingdom. This is a special time when God will intervene directly in judgment, called 'the Day of the Lord.' The judgment of God is not to be confused with the curse or automatic negative consequences of sin, which man has always experienced. Rather these are direct actions God personally makes in response to man's sin. Generally, the Church Age is a time of mercy, rather than judgment (although a man faces immediate eternal judgment after his death, if he dies in his sins). In the Day of the Lord however, God will move in history, with ever-intensifying judgments, and therefore it will be a time of darkness (Zephaniah 1), the worst time that man has ever experienced on earth (Jeremiah 30:7, Daniel 12:1, Matthew 24:21).

In Part 2, we established that the Rapture of the Church takes place before the Tribulation. This is the doctrine of the Pre-Tribulation Rapture. A major key to understanding Bible Prophecy and especially the necessity for the Pre-Tribulation Rapture is comprehending the nature of the Tribulation. In Part 3, we will study the Tribulation in great detail. Unlike the Rapture, which was a Mystery previously hidden in God (1Corinthians 15:51), the special period of time that we call the Tribulation was revealed in the Old Testament. However, the primary name used by the prophets for the Tribulation was 'the Day of the Lord'. This terminology is also used in the New Testament. Although 'the Tribulation' is a valid Biblical name used by Christ for this unique time of great suffering leading up to the 2nd Coming (Matthew 24:9, 29), with its final 3.5 years being called 'the Great Tribulation' (v21), which corresponds to 'the Time of Trouble (Tribulation)' (Jeremiah 30:7, Daniel 12:1) in the Old Testament, it should not be seen as the primary Biblical name for this time. That honour belongs to 'the Day of the Lord.' However, the 'Tribulation' has become the standard theological term used for this period of time, instead of 'the Day of the Lord', and this leads to the problem of people not understanding the essential defining nature of the Tribulation, as being a time of Divine Wrath, which is what the name 'the Day of the Lord' communicates.

Describing this time as the Tribulation his points to the fact that this will be a time of great persecution of the saints, much of which is caused by the antichrist. Although it is valid, the better and more definitive term is 'the Day of the Lord', because the primary distinguishing aspect of this time is that it is when God directly intervenes in world-wide judgment. The trouble with merely calling it 'the Tribulation' is that it gives the impression that it is simply a time of great persecution, but since there is also much trouble and persecution in the Church Age, people do not understand its fundamental difference with the Church Age. In this way, many confuse it with the Church Age, because one of the characteristics of the Church Age is 'tribulation' (John 16:33). As a result, many Christians have no real concept of the Tribulation as a distinct period of time of Divine Judgment upon the whole world, but rather see it as just part of the Church Age, in which life on earth is a bit worse than usual. It seems to them that the Tribulation is just an intensified continuation of the Church Age, so they don't understand why the Church should be raptured before it begins. This in turn causes them to think the motivation for the Pre-Tribulation Rapture is the desire to avoid the persecution of the antichrist, which they see as a baseless hope, because we are all called to suffer persecution for our faith (2Timothy 3:12). However, the reason and basis for the Pre-Tribulation Rapture is that we are not called to endure the Wrath of God in the Day of the Lord (1Thessalonians 1:10, 5:2-9).

Moreover, not understanding that 'the Day of the Lord' is 'the Tribulation' results in missing out on much of the Old Testament teaching on the Tribulation, and in misinterpreting the New Testament references to 'the Day of the Lord', by equating it to the 2nd Coming of Christ, which in fact is called 'the Great and Awesome Day of the Lord', the climactic day of 'the Day of the Lord.' This simple error of terminology, which ignores the Old Testament teaching on the Day of the Lord, as an extended time of temporal Divine Judgment, has resulted in a multitude of wrong interpretations of New Testament prophetic Scriptures.

NAMES for the TRIBULATION

The most common term denoting the Tribulation and marking it out as a time of Divine Judgment is: 'The Day of the Lord.' This refers to a special time when God will intervene directly in history to punish the rebellious on a world-wide scale, and bring salvation to His people, this bringing things to a conclusion in order to establish a new order. The term refers to the whole Tribulation, although often the climax is primarily in view - namely the last few days leading up to the Return of Christ (Joel 2:1-11, 3:14, Zechariah 14:1-3). The same applies to 'the Day of Vengeance', where the focus is on the climax of the Day of the Lord - the 2nd Coming of Christ (Isaiah 34:8, 35:4, 61:2, Jeremiah 46:10). The New Testament reveals that the Day of the Lord begins as a Thief in the Night, a reference to the imminent Coming of the Lord in the Rapture, initiating a time of Darkness on the earth (1Thessalonians 5:2, 2 Peter 3:10).

It is a time of Divine Judgment: **"For the Day of the Lord of hosts shall be upon every one that is proud and lofty, and upon every one that is lifted up; and he shall be brought low"** (Isaiah 2:12). **"Howl, for the Day of the Lord is at hand; it shall come as a destruction from the Almighty"** (Isaiah 13:6). **"Behold, the Day of the Lord comes, cruel both with wrath and fierce anger, to lay the land desolate: and He shall destroy the sinners thereof out of it"** (Isaiah 13:9). **"Woe to you who desire the Day of the Lord! to what end is it for you? the Day of the Lord is darkness, and not light. It will be as though a man fled from a lion, and a bear met him! Or as though he went into the house, leaned his hand on the wall, and a serpent bit him! Shall not the Day of the Lord be darkness, and not light? even very dark, and no brightness in it?"** (Amos 5:18-20).

The **'Day of the Lord'** in Zephaniah 1:7-13 is **'a time of Trouble for Israel.'** It is: **'the Day of Israel's calamity'** (Deuteronomy 32:35, Obadiah 12-14). Zephaniah 1:14 - 2:3 describes it as also being a time of judgment upon the whole world.   It is: **'the Day of wrath, trouble, distress, wasteness, desolation, gloominess, darkness and clouds, of thick darkness'** (1:15; also, Amos 5:18-20; Joel 2:2). It is **'the Day of the trumpet and alarm'** (1:16). It is **'the Day of the Lord's wrath' (1:18), 'the Day of the Lord's anger'** (2:2,3).

Often the prophets would refer to a judgment of God in history as a foretaste, picture and warning of the DAY of the LORD when God's judgments on the nations will be brought to their conclusion. After describing a judgment on Israel (Joel 1:1-14), he warns: **"Alas for the Day! for the Day of the Lord is at hand, and as a destruction from the Almighty shall it come"** (1:15). Then in Joel 1:15 – 3:16, he describes this Day of the Lord in detail: **"Blow the trumpet in Zion, and sound an alarm in my holy mountain: let all the inhabitants of the Land tremble: for the Day of the Lord comes, for it is nigh at hand"** (Joel 2:1). After describing judgments on Edom, Obadiah warns all nations: **"the Day of the Lord is near upon all the nations: as you have done, it shall be done unto you: your reward shall return upon your own head"** (v15, see also v16-21).

The Tribulation is also called: **'the wrath to come'** (1Thessalonians 1:10), **'wrath'** (1Thessalonians 5:9, Revelation 11:18), **'the wrath of God'** (Revelation 15:1,7; 14:10, 19; 16:1), **'the Hour of Judgment'** (Revelation 14:7), **'the Indignation'** (Isaiah 26:20,21; 34:2; Daniel 11:36). These terms confirm that the whole Tribulation is a time of Divine Wrath and Judgement, starting with the breaking of the first 6 Seals (Revelation 6), which increases in intensity in the Great Tribulation (at the 7th Trumpet), and then again with the Bowls of Wrath leading up to the climax in the Second Coming – the Great and Awesome Day of the Lord.

The Day of the Lord is described in detail in Matthew 24:7-30, where it is also described as the End of the Age (v3), and the Tribulation (v9,29), concluding with the Great Tribulation (v21), as well as a time of 'Birth Pains' for the whole world (v8), leading up to the birth of God's Kingdom on earth. Therefore, it is a time of world-wide Judgement. It includes the 7 years of 'Daniel's 70th Week' (the final 7 years of the Tribulation). It is also: 'the Time of the End' (Daniel 12:9) and 'the End (Consummation) of the Age' (Matthew 13:40,49; 24:3,6). It is: 'Jehovah's Strange Work and Act - a destruction upon the whole earth' (Isaiah 28:21-22). It is 'the Hour of Trial which will come upon the whole earth' (Revelation 3:10). This time is also described in great detail in Revelation 6-19, which emphasises that it is primarily a time of Divine Judgment upon the unbelieving world, as well as great persecution and tribulation for the saints.

The Tribulation is a time of 'distress of nations' (Luke 21:25,26), a time of shaking for all nations: **"Thus says the Lord of hosts: Once more (it is a little while) I will shake heaven and earth, the sea and dry land; and I will shake all nations, and the Desire of all Nations (Christ) shall come ... I will shake heaven and earth. I will overthrow the throne of kingdoms; I will destroy the strength of the Gentile kingdoms. I will overthrow the chariots and those who ride in them; the horses and their riders shall come down, every one by the sword of his brother"** (Haggai 2:6,7,21-22). This is God moving in judgment removing all things that are not of Him, so that only His Kingdom remains and stands upon the earth: **"Yet once more I shake not only the earth, but also heaven. Now, yet once more, indicates the removal of those things that are being shaken, as of things that are made, that the things which cannot be shaken may remain. Therefore, since we are receiving a Kingdom which cannot be shaken, let us have grace, by which we may serve God acceptably with reverence and godly fear, for our God is a Consuming Fire"** (Hebrews 12:26-29).

Many Old Testament passages describe the general, world-wide nature of this time, for example, the Little Apocalypse of Isaiah (Isaiah 24:1 - 27:13), and the Day of Jehovah passages relating to the whole world (Isaiah 2:12-22; 13:6-16, Ezekiel 30:1-9, Joel 1:15-20, Obadiah 10-20; Zephaniah 1:14-2:3). However, it is especially a time of Tribulation for Israel (Matthew 24:9-12). In fact, all her sufferings thus far, including the Holocaust, will not compare to the Tribulation. In this connection, it is called: 'the Time of Jacob's Trouble' (Jeremiah 30:7) and 'the Time of Trouble' (Daniel 12:1, Zephaniah 1:15). The Tribulation is the consequence of Israel's rejection of Christ (AD 26-33), causing Daniel's 70th Week to rerun. (In Zechariah 11:12-13, Israel's rejection, illustrated in the prophecy of the 30 pieces of silver, leads to her suffering under the antichrist in v14-17. This same theme is picked up in 13:7-9). Many Scriptures speak of the special relationship that the Tribulation has with Israel (Deuteronomy 4:30; Ezekiel 13:1-7, 20:37; Daniel 12:1; Zechariah 13:8,9, Matthew 24:7-26; Revelation 7 and 12; Isaiah 3:1 - 4:1; Joel 2:1-11; 3:14-17; Amos 5:18-20; Zephaniah 1:7-13).

In Revelation 1:10, John was caught up in the Spirit on 'the Lord's Day.' One possible interpretation is that this signifies that John was transported forward in time to witness first-hand 'the Day of the Lord', and then write it down for us as an eyewitness testimony in Revelation chapters 4-19. However, it should be noted that: 'the Day of Christ' and 'the Day of the Lord Jesus', refers to the Rapture (1Corinthians 1:8, 5:5; 2Corinthians 1:14, Philippians 1:6,10; 2:16), not to the Tribulation.

The Great and Awesome Day of the Lord

It is worth emphasising that although 'the Day of the Lord' refers to the Tribulation as a whole or any part of it, the actual 24-hour day of Christ's Coming in power and glory is called: 'the Great and Terrible Day of the Lord' or 'the Great and Awesome Day of the Lord': **"The LORD shall utter his voice before His army: for His camp is very great: for He is strong that executes His word: for the Day of the Lord is Great and very Terrible; and who can abide it?"** (Joel 2:11). **"The sun shall be turned into darkness, and the moon into blood, before the Great and the Awesome Day of the Lord come"** (Joel 2:31). **"Behold, I will send you Elijah the prophet before the Coming of the Great and Awesome Day of the LORD"** (Malachi 4:5). The Hebrew word is 'fearful', as in the reverential fear and awe of the Lord, resulting from the revelation of His awesomeness. It is sometimes used in the sense of 'awesome', when God manifested His glory in a special way (Judges 13:6, Exodus 15:11). So, the English translations of these Old Testament verses vary between 'terrible' or 'dreadful' verses 'awesome'. Both are valid, but the better translation is 'awesome', and this is confirmed by the way this word is quoted and translated into Greek, and interpreted in the New Testament in Acts 2:20: **"The sun shall be turned into darkness, and the moon into blood, before the coming of the Great and Awesome** (epiphaneia) **Day of the Lord."** Epiphaneia means a Divine Appearance or Manifestation in Glory. It is where we get the word 'Epiphany' from, which refers to the Manifestation of Jesus Christ to the world. So, the Old Testament speaks of the Great and Awesome Day of the Lord, and implies this is because it is the Day of His Manifestation in Glory. This understanding is confirmed and made explicit by the way the New Testament interprets this word, by translating it into Greek as epiphaneia, which means 'manifestation', 'appearing', 'glorious display', the word used for the glorious Appearing of Christ (Titus 2:13 1 Timothy 6:14; 2 Thessalonians 2:8, 2 Timothy 4:1,8). So, applying the New Testament interpretation to Joel 2:31 and the other verses, we conclude that it should be called **'the Great and Awesome Day of the Lord'** and its full meaning is: **'the Great and Manifest Day of the Lord'**, or **'the Great Day of the Lord's Manifestation in Glory'** (Acts 2:20). Finally: **"the Great Day of His Wrath"** (Revelation 6:17) also refers to the day of the 2nd Coming of Christ.

*There are 3 main PURPOSES of the TRIBULATION

*The 1st Purpose of the Tribulation is to end wickedness and wicked ones. Evil is allowed to come to its fullness, so it can be revealed and judged. It is the Day of the Lord, a time of world-wide judgment, as Isaiah 13:9 says: **"Behold, the Day of the LORD comes, cruel, with both wrath and fierce anger, to lay the earth desolate and He will destroy its sinners from it."** By the end of the 7 years, God will have fully separated the righteous from the wicked and judged all the evil ones on the earth. Often people ask why doesn't God intervene and stop evil. Well, in the Tribulation He will. This is where God's Kingdom forcibly comes into confrontation with the kingdoms of this world.

*The 2nd Purpose of the Tribulation is to bring a world-wide soul-harvest. In context, Matthew 24:14 refers to evangelism in the Tribulation: **"This Gospel of the Kingdom will be preached in all the world as a witness to all the nations, and then the end will come."** This will be spearheaded by the 2 Witnesses and the 144,000 Jewish Evangelists. In the midst of all the judgments, many will repent and be saved. Often when everything is comfortable people forget God. But when everything is shaken many realise that they need God.

*The 3rd Purpose of the Tribulation is the Salvation of Israel. Romans 11:25-26 says that after the fullness of the Church-Age harvest has come in, all Israel will be saved in the Tribulation. The terrible troubles of the Tribulation will break the stubborn unbelief and pride of Israel, so that by its end, all Israel will receive Jesus as her Messiah-King, enter the New Covenant and be saved. She will also call on the Name of the Lord to save her from those trying to destroy her at Armageddon. This faith will qualify her to possess the promised Messianic Kingdom. Daniel 12:7: **"He swore by Him who lives forever, that it** (the Great Tribulation) **shall be for a Time, Times, and half a Time** (3.5 years); **and when the power** (stubborn pride, self-righteousness and self-sufficiency) **of the holy People** (Israel) **has been completely broken, all these things shall be finished** (accomplished)."

The Day of the Lord is a Time of Trouble, especially for Israel (Jeremiah 30:7), but in it she will turn back to God, and He will save her and restore her: **"When you** (Israel) **are in DISTRESS (Tribulation), and all these things come upon you in the latter days, when you turn to the Lord your God and obey His voice**

(for the LORD your God is a merciful God), He will not forsake you nor destroy you, nor forget the covenant of your fathers which He swore to them" (Deuteronomy 4:30,31).

Hosea 5:14 describes the first Coming of the Messiah to Israel as a lion (her King), but this results in His judgment coming upon her, because she rejects Him. Then He says: **"I (the Messiah) will return again to My Place** (Heaven) **UNTIL they** (Israel) **acknowledge their offense** (of rejecting Christ). **Then they** (Israel) **will seek My face; in their AFFLICTION** (in the Tribulation) **they will earnestly seek Me"** (5:15). Then Hosea 6:1-2 describes Israel returning to the Lord, expecting Him to save and restore her, so that she will live in His Presence. It even gives a hint as to when this will happen: **"After 2 DAYS He will revive us; on the 3rd DAY He will raise us up, that we may live in His sight"** (6:2). Assuming a DAY represents 1000 years (Psalm 90:4, 2Peter 3:8), this implies Israel's repentance and restoration will take place 2000 years after Christ's ascension to Heaven after she rejected Him as her Messiah-King. Also, it points to 1000 years, when Christ will abide with Israel (the 3rd DAY = the Millennium). This is initiated by His Return from Heaven at the end of the Tribulation, in response to Israel's repentance and calling on His Name: **"Let us know the Lord. His going forth** (from Heaven) **is established as the morning** (sunrise)" (6:3, see Malachi 4:2).

This is confirmed by Jesus. In Matthew 23:37-38, He announces the judgment upon Israel for rejecting Him: **"O Jerusalem, Jerusalem, the one who kills the prophets and stones those who are sent to her! How often I wanted to gather your children together, as a hen gathers her chicks under her wings, but you were not willing! See! Your House** (Temple) **is left to you desolate** (it was destroyed in AD 70)." But then in v39 He announces that He will return to Jerusalem, when she repents as a nation, and receives Him as her Messiah, calling upon Him to return to save her: **"for I say to you, you shall see Me no more till you say: 'Blessed is He who comes in the Name of the Lord!"** This is the Messianic Greeting Israel will give Jesus, which He declared would be the basis for His 2nd Coming. In other words, Jesus will return for Israel's sake, for Israel is still God's elect, chosen nation (Isaiah 41:8, 44:1, 45:4). Then in Matthew 24:21,22, Jesus says that this will happen at the end of the Tribulation: **"then there will be Great Tribulation, such as has not been since the beginning of the world until this time, no, nor ever shall be. And unless those days were shortened** (by His Return) **no flesh would be saved; but for the ELECT'S** (Israel's) **sake those days will be shortened."** Jesus will return to deliver the believing remnant of Israel, the elect, who are in great danger, even facing imminent annihilation (see also Jeremiah 30:7 and Daniel 12:1). In other words, He will bring the Tribulation to an end by His Return, as described in Matthew 24:29-30:

"Immediately after (at the end of) **the Tribulation of those days the sun will be darkened, and the moon will not give its light; the stars will fall from heaven, and the powers of the heavens will be shaken. Then the sign of the Son of Man will appear in heaven, and then all the tribes of the earth will mourn, and they will see the Son of Man coming on the clouds of heaven with power and great glory."** He will deliver her from the antichrist at Armageddon, and then complete her regathering to the Land from all nations, in order to fully restore and establish her as His chief nation in the Millennium: **"And He will send His angels with a great sound of a trumpet, and they will gather together His ELECT from the 4 winds, from one end of heaven to the other"** (see Isaiah 27:13 for confirmation of this interpretation).

It will be a combination of things that will bring Israel to faith in the Tribulation:

(1) The Rapture will be a major Sign confirming the truth of the New Testament.

(2) The spectacular ministry of the 2 witnesses, who will preach Jesus as the Messiah, with their death and resurrection giving Israel a 3rd Sign of Jonah.

(3) The ministry of the 144,000 Jewish Evangelists

(4) The way all the New Testament prophecies of the Tribulation will be coming to pass.

(5) Their great affliction will cause them to stop depending on self, and instead turn to God.

(6) Also, God will lift the judicial blindness that had been on Israel since her rejection of Christ.

In summary, as well as seeing the Coming of the Messiah in power and glory to judge the world and establish His Kingdom on the earth, the Old Testament prophets saw that there would be a special time of unparalleled evil and distress on the earth, especially for Israel, as well as a world-wide outpouring of Divine Wrath, in the time leading up to the personal Appearance of the Lord. Thus, the prophets describe this time as being a time of Divine Wrath, called the DAY of the LORD, as well as describing it as being a unique time of TROUBLE or TRIBULATION. The New Testament confirms that after the Church Age, evil is allowed to come to its fullness (in the antichrist), and God's Wrath will be poured out upon this evil world-system. Thus, the TRIBULATION is also a special time of Divine Judgment, called the DAY of the LORD, for then the Lord will directly intervene in judgment. It's the climax in the war between good and evil. This time is brought to its climax and end by Christ's Return to destroy all evildoers from the earth and establish His Kingdom (2Thesssalonians 2:8, Revelation 19). This time is also described as the time of BIRTH PAINS, as well as being called 'the END (consummation) of the AGE' (Daniel 11-12, Matthew 13:39-40,49, 24:3, 28:20), because it brings this present Age to its close, just as the period of a woman's birth pains brings her time of pregnancy to its close.

Chapter 2: The Day of the Lord
in the Old Testament

Since the New Testament is built on the foundation of the Old, in order to understand what God has revealed about the Day of the Lord, it is necessary for us to start by summarising what the Old Testament revealed about this unique time leading up to Messiah's Return in power and glory. Only then are we position to understand and harmonise the New Testament Scriptures on the Rapture and Tribulation, which we will do in detail in chapters 4-6 (the Rapture, being a Mystery hidden in God, was not revealed in the Old Testament). We need to know what end-time truths were already established, as Jesus would have taken them as understood, and built His teaching on the basis of their truth, without necessarily recapitulating them. In this way, we will understand the difference between when (1) He was reaffirming these truths and perhaps adding more detail to them, and when (2) He was introducing brand new truth (the Mystery).

The prophets saw a future time of world-wide Judgment called 'the Day of the Lord', which would be at the End of the Age, just before the Messiah personally comes to establish His glorious Kingdom on the earth. It will be a time of great darkness, which included judgment on Israel, as well as on all the nations (Amos 5:18-20). This concept runs through the prophetic writings, as a unifying theme, and it refers to the complex of events leading up to the personal Coming of the Lord in judgment to conquer His foes and establish His Kingdom on the earth, with Israel as the head nation. So, the Day of the Lord will start with a time of judgment of God's enemies (darkness), which will lead to a time of blessedness (light) for the righteous – the Messianic Kingdom. This Day of the Lord is the future time of God's decisive action and intervention into human history. Whilst any time of judgment in history could be called 'a Day of the Lord', these all foreshadow the ultimate, climactic and final eschatological Day of the Lord, that will usher in God's Kingdom on earth. The phrase 'the Day of the Lord' is found 15 times in the Old Testament, and there are many more times that variations of this phrase are used, such as 'the Day of the Wrath of Yahweh', 'that Day', 'Yahweh has a Day', 'the Day' or 'the Great Day.' These all speak of a climactic outpouring of Divine Wrath, when God wages war on the wicked, and removes them from the earth (Isaiah 2:6-22, 13:1-22, 24:1-23, 26:16-21, 34:1-17, Jeremiah 30:5-11, Zephaniah 1:2-3:8, Joel 2-3, Malachi 4:1-6 are some examples).

Isaiah 24 says the Day of the Lord will result in the devastation of the whole earth and the wholesale emptying of its population (v1-4,19-20) for: **"the earth is defiled under its inhabitants because they have transgressed the laws,**

changed the ordinance, broken the everlasting covenant. Therefore, the curse has devoured the earth, and those who dwell in it are desolate. Therefore, the inhabitants of the earth are burned, and few men are left" (v5,6). God's judgment will be upon all the wicked of all the nations (Isaiah 34:2, Jeremiah 25:31). Likewise, Jesus said: **"unless those days were shortened, no flesh would be saved"** (Matthew 24:22).

This Day of the Lord's Wrath will come to its climax on its final 24-hour day, called **'the Great and Awesome Day of the Lord'** (Joel 2:11, 31, Malachi 4:5), when Christ will personally return in power and glory to complete His Judgment of the world (Isaiah 2:10,19,21, 26:21, Malachi 4:2), and to establish His Kingdom over the whole earth, bringing in a new Age, when the Lord Himself will reign in glory over all the earth (Zechariah 12-14). Thus, Christ will return immediately after the Tribulation, bringing it to its climax, which is exactly what Jesus affirms in Matthew 24:29-30. This Messianic Kingdom is the 'light' phase of the Day of the Lord (which follows the 'darkness' phase of the Day of the Lord), when His glory will cover the earth, which will last for 1000 years (Revelation 20:1-6, Psalm 90:4, 2Peter 3:8). The Great and Awesome Day of the Lord (the 2nd Coming of Christ) will be heralded by Signs in the Heavens (Isaiah 13:10, 34:4, Joel 2:31, 3:15), as Jesus confirmed (Matthew 24:29, Mark 13:24-25, Luke 21:25).

The DAY of the LORD will be a time of Trial and TRIBULATION for all upon the earth. One purpose of these judgments is that men would repent before it is too late, and those who do repent are promised life and blessing. By the end of the Day of the Lord, all unrepentant sinners will be removed from the earth, leaving the remaining believers to inherit the Kingdom, as Jesus confirmed in Matthew 13:38-42, 25:31-46. It is especially a Time of Trouble for the Jews and Israel (Jeremiah 30:7), which will have been regathered back to the Land as a nation (30:3), due to the targeted persecution by the antichrist (Daniel 7:21,25, 12:1,7, confirmed by Jesus in Matthew 24:9). However, in this time of Affliction, Israel will repent, and put her trust in Christ for salvation (Zechariah 12:10 – 13:9, Malachi 4:4-6, Hosea 5:14 - 6:2), and will call on Him to return to deliver her from her enemies (Joel 2:32), for the armies of all the nations will be gathered together to invade and destroy Israel (Zechariah 12:2-3, 14:2, Joel 3:2,9-14, confirmed in Matthew 24:28, Revelation 16:14-16, 19:16). In response to this request from His elect covenant nation Israel, Christ will speedily return in glory, for Israel's sake, to rescue her, and restore her to full blessing at His Return (Zechariah 14:1-7, Hosea 6:3, as confirmed by Christ in Matthew 24:22,31), and establish His Kingdom on the earth (Zechariah 14:8-21, Hosea 6:3, as confirmed by Christ in Matthew 25:31,34). Thus, Israel will be saved out of this unique time of Trouble, by Christ's Return, when He brings it to its end (Jeremiah 30:7, c.f. Matthew

24:13,22). Thus, the final outcome of this time of Tribulation will be the Messianic Kingdom (Isaiah 24:23 - 25:12, 2:1-5, Zephaniah 3:9-20, Jeremiah 30:8-11), under the reign of the exalted Son of Man, who will destroy the antichrist, when He comes back to the earth (Daniel 7:13-14, 21-22, 26-27).

The prophets also warn that this Day is 'near' (Isaiah 13:6, Zephaniah 1:14, Obadiah 1:15), which means the start of this Day is imminent (it could come at any time, and when it does, it will come suddenly and without warning) - an emphasis strongly repeated in the New Testament.

The BIRTH PAINS

The eschatological DAY of the LORD is not a 24-hour day, but an extended, but well-defined, period of time of Divine Wrath, which comes to its climax with the Great Awesome Day of the Lord (the Coming of the Messiah in power and glory). This is clear from the fact that the prophets often described this period in terms of BIRTH PAINS, the travail of childbirth, which combines the experience of intense suffering with the expectation of something new and wonderful coming forth after the labour is over (Isaiah 13:6-11, 26:16-18, Jeremiah 30:5-7, Hosea 13:13, Micah 4:9-10). It describes the experience of end-time judgment in the Tribulation, leading up to the manifestation of the Messiah and the birth of His Kingdom on the earth, which Jesus called 'the regeneration' – that is, the rebirth of the earth (Matthew 19:28). The Jewish Rabbis called this time 'the Birth Pains of the Messiah', because at the end of this time of Tribulation, Messiah will personally appear in power and glory and His Kingdom will be established (born) on earth. The sudden beginning and involuntary and uncontrollable nature of birth pains, and the way that, once begun, they continually intensify until the time of deliverance and birth, perfectly pictures this time of Divine Judgment that will run its course until Messiah appears in glory to bring deliverance and establish His visible Kingdom on earth. Thus, just before God's Kingdom is brought to birth on the earth at Christ's Return, there will be a time of Birth Pains, which once started will continue and intensify until the Birth of the Kingdom.

One reason why BIRTH PAINS is an appropriate description of the experience of the Tribulation is because the helpless state of women in their suffering, just before giving birth describes the helpless, suffering state of people in the Tribulation, especially the nation of Israel: **"Wail, for the DAY of the LORD is at hand! It will come as DESTRUCTION from the Almighty. Therefore, all hands will be limp, every man's heart will melt, and they will be afraid. PANGS and SORROWS will take hold of them, they will be in PAIN as a WOMAN in CHILDBIRTH; they will be amazed at one another... Behold, the DAY of the LORD** comes, cruel, with both **WRATH** and fierce **ANGER**, to lay the land (earth) desolate; and He will destroy its sinners from it... I will PUNISH the world for its evil, and the wicked for their iniquity; I will halt the arrogance of the proud, and will lay low the haughtiness of the terrible (cruel)" (Isaiah 13:6-11). Notice that this clearly describes the DAY of the LORD as a time of Divine Wrath, Judgment, Punishment and Destruction, and also of BIRTH PAINS.

Jeremiah 30:3-11 describes this time that leads up to Israel's salvation and her restoration in the Messianic Kingdom. v3: **"Behold, the days are coming, says the Lord, that I will bring back from captivity My people Israel and Judah,' says the Lord. "And I will cause them to return to the Land that I gave to their fathers, and they shall possess it."**

This is one of many prophecies that predict the Regathering of Israel from captivity in the nations. These prophecies generally present this Regathering from the nations as taking place in 2 Stages. First, there will be a partial regathering of Israel to the Land in unbelief, and then when Messiah returns there will be a final and complete regathering at the start of the Messianic Kingdom and this time Israel will be in faith. As we read on it will become clear that Jeremiah 30 is describing the initial partial regathering of Israel in unbelief, for having returning to the Land she still has to go through 'the Time of Jacob's Trouble' (v7). The fact God calls the nation 'Jacob' rather than 'Israel' indicates that she is still in unbelief concerning Messiah. When in unbelief the nation is called Jacob, when in faith it is called Israel. So, Jeremiah 30:3 has been fulfilled in recent times with Israel returning to her Land and being reborn as a nation in 1948. God did not regather her because she repented. It was a sovereign act of God to vindicate His Name and fulfil His Unconditional Covenant with Abraham. His Plan is to restore Israel to the Land and to deal with her there as a nation, in order to bring her to repentance and restore her to Himself. He first restores her to the Land, and then to the Lord.

v4-5: **"Now these are the words which the Lord spoke concerning Israel and Judah: For thus says the LORD: "I have heard a voice of trembling, of fear, and not of peace."** This predicts that even when God has regathered Israel to the Land, she will still face dangerous times. Therefore, there's still much trouble for Israel ahead, because she is still in unbelief.

v6: **"Ask now, and see, whether a man is ever in LABOUR with CHILD? So why do I see every man with his hands on his loins like a WOMAN in LABOUR, and all faces turned pale?"** Here we see this time compared to a time of BIRTH PAINS, because a baby, the Kingdom of God, is going to be born on the earth. The rabbis called this time of Tribulation before the manifestation of the Messiah's glorious Kingdom 'the Birth Pains of the Messiah'. The presence of sin and the curse sets up a resistance to every birth, resulting in birth pains just before the birth. So as the baby pushes through to be born it causes birth-pains in the mother. Likewise, in the Tribulation God's Kingdom starts to force itself into manifestation in the earth. As is does it comes into conflict with the kingdoms of this world which are under sin, the curse and the kingdom of darkness. This will result in the sudden onset of world-wide birth-pains, which will grow in intensity until the baby, that is the Kingdom, is born on the earth. Like a woman in pregnancy, the earth has been moving towards the birth of the Messianic Kingdom upon the earth. The Tribulation is the relatively short time of birth pains just before the birth. As 1 day is to 9 months, so 7 years is to 2000 years.

   v7: **"Alas! for that DAY** (of the Lord) **is GREAT, so that none is like it, and it is the TIME of Jacob's TROUBLE** (or TRIBULATION)**, but he shall be SAVED out of it."** This is a unique time, for there is 'none like it.' This key verse combines the 2 main descriptions of this time, as well as identifying it as the time of BIRTH PAINS (v6). First, 'that DAY' can only refer to 'the DAY of the LORD', a time when God directly intervenes in human history, either by judging or reigning. So here, as in many places, 'that Day' is shorthand for 'the Day of the Lord.' Second, this time (the Day of the Lord) is also called 'the Time of Jacob's TROUBLE.' 'Trouble' is equivalent to 'Tribulation.' So, this is the origin of our normal name for this time: 'the Tribulation.' Now it is true that Jesus told us in John 16:33: **"In the world you will have tribulation."** In other words, we face troubles and persecution in the Church Age, but they are nothing compared to what will happen in the Tribulation. This is confirmed by the parallel verse of Daniel 12:1 says: **"There shall be a TIME of TROUBLE** (TRIBULATION)**, such as never was since there was a nation, even to that time, and at that time your people** (Israel) **shall be delivered."** This unique time will be far worse than any other period of history. Jesus used the very same language as Jeremiah and Daniel to describe the final years leading up to His 2nd Coming: **"For then there will be GREAT TRIBULATION, such as has not been since the beginning of the world until this time, no, nor ever shall be"** (Matthew 24:21).

   So, when Jesus used the term 'the TRIBULATION' to describe the special time of trouble for the whole world, and especially Israel, at the End of the Age, just before His Return (Matthew 24:9,21,29), He was referring to Jeremiah 30:7 and Daniel 12:1, which describe it a unique 'Time of Trouble', worse than any other. Although the whole Tribulation is a time of Birth Pains, in the final 3.5 years these Pains come into full manifestation, so that this final period of the TRIBULATION is called the GREAT TRIBULATION, and it is this period that is especially in view in Jeremiah 30:7, Daniel 12:1 and Matthew 24:21 (see Daniel

9:27, 12:11, Matthew 24:15-21). Jeremiah's description of that TIME of TROUBLE being 'GREAT' is the basis for Jesus' description of it as being the GREAT TRIBULATION. But Jeremiah 30:7 concludes with a promise saying: **"but he (Jacob) will be saved from it."** So, by the end of the Time of Jacob's Trouble, Israel will repent of her unbelief and receive Jesus as her Saviour-Messiah, and so Israel, as a whole, as a nation, will be saved (Romans 11:26), and she will call upon Him to return as her Messiah-King (Matthew 23:37-39), and deliver her from the armies of antichrist. In response Christ will return at the Battle of Armageddon and deliver Israel, and establish His Kingdom through her. Similarly, <u>Daniel 12:1 says</u>: **"at that time your people** (Israel) **shall be delivered."** Likewise, after describing the Great Tribulation in Matthew 24:21, Jesus said: **"And unless those days were shortened, no flesh would be saved; but for the elect's** (Israel's) **sake those days will be shortened** (by the 2nd Coming of Christ)**"** (v22).

Then, <u>Jeremiah 30:8 describes this deliverance at the 2nd Coming</u>: **"For it shall come to pass in THAT DAY", says the Lord of hosts: "that I will break his yoke from your neck, and will burst your bonds; foreigners shall no more enslave them."** God promises deliverance at the end of the Tribulation with the 2nd Coming of Christ. Then <u>v9</u> describes Israel in the Messianic Kingdom: **"But they shall serve the LORD their God, and David their king whom I will raise up for them."** Then <u>v10</u> describes the final and complete Regathering of Israel from the nations by the Messiah: **"Therefore do not fear O My servant Jacob"** says the LORD, **"Nor be dismayed, O Israel; for behold, I will save you from afar, and your seed from the land of their captivity. Jacob shall return, have rest and be quiet, and no one shall make him afraid. For I am with you,"** says the LORD, **"to save you; though I make a full end of all nations where I have scattered you, yet I will not make a complete end of you."**

Thus Jeremiah 30 reveals that the DAY of the LORD is a unique specific future TIME of TRIBULATION, worse than any other time (v7), especially for Jacob (Israel), regathered to her Land as a single national entity (v1-3), and a time of BIRTH PAINS (v5-6), at the end of which will be the manifestation of Israel's national regeneration, salvation, deliverance and irreversible restoration in the Messianic Kingdom under the reign of Christ (v7-11). Taken literally, this prophecy can only be fulfilled by the ultimate DAY of the LORD, rather than by some event that has already taken place in history. Jesus confirmed this when He alluded to v7 in Matthew 24:21, when He described the events that would lead immediately up to His 2nd Coming, which confirms His prophetic teaching on the Tribulation and 2nd Coming is built upon an Old Testament foundation. Moreover, in agreement with Jeremiah 30, He described Israel's full regathering after the 2nd Coming (Matthew 24:31), and her possession of the Messianic Kingdom, under the reign of Christ, as the brethren of Jesus, along with the believing Gentiles (Matthew 25:31-46).

Daniel 12:1 and Matthew 24:21-22 agree with Jeremiah 30:6-7, that this time of intense BIRTH PAINS is a unique time, worse than any other time of history (this refutes the preterist view that all these prophecies were fulfilled in AD 70, when a million Jews were killed by the Romans, because the Holocaust was far worse). It will be a Time of Trouble for the whole world, but especially for Israel, as she is the main target for antichrist's persecution. Israel opened the door for this by her national rejection of Christ, compounded by her trusting in and making a covenant with the antichrist early in the Tribulation (Daniel 9:27). However, by the end of the Tribulation, Israel will repent and receive Jesus as her Messiah, and call upon Him to deliver her from the antichrist, which He will do by returning to Jerusalem in power and establishing His Kingdom (Zechariah 14, Matthew 23:37-39).

Jeremiah 4:31 also talks about this time of BIRTH PAINS, describing it as a special time of TROUBLE or TRIBULATION: **"For I have heard a voice as of a woman in LABOUR, the ANGUISH** (Hebrew: *sar* –the same word that is translated TROUBLE in Daniel 12:1 and Jeremiah 30:7), **as of her who brings forth her first child. The voice of the daughter of Zion bewailing herself; she spreads her hands, saying: 'Woe is me now, for my soul is weary because of murderers!"** Likewise, we will see that Jesus also links the terminology of TRIBULATION with LABOUR PAINS, confirming that the TRIBULATION is exactly the same as the time of LABOUR PAINS. Moreover, 1Thessalonians 5:2-3 defines the DAY of the LORD as the time of LABOUR PAINS. Thus all 3 terms must describe the same time-period.

Isaiah 26 is Israel's Song of Salvation, that they will sing at the start of the Millennium (described in Isaiah 25). It looks back on the TRIBULATION (described in Isaiah 24), from which they have just been saved, and describes their recent experience in terms of the pains of childbirth: **"Lord, in TRIBULATION they have sought You, they poured out a prayer when Your chastening was upon them. As a WOMAN with CHILD is in PAIN and cries out in her BIRTH PANGS, when she draws near the time of her delivery, so we were, because of You, O Lord. We have been with child, we have been in pain; we have, as it were, brought forth wind; we have not accomplished any deliverance in the earth, nor have the inhabitants of the world fallen"** (v16-18). Having acknowledged that their salvation was not of themselves, in v19-21 they proclaim the Lord alone is the Deliverer, who personally: **"comes out of His Place** (Heaven) **to punish the inhabitants of the earth for their iniquity"** (v21). This takes place at the end of the time of INDIGNATION (the Day of the Lord) – see v20. The birth of God's Kingdom on earth will be heralded by the resurrection of all the remaining righteous dead (v19, see Revelation 20:4-6). (The same sequence of Tribulation followed by deliverance and resurrection is found in Daniel 12:1-3,13 and Hosea 5:15 - 6:2). Thus, Isaiah 26:16-21 confirms that before the Lord personally returns to judge the earth there will be an extended time of special TRIBULATION, described also as a time of LABOUR PAINS.

The New Testament confirms and develops this Old Testament description of the DAY of the LORD as being a time of world-wide BIRTH PAINS. When Jesus was asked for the Signs of His Coming, which would take place in the END (*suntelia*, the Consummation or Closing Period) of the AGE (Matthew 24:3), the time leading up to His Coming in power and glory, also known as the Tribulation, He first described the start of the period as the sudden onset of intense BIRTH PAINS, manifesting as world-wide war, famine, disease and disturbances in nature: **"For nation will rise against nation, and kingdom against kingdom. And there will be famines, pestilences, and earthquakes in various places. All these are the BEGINNING of SORROWS** (*odin* - literally: BIRTH PAINS)**"** (v7-8). These events Jesus describes are agonies that can be compared to Birth Pains, which signify that a new Age in human history is about to be born – God's Kingdom visibly manifested on earth. The fact that these are called "the BEGINNING of Birth Pains" signifies that all these things will suddenly break out together at the start of the Tribulation and will continue and intensify over a period of time (the whole Tribulation), until Christ returns to bring the Tribulation (time of travail) to an end (v30), just as once birth pains have started, they continue and intensify until the baby is born (see also 1Thessalonians 5:2-3). Thus, Jesus described the End *(suntelia)* of the Age' (Matthew 24:3) as a time of Birth Pains (v7-8) leading up to His Coming, which is the final End *(telos)* (v13, 14). Thus, the Birth Pains and other events of the End of the Age will function as signs of the final End (the 2nd Coming).

Jesus then described this time of BIRTH PAINS as a time of TRIBULATION, in which there will be great persecution of the saints alive at that time: **"Then they will deliver you up to TRIBULATION and kill you, and you will be hated by all nations for My Name's sake"** (v9). In fact, the word used for TRIBULATION is also used for the TRAVAIL of child-birth. Our word *tribulation* translates the Greek word *thlipsis*, which can be used to describe the anguish of childbirth. It was used that way by Jesus Himself in John 16:21: **"A woman, when she is in labour, has sorrow because her hour has come; but as soon as she has given birth to the child, she no longer remembers the anguish** *(thlipsis)***, for joy that a human being has been born into the world."** Thus, the two phrases used by

Jesus to describe this time 'Tribulation' and 'Labour Pains' are connected. So, we could call the Tribulation and the Great Tribulation, the Travail and the Great Travail.

Jesus' description of the various kinds of Birth Pains in Matthew 24:7-13 correspond perfectly to John's description of the first 6 Seals in Revelation 6. He also characterises this as a special time of TRIBULATION (v9,29), which ends with His Coming in power and glory (v27,29-30). By using the phrase: **"All these are the BEGINNING of BIRTH PAINS"** (v8), and by their very nature, Jesus made it clear that these Birth Pains take place over an extended period of time (not just a single day). However, this time will come to an END (v13,14), when God will provide a salvation for the surviving believers, at the 2nd Coming of Christ.

Paul summarises the Old Testament teaching and Jesus' teaching, by equating the DAY of the LORD with the time of world-wide BIRTH PAINS, which proves that the Day of the Lord is an extended period of time, and not limited to the 24-hour day of His 2nd Coming: **"the DAY of the LORD so comes as a thief in the night. For when they say: "Peace and safety!", then sudden DESTRUCTION comes upon them, as LABOUR PAINS upon a pregnant woman"** (1Thessalonians 5:2-3). Paul also emphasises the imminence of the Start of the Day of the Lord, that it will come suddenly upon the world, as a thief, taking them by surprise, while normal life is going on, with people saying 'all is well, peace and safety.' The imminence of the Day of the Lord is a summary of Jesus' teaching in Matthew 24:36-44.

The Birth Pains of v7-8 are just 'the beginning' of the time of Travail or Tribulation. They are followed by more severe agonies, which will reach an intensity that will be without parallel in world-history (v15-21). The initial Labour Pains are intense enough to show that God's judgments have begun, but they are only the start, as Jesus said: **"For then** (when the Abomination of Desolation is set up, half-way through Daniel's 70th Week, see Daniel 9:27, 12:11), **there will be GREAT TRIBULATION** (Great Travail), **such as has not been since the beginning of the world until this time, no, nor ever shall be. And unless those days were shortened** (by Christ's Return), **no flesh would be saved"** (Matthew 24:21-22).

Daniel's 70th Week

The primary Tribulation text cited by Jesus in the Olivet Discourse (Matthew 24:15, Mark 13:14), and alluded to by Paul in His Day of the Lord discourse (2Thessalonians 2:4) is Daniel 9:27, which indicates that this time will last for at least 7 years (Daniel 9:27). It describes the 7 years known as Daniel's 70th Week, which are the final 7 years allocated by God to Daniel's people, Israel (v24), for the fulfilment of all His purposes and promises to Israel, through the establishment of the Messianic Kingdom (Daniel 9:24). Thus, its purpose is to bring in the Kingdom of God on earth (v24). It's not part of the Mystery Church Age, as it is the last 7 years allocated to Israel before the Messiah establishes His Kingdom. Therefore, this unique time is revealed by the Old Testament prophets, and God's purposes in it centre on Israel, not the Church. In Part 1, we saw that the origin of these 7-years of judgment is the 7-years of grace (AD 26-33) when the Kingdom was presented to Israel. When she rejected Christ and His Kingdom (after these 7 years had run their course), God could not establish the Kingdom, so He cancelled these 7-years in order to rerun them after the Church-Age as the Tribulation, after which He will establish His Kingdom on earth. Because Israel rejected the 7-years of grace under Christ, they must now suffer 7-years of judgment under Antichrist.

Daniel 9:27 marks the (1) beginning, (2) midpoint and (3) end of this 70th Week: "(1) **He** (the prince to come, see v26) **will confirm a covenant with many for one 'Seven'** (or 'Week'). (2) **In the middle of the 'Seven' he will put an end to sacrifice and offering. And at the Temple, he will set up an Abomination that causes Desolation, until** (3) **the end that is decreed is poured out on him** (for this decree see Daniel 7:11,22,26)" (NIV translation).

*(1) The beginning of these 7 years is when Israel enters into a covenant with the antichrist, called 'the prince to come' (v26), since he was predicted to come in a number of other prophecies in Daniel 7,8,11,12 - we will show later that this covenant happens at the same time as the 7th Seal. This covenant that Israel makes with the antichrist (Daniel 9:27) is also referred to as a covenant with death, whereby Israel is deceived into trusting in the antichrist as her saviour, for her protection, in Isaiah 28:14-15: **"Hear the word of the Lord you scornful men, who rule this people who are in Jerusalem, because you have said: 'We have made a covenant with death, and with Sheol we are in agreement. When the overflowing scourge passes through, it will not come to us, for we have made lies our refuge, and under falsehood we have hidden ourselves.'"** Israel trusts antichrist for protection, thinking it will protect them from invasion and death, but it is a deceptive covenant, which the antichrist will break.

Israel should trust in Christ for salvation, rather than in antichrist, but the majority of Israel (the 'many' of Daniel 9:27), who don't believe in Christ, rush hastily into this false covenant, however there is a remnant who believe: **"Therefore, thus says the Lord God: Behold, I lay in Zion a STONE (Christ) for a FOUNDATION, a tried stone, a precious cornerstone, a sure foundation; whoever believes will not act hastily"** (v16). Through this covenant, Israel submits to antichrist, trusting in him for protection, instead of receiving the true

Christ, as Jesus warned in <u>John 5:43</u>: **"I have come in My Father's Name, and you do not receive Me; if another comes in his own name, him you will receive."** This trusting in antichrist will result in Israel facing 7 years of judgment before she repents and receives her true Messiah. Thus, this climactic manifestation of her rejection of the Christ as her Foundation Stone, results in the judgment, that has come upon national Israel for her rejection of Christ, coming to its climactic manifestation in the 70ᵗʰ Week (v17-22). We will see that on the very same day as this covenant, the 2 witnesses will appear in the Temple clothed in sackcloth, calling Israel to repentance and faith in her Messiah, Jesus, and calling down judgments from God (Revelation 11:1-6). At the same time God will judge the unbelieving world for their rejection of Christ and His New Covenant, and the Gentile nations for their domination and oppression of Israel, which is why Isaiah speaks of the: **"destruction determined even upon the whole earth"** at this time (v22).

This judgment includes the breaking of this covenant by the antichrist: **"Also, I will make justice the measuring line, and righteousness the plummet; the hail will sweep away the refuge of lies, and the waters will overflow the hiding place. Your covenant with death will be annulled, and your agreement with Sheol will not stand; when the overflowing scourge passes through, then you will be trampled down by it"** (v17-18). This covenant will not protect Israel, for antichrist will invade her after 3.5 years (Daniel 9:27), resulting in great suffering and death, and he will trample her down during the Great Tribulation – Revelation 11:2). The judgments released at this time will not just be upon Israel (v19-20), but upon the whole earth (v21-22), reaching their climax at the Second Coming.

Thus, the start of the 70ᵗʰ Week also marks the start of a special time of judgement upon Israel for her rejection of her Messiah and the New Covenant in His atoning Blood (Daniel 9:24). However, Daniel 9:24-27 predicts that during this time of Tribulation and Judgment, Israel will repent, be saved, and then be fully restored as a nation. Then through Israel's restoration all the nations will be blessed under Christ's reign in the Messianic Kingdom (Romans 11:12,15).

*<u>(2) The Mid-Point of the 70ᵗʰ Week</u> (3.5 years before the end) is marked by the antichrist violating this covenant, by invading Israel, stopping the Jewish sacrifices and desecrating the Temple of God with the Abomination of Desolation (this implies the Jewish Temple will be rebuilt and that this covenant will endorse its institution and allow it to function in the first half of the 70ᵗʰ Week). (See also 2Thessalonians 2:4, Revelation 13:6,14). This Abomination refers to the erection of an idol in the sacred space of the Temple, by a foreign power which desecrates

it, forcing the cessation of the sacrificial system, just like what happened in the time of the Maccabees (Daniel 11:31). This desolating Abomination calls forth desolating judgments from God. It is this event, that Jesus pointed to in Matthew 24:15, as a major sign of being in the Tribulation, marking the start of the Great Tribulation (v21), and giving the signal for the believing Jews to flee to Jordan: **"When you see the 'Abomination of Desolation' spoken of by Daniel the prophet (Daniel 9:27), standing in the Holy Place...then let those who are in Judea flee to the mountains... For then there will be GREAT TRIBULATION, such as has not been since the beginning of the world until this time, no, nor ever shall be"** (v15-21).

Thus, the Great Tribulation is the 2nd half of the 70th Week, the last 3.5 years of the Tribulation leading up to Christ's Return, and it will be the worst time ever. This description agrees with the language of Daniel 12:1 and Jeremiah 30:7. Also Revelation 7:14 describes multitudes of martyrs coming out of the Great Tribulation. It is a time of Great Trouble especially for Israel, but by its end all Israel will have come to faith in Christ, and will be saved by Him at His Return from total destruction by antichrist (Romans 11:26, Daniel 12:1, Jeremiah 30:7, Matthew 24:22, 27-28, 31). The Great Tribulation will last exactly 1,290 days (Daniel 12:11). Therefore, the Abomination is the sign by which the exact day of the 2nd Coming can be known. The context in which Jesus quotes Daniel 9:27 (Matthew 24:15-30) proves that Daniel's 70th Week must be the final 7 years before His 2nd Coming. The fact these predicted events have not yet literally taken place, for example in AD 70, confirms they still await their future fulfilment.

*(3) The 70th Week ends with the destruction of antichrist, which has been decreed by the Court of Heaven (7:22,26). This takes place at the 2nd Coming of Christ, when He defeats antichrist at Armageddon (Revelation 19:11-21). Following the 2nd Coming the Messianic Kingdom, the Age of Righteousness, will be established in fulfilment of all the Old Testament covenants and prophecies (Daniel 9:24).

Daniel 11:35 – 12:11

Daniel 11:35b–12:11 gives us more detail about the 70th Week, describing the activity of the antichrist, as he rises to world-power (see also 7:7-8,11,19-25), and then invades Israel at its midpoint, and breaks the covenant by taking over the Temple Mount (11:41,45). This initiates **"a TIME of TROUBLE (Tribulation), such as never was since there was a nation, even to that time. And at that time your people (Israel) shall be delivered** (by Messiah's Return, who brings it to an end)**, everyone who is found written in the Book** (of Life)**"** (12:1). This is a parallel verse with Jeremiah 30:7, which gives the same revelation, promising the salvation of believing Israel at the end of a Time of Trouble, unparalleled in all history. This time of Tribulation, especially the last 3.5 years, are described as being unique and far worse than any other time in all history: **"Alas! For that DAY** (the Day of the Lord) **is GREAT, so that none is like it, and it is the time of Jacob's TROUBLE, but he** (Jacob) **shall be saved out of it** (by Messiah's Return)**"** (Jeremiah 30:7). Jesus referred to both of these verses in Matthew 24:21, when He repeated this description, and called it the GREAT TRIBULATION (the time of GREAT TROUBLE), and in v22, He confirmed He would return to save the ELECT (believing Israel, see also v13) from complete destruction. Thus, Jeremiah, Daniel and Jesus describe the last 3.5 years (the Great Tribulation) as being far worse than the first 3.5 years, especially for the Jews, for they will be the main target for antichrist's persecution.

Daniel 11 initially predicts events which have been fulfilled in the 2 centuries before Christ (v1-35a), then the prophecy jumps to 'the Time of the End', when it describes the Tribulation (especially the activity of the antichrist) in detail from Daniel 11:35b – 12:11. The name used most for this time is 'the Time of the End' (Daniel 11:35,40, 12:1,4,9). In fact, the way God signifies the prophecy is now transitioning to describe the Tribulation is by saying: **"The TIME of the END - because it is still for the appointed time."** In the Septuagint (the translation into Greek, which was often used by the New Testament writers), the word used for END in all these verses is *suntelia*, signifying the closing period of the Age, leading up to Messiah's Return. So, when Daniel 12:1 says: **"At that time...there shall be a TIME of TROUBLE** (Tribulation)**, such as never was since there was a nation, even to that time."** 'At that time' refers firstly to 'the Time of the End (*suntelia*)', from the preceding context (see 11:35,40), and more precisely to the time of antichrist's invasion of Israel, mid-way through the last 7 years (11:41,45).

This is confirmed by Daniel 7:25, which says he will oppress God's holy people and they will be delivered into his hands for a Time, Times and half a Time, before he is destroyed by God (v26-27). During these 3.5 years, the antichrist will shatter the power and stubborn pride of Israel by his merciless persecution. This must be the 2nd half of Daniel's 70th Week, confirming that it describes the last 7 years before Christ returns. Moreover, Daniel 12:11 puts the issue beyond doubt, by connecting the final events of the Great Tribulation as described in Daniel 12 with Daniel 9:27, saying: **"And from the time that the daily sacrifice is taken away, and the Abomination of Desolation is set up, there shall be 1,290 days."** This says the Abomination of Desolation (the very end-time sign to which Jesus pointed in Matthew 24:15) will be a marker, whereby those in the Tribulation will be able to know when it will end, for Christ must return 1,290 days after this Abomination is set up in the Temple. This proves that the Great Tribulation lasts

1,290 days (Matthew 24:15,21), until Christ's Return (v30), being the 2ⁿᵈ half of Daniel's 70ᵗʰ Week. Also, the Old Testament saints will be resurrected at Christ's Return at the end of this time of Tribulation (Daniel 12:2-3,13, Isaiah 26:19, c.f. 26:16-18, Jeremiah 30:9, Revelation 20:4).

Thus, one name for the Tribulation (used in this passage of Daniel 11:35-12:11, describing the events of the Tribulation) is 'the Time of the END (*suntelia*).' This provides the origin for a key term for the Tribulation, used by Jesus (Matthew 13:39,40,49, 24:3, 28:20): 'the END *(suntelia)* of the Age.' There are 2 Greek words for END: (1) *Telos* meaning the final end, and this is used to describe the 2nd Coming of Christ, and (2) *suntelia* which means 'consummation', a period of time during which all things are brought to a close. So, when a school talks about the end of term, it usually means the last few days. Likewise, when a teacher wraps up his message and brings all his main points together in his conclusion in the final few minutes of his lesson, he might call this the 'end of the lesson.' When the Bible speaks of 'the End of the Age', the word translated 'End' is *sun-telia*, which means the closing period or consummation, rather than the final end (*telos*). *Sun-telia* literally means *'with the end'* – the period associated with the final end. This naturally points to the Tribulation, whose end (*telos*) is the 2ⁿᵈ Coming. So, a better translation would be 'the Consummation of the Age', a special time when all things are brought to their head and conclusion, a perfect description of the Tribulation. Sadly, most people, unaware of the difference between *suntelia* and *telos* assume that the End of the Age simply refers to the 2ⁿᵈ Coming.

The first time Jesus used the phrase: 'the END *(suntelia)* of the AGE' was in the Parable of the Wheat and Tares (Matthew 13:24-30, 36-43). He compared the world during the course of this present Age to a field, between the time of sowing and reaping. The Age is characterised by Christ and His apostles sowing good seed (His word) through His people, producing sons of the Kingdom (golden wheat), and His enemy, the devil, sowing evil seed through his people, producing sons of the wicked one (tares, that turn black): **"He who sows the good seed is the Son of Man. The field is the world, the good seeds are the sons of the kingdom, but the tares are the sons of the wicked one. The enemy who sowed them is the devil"** (v37-39). This Parable confirms the main purpose of the Church Age is the bringing forth of a harvest of souls for God. The main part of the Age (which we call the Church Age) is when both the wheat and tares are growing together. This is not the ordained time for the judgment of the tares (v26-30a). But then by way of complete contrast to the main part of the Age, the closing period of the Age will be a time of judgment: **"Let both** (wheat and tares) **grow together until the HARVEST, and at the TIME of HARVEST, I** (Christ) **will say**

to the reapers (angels)**: "First gather together the tares** (wicked) **and bind them in bundles to burn them, but gather the wheat** (righteous) **into my barn"** (v30). This Age will end with HARVEST TIME, when the tares will come under Divine Judgment (v30b, 39-43). Notice that although the Time of Harvest is much shorter than the time in which the wheat was growing, it is nevertheless a period of time, rather than a single event. In other words, it corresponds to the whole Day of the Lord, rather than just the 2nd Coming. This is confirmed by the fact that during this time: **"the reapers are the angels"** (v39), rather than Christ Himself. He uses the angels as His instruments of judgment, which is exactly what we see in the Tribulation, as described in Revelation. Jesus called this period of time: 'the END of the AGE': **"The HARVEST is the END** (suntelia) **of the AGE"** (v39).

Thus, this prophetic Parable of Jesus tells us clearly that 'the END (Consummation) of the AGE' is a name for the Tribulation, and that the primary characteristic differentiating the Tribulation from the Church Age is that it is a time of Divine JUDGMENT, unlike the Church Age. Jesus described how the judgments of the Tribulation carried out by angels will result in the deaths of multitudes of unrepentant unbelievers, whereby their souls will enter into an everlasting punishment of fire, first in Hades (Luke 16:23-24), and then in the Lake of Fire (Revelation 20:15): **"Therefore as the tares are gathered and burned in the fire, so it will be at the END of this AGE. The Son of Man will send out His angels, and they will gather out of His Kingdom all things that offend, and those who practice lawlessness, and will cast them into the furnace of fire. There will be wailing and gnashing of teeth"** (v40-42).

In conclusion, God is withholding His judgment on the tares for a long time, until the time of harvest, called 'the End of the Age' (Matthew 13:28-30, 39-42). This signifies that the present Church Age will continue for a significant time, during which God withholds His judgment, but eventually history will enter a new phase called 'the End of the Age', during which He brings all things to their conclusion, through a time of Divine Judgment. Thus, the End or Consummation or Closing of the Age is a special final period of time leading up to the final end at the 2nd Coming of Christ. Thus 'the End of the Age' is another name for 'the Day of the Lord.'

So, it is the aspect of Divine Judgment, which primarily differentiates the Tribulation from the Church Age. In conclusion, there is a unique time that is yet to come called the Tribulation. Its uniqueness is not just because evil is allowed to come to its fullness through the antichrist, but also because it is a time of Divine Wrath - hence it is called the Day of the Lord. This is why it must be distinguished from the Church Age, for in the Church Age, God is not generally moving in judgment, as we see from the Parable of the Tares, where we saw that the Lord is withholding His judgment until the End or Consummation of the Age.

The key term used to describe the TRIBULATION in Daniel 12:1 is 'Time of TROUBLE.' The Hebrew word translated 'Trouble' expresses a constricted condition, suffering tribulation and distress, often as a result of Divine judgment. It is first used in relation to the end-time Tribulation in Deuteronomy 4, when Moses predicted that Israel would sin and be cast out of her Land, and be scattered to the nations, but that, in the latter days, when she will be in a time of special DISTRESS, she will repent and turn to God for mercy, and He will hear and restore her (v29-31). We know that Daniel studied Jeremiah's prophecies, for they were the basis for his prayers in Daniel 9:2-19, which led to the revelation of the 70 Weeks (v24-27). So, it is evident that Daniel's use of the phrase: 'the TIME of TROUBLE' in Daniel 12:1 derives from <u>Jeremiah 30:7</u> (a parallel verse), which also connects it both with 'the DAY of the LORD', and the time of 'BIRTH PAINS' (v6): **"Alas! For that DAY is great, so that none is like it; and it is the Time of Jacob's TROUBLE, but he shall be saved out of it."**

Both Jeremiah 30:7 and Daniel 12:1 describe a unique time of Trouble, worse than any other time of history, especially for Israel, and both promise that God will provide Israel a national salvation at the end of it. Clearly both these Scriptures describe the same well-defined period of time. They are both clearly set right at the End of the Age, just before Messiah establishes His Kingdom on earth, and their description of this time as a unique 'TIME of TROUBLE' is the basis for Jesus' description of this time as being 'the TRIBULATION', the unique Time of Trouble leading up to the 2nd Coming (Matthew 24:9,21,29), the Greek *Thlipsis* (Tribulation) being the equivalent of the Hebrew word for 'Trouble' in Jeremiah 30:7 and Daniel 12:1. Although the main focus in these verses is on the 2nd half of the 70th Week, which Jeremiah 30:7 describes as GREAT TROUBLE, the continuity between the 2 halves of the 70th Week, and the clear connection between their events (the antichrist's covenant at its start and its violation at the mid-point, centred on the Temple), as reflected in Daniel $11:35 - 12:11$, which covers both halves of the 70th Week, means that the term TROUBLE or TRIBULATION should apply to the whole of the 70th Week, just as 'the End of the Age' does. Then, because of antichrist's actions at the mid-point of the 70th Week, the Tribulation turns into the Great Tribulation, a time that is worse than any other time in history.

This agrees with Jesus' description of the Tribulation in Matthew 24, where He describes the events of the End of the Age (v3). He defines and describes it as a period of world-wide Birth Pains leading up to the Birth of God's

Kingdom (at the 2nd Coming), comparing its start with the sudden onset of Birth Pains (v7-8). This results in a special time of Tribulation (v9,29), quite distinct from the normal tribulations of life in this Age. As birth pains escalate and intensify, so it will be in the Tribulation, until in the Middle of the 70th Week, when the Abomination appears (v15), the world enters into the Great Tribulation (v21), corresponding to full labour pains. Finally, as birth pains come to their climax just before the birth, so immediately before the 2nd Coming (v30), there will be the greatest and most dramatic signs in the earth and the heavens (v29). Thus, the Tribulation (the End of the Age, the Time of Birth Pains, the Day of the Lord) includes the whole of the 70th Week, and is not just the last 3.5 years as some say. The last 3.5 years is the Great Tribulation, but the Tribulation is at least 7 years, if not more.

Chapter 3: The Day of the Lord in the New Testament

So far, we have mainly focused on the teaching of the Old Testament on the Day of the Lord. The teaching of the New Testament, starting with Christ's own teaching, is consistent with it. In fact, the New Testament takes the revealed knowledge of the prophets for granted and builds on it, confirming and adding more detail to the Old Testament revelation, as well as bringing forth an entirely new area of revelation, which had previously been hidden from mankind (the Mystery, which includes the imminent Rapture – 1Corinthians 15:51). In His conclusion to His prophetic Parables describing this present Age, Jesus described this combination of old and new revelation, which He and correctly taught Bible Teachers bring forth: **"Therefore, every Scribe instructed concerning the Kingdom of Heaven is like a householder, who brings out of his treasure things NEW and OLD"** (Matthew 13:52).

The key issue is how the NEW revelation of the CHURCH and the RAPTURE is connected to the OLD revelation of the DAY of the LORD. In the next chapters, we will see how this connection runs like a golden thread throughout the whole prophetic teaching of the New Testament, starting with Jesus and including all of His apostles. We will see that this key truth is that the DAY of the LORD is initiated by the RAPTURE of the CHURCH. That is, when Jesus comes to initiate the Day of the Lord, His initial act is to rescue His Church in the Rapture from this coming time of WRATH on the earth, for we are **"to wait for His Son from Heaven, even Jesus who DELIVERS us from the WRATH to COME"** (1Thessalonians 1:10). He will do this: **"for God did not appoint us to WRATH, but to obtain SALVATION** (through the Rapture) **through our Lord Jesus Christ"** (5:9). Thus, His Coming for His Church in the Rapture will initiate the Day of the Lord on the earth. In other words, the judgments of the Day of the Lord will start to be released immediately after the Rapture (even on the very same day). One way this truth is manifested in the Scriptures is through the fact of Dual Imminence – that both the Rapture of the Church and the Start of the Day of the Lord are presented as imminent events – something that can happen suddenly at any time. They are both imminent simply because they are simultaneous. In addition, both the imminent Start of the Day of the Lord and the Rapture are described in connection with the Coming of the Lord (Matthew 24:37-39, 42-44, Luke 12:39-40, 1Thessalonians 1:10, 4:15-17, 5:2-10, 1Corinthians 15:23,51-52, 2Peter 3:10, Revelation 3:3,10-11, 16:15). In other words, when the Lord comes, He will first rapture His own, and then immediately initiate the Day of the Lord judgments on the earth, just as in the days of Noah and of Lot, when as soon as the believers were removed from the scene of judgment, God's judgments were released upon those who were left (Luke 17:26-30). In fact, the Rapture of the Church is the initiating event of the Day of the Lord.

This agrees with 2Thessalonians 2:6-8, which describes the Spirit-filled Church as being the Restrainer, holding back the manifestation of the antichrist, so that as soon as the Church is taken out of the way (literally: 'out of the midst') in the Rapture (v1,7), the lawless one will be revealed (v6,8). The initial rise and revelation of the antichrist on the world-stage will be the opening event of the Day of the Lord, once it has been initiated by the Rapture. This is made clear by 2Thessalonians 2:4, once it is translated correctly. We will see that a correct literal translation reads: **"that DAY** (of the Lord) **will not be present unless the Departure** (of the Church in the Rapture – see v1) **comes first, and the man of sin is revealed."** This agrees with Revelation, which describes the first event of the Tribulation (under the 1st Seal) as the Rider on the white horse going forth to conquer (Revelation 6:1-2).

In fact, the Tribulation exactly coincides with the public career of the antichrist.

*(1) The first Seal, right at the start of the Tribulation, releases the rider on the white horse, the antichrist, who rises to power and starts to go forth to conquer the world (Revelation 6:1-2). This is his initial revelation in 2Thessalonians 2:3,8.

*(2) After a time, he will be further revealed and clearly identified, by making his move to gain control of Israel and the Middle-East through making a 7-year covenant with Israel, as Daniel 9:27 says: **"Then he** (antichrist) **shall confirm a covenant with many for one Week** (that is 7 years)**."** These 7 years are called Daniel's 70th Week, the last 7 years of the Tribulation, which Christ will bring to an end when He returns to destroy the antichrist. Thus, the Tribulation will last at least 7 years, as it concludes with Daniel's 70th Week, and since the antichrist is active throughout the 70th Week, the whole 70th Week must be part of the Tribulation. This covenant, which initiates the final 7-Times of Gentile dominion over Israel gives antichrist a measure of authority over Israel, and in return he gives her promises of protection, peace and security, and this covenant will provide for a sharing of the Temple Mount between Jews and Gentiles (Islam), with Israel receiving permission to worship in her rebuilt Temple there (Revelation 11:1-4). We will see that this covenant coincides with the 7th Seal and the appearance of the 2 witnesses.

*(3) The antichrist is even more clearly revealed 3.5 years later, in the middle of the 70th Week, when he breaks the covenant and invades Israel, kills

the 2 witnesses and desecrates the Temple by setting up the Abomination of Desolation there (an idol to himself – the image of the beast). This marks the start of the Great Tribulation (Daniel 9:27, 12:11, Matthew 24:15-21), the Time of Jacob's Trouble (Jeremiah 30:7). This is when he proclaims himself to be 'god' in the Temple of God, confirmed by signs and wonders, through the power of Satan, causing the whole world to follow after him. At this point he becomes the world-dictator of a one-world government and sets up the Mark of the Beast to enforce his control, requiring all people to worship him (2Thessalonians 2:4,9, Revelation 13).

*(4) Finally, at the end of the Tribulation both he the false prophet will be destroyed by the personal Appearance of Christ in power and glory (2Thessalonians 2:8, Revelation 19:20).

The Tribulation is a Time of Divine Wrath

One reason the Church must be raptured before the Tribulation is that it is a time of Divine WRATH, and the Church has been promised deliverance from the Wrath of God (Romans 5:9, 1Thessalonians 1:10, 5:9). In Matthew 24:36-44, Jesus compared the time before and after His Coming in the Rapture, to the days of Noah, saying: **"as the days of Noah were, so also will the Coming of the Son of Man be"** (v37). The outstanding event in the days of Noah was the FLOOD - a world-wide JUDGMENT, in which all unbelievers were killed. Likewise, the whole TRIBULATION is a world-wide JUDGMENT, leaving only believers alive at its end to repopulate the earth in the Millennium. Jesus was comparing the TRIBULATION to Noah's FLOOD – a time of world-wide JUDGMENT. Before the Flood, life was going on as normal, as Jesus said in v38: **"as in the days before the Flood, they were eating and drinking, marrying and giving in marriage."** The people had no idea that judgement was about to fall even though Noah warned them. Likewise, as in the days of Noah, just before the Tribulation, life will carry on normally, and they will even be saying: "peace and safety" (1Thessalonians 5:3). This is one reason why the FLOOD is a TYPE of the whole TRIBULATION, and not just the 2nd Coming, for in the days just before the 2nd Coming, described in detail in Revelation, anything but normal life is going on. This is the Great Tribulation, the worst time ever, including the 7 Bowls of Wrath, and Jesus said if He did not cut it short all flesh would be destroyed.

The final event before the Flood fell was the disappearance of believers into the Ark, when God removed them from the scene of judgement and lifted them above it, as v38-39 says, they were living their normal life: **"until the day that Noah entered the Ark, and did not know until the Flood came and took them all away, so also will the Coming of the Son of Man be."** Likewise, the final event before the Tribulation-Flood falls will be the disappearance of all believers into Christ at the Rapture. He will remove the true Church from the earth by lifting us above the scene of judgment, before pouring out His Tribulation Judgments. Jesus then described this Rapture of believers that happens in conjunction with His Return: **"Then 2 men will be in the field: one will be taken** (to Heaven in the Rapture) **and the other left** (on earth to enter the Day of the Lord). **2 women will be grinding at the mill: one taken and the other left. Watch therefore, for you do not know what hour your Lord is coming"** (v40-42).

Then in, Jesus compared His Coming in the Rapture to a thief coming suddenly in the night to bring judgment to the house (world) and to take the valuable things from it: **"But know this, that if the master of the house had known what hour the THIEF would COME, he would have watched and not allowed his house to be broken into. Therefore, you also be ready, for the SON of MAN is COMING at an hour you do not expect"** (v43-44). The coming of a thief results in loss to a house, thus it is a picture of judgment as far as the world is concerned. But why would He use the image of a thief for Himself, as it carries negative overtones? If He was describing the 2nd Coming, there would be better images to use, such as a conquering King, coming to take over the house of this world. But His Coming as a THIEF perfectly fits the imminent Rapture, when He does not come to take over the house, but rather to TAKE the precious things (His own people) from the house, and thereby inflict a loss (judgment) upon the house, for it will appear to the world after the Rapture has happened - that a thief has come and taken multitudes of people. Thus, using the image of a THIEF perfectly combines the dual aspect of His imminent Coming: (1) to REMOVE His people from the house, and (2) initiate a JUDGMENT (loss) upon those remaining in the house. Since both these aspects necessarily happen at the same time, this imagery teaches that when Jesus comes in the Rapture, He simultaneously initiates the Day of the Lord on the earth, and that both these events are imminent. Now of course Jesus is not really a thief because He will only take what belongs to Him (His own people). To the world, He will come as a thief, but for us He comes as the Bridegroom for His Bride, to rescue her from danger before waging war on the world-system under the power of the evil one. Thus, when He returns, He will take all the true believers to Himself, which in itself will be the first act of judgment, which opens the Day of the Lord. So as far as the world is concerned, the initial act of judgment of the Day of Lord is when Jesus gets up from sitting at the right hand of the Father and returns to receive His own to Himself. By removing the Church, He is removing His restraint upon evil, allowing it to come to fullness in order for it to be judged. This action also allows Him to move in greater judgment. Thus, the Day of the Lord begins with the Coming of the Lord to rapture His Church, and then continues to the end of the Tribulation as He continues to pour out His judgments. Thus, His Coming in the Rapture for His Church will also be His Coming as a thief to the world, initiating a time of judgment on earth. His Coming as a thief does not represent the completion of His judgment of the world, which only happens at His 2nd Coming, because a thief does not come to destroy a house. Instead, His Coming as a thief initiates the time of judgment - even the world-wide judgment of the Day of the Lord.

In a parallel passage in Luke 21:34-36, after describing the events of the Tribulation, Jesus said: **"Take heed to yourselves lest that DAY** (the DAY of the LORD) **come on you unexpectedly. For it will come as a snare on all those who dwell on the face of the whole earth** (it will be a world-wide judgment). **Watch therefore and pray always that you may be counted worthy to escape** (in the Rapture) **all these things that will come to pass** (in the Day of the Lord) **and to stand before the Son of Man."** Since the events of the Tribulation come upon all those on the earth, the only way to escape all these things is to be removed from the earth and this is exactly what Jesus will do in the Rapture for those counted worthy (righteous) through their faith in Him, because it is not fitting for them to face His wrath. They will be lifted up from the earth and find themselves standing before the Son of Man in their glorified bodies.

In 1Thessalonians 5:2-4, Paul defined the DAY of the LORD (the coming time of Divine Judgment, according to the Old Testament prophets) as being the time of LABOUR PAINS (a description of the TRIBULATION, according to the prophets and Jesus in Matthew 24:8): **"the DAY of the LORD, so comes as a THIEF in the night.   For when THEY say: "Peace and safety!" then SUDDEN DESTRUCTION comes upon THEM** (on the world, not the Church), **as LABOUR PAINS upon a pregnant woman. And THEY shall not escape** (it will be a world-wide judgment). **But YOU, brethren, are not in** (the kingdom of) **darkness, so that this DAY** (of the LORD) **should overtake YOU as a THIEF."** This refutes the common mistake that the DAY of the LORD refers to the 2nd Coming – in fact, the 2nd Coming is the climax of the Day of the Lord. This scripture also confirms that the TRIBULATION is also the DAY of the LORD (a time of Divine Judgment), and that it will come suddenly, without warning, upon the unbelieving world (not the Church), out of the blue (imminence), while normal life is going on ('peace and safety', as in the days of Noah), as the COMING of a THIEF, in agreement with the teaching of Jesus (Matthew 24:36-44). The THIEF, as Jesus pointed out, will be Christ Himself coming suddenly to break into the world and cause it to suffer loss, in other words, this will be the initial judgement of the Day of the Lord (Matthew 24:43-44). In His action as the thief, Jesus will remove His true Church in the Rapture (1Thessalonians 4:15-17), which is His initial judgment on the world, preparing the way for the remaining judgments, since it removes the major reason why God would withhold His wrath (as with Noah and Lot), as well as removing the Restrainer. The removal of the Church, before the remaining judgments are released, explains why the sudden destruction of the Day of the Lord only comes on 'THEM', but not on the Church ('YOU'). Again, we see that the imminent Coming of the LORD in the Rapture (4:15-18), will initiate the DAY of the LORD on the earth (5:2), a time of Divine Judgment, also described as the time of BIRTH PAINS (5:3), an equivalent term to the TRIBULATION. Thus, Paul's language agrees with that of Jesus and the prophets, and His teaching expounds that of Jesus.

Notice the DAY of the LORD is described as a time of sudden TROUBLE and DESTRUCTION initiated by the LORD, coming on the whole world, confirming that it is a time of world-wide JUDGMENT. The world (but not the Church) experiences it as the COMING of a THIEF (v2,4) who brings loss to the house, confirming that the imagery of a THIEF speaks of unexpected, sudden JUDGMENT, but at the same time revealing the removal of something of great value. Jesus identified Himself as the thief, so the Tribulation will be initiated by the Coming of the Lord as a thief to take His own in the Rapture.

The world will experience the Rapture as if a thief has come, when a billion or so people are suddenly taken from the earth (v2-3). The world will not escape the Day of the Lord judgments, for they will suddenly come upon them and overtake them. On the other hand, the believers will not experience the Rapture as the coming of a thief, but as an escape from the DARKNESS of the DAY of the LORD (v4-5), being rescued from this time of WRATH by our Heavenly Bridegroom, for it is not right that the sons of the light should endure the darkness of God's wrath (v4-5), for we have been saved from wrath by the Blood of Christ (Romans 5:9). Paul concludes this teaching on the Day of the Lord by saying that in the light of the Pre-Tribulation Rapture, believers are to: **"put on as a helmet the hope** (confident expectation) **of** (future) **SALVATION, for God did not appoint us to WRATH** (the wrath of the Day of the Lord), **but to obtain SALVATION** (in the Rapture) **through our Lord Jesus Christ"** (v8-9). The context of this reference to WRATH (v9), tells us that it must be the WRATH of the DAY of the LORD, confirming that the TRIBULATION is also a time of Divine WRATH. Paul assures us that believers are not appointed to the WRATH of the DAY of the LORD (v9, confirming v3-4), but instead the Lord Jesus will deliver (save) them from this time of wrath, by completing their salvation (the transformation of their bodies) in the Rapture (see 4:15-17). This agrees perfectly with what Paul says earlier in the same letter, when he says believers are those who: **"wait for His Son from Heaven, even Jesus, who DELIVERS** (rescues) **us from the WRATH to COME** (in the Day of the Lord)" (1Thessalonians 1:10). In the Rapture, Jesus will come from Heaven to deliver us from this this time of WRATH that is coming upon the earth. It is clear that the 'wrath' in this verse cannot be the wrath of Hell, but a wrath that will come upon mankind while they are living on the earth, necessitating the Lord's Coming to earth to rescue His own from this coming wrath, which is the coming Day of the Lord (5:2). Our deliverance from the everlasting wrath of Hell, secured by the Blood of Christ, does not require the Lord's Coming. Thus, the language of this verse fits the Day of the Lord Wrath, not the Wrath of Hell.

The Book of Revelation

Revelation 4-19 gives us the fullest and most detailed description of the Day of the Lord in the whole Bible, bringing the whole Biblical revelation of this time together into a coherent chronological account of the main events of this whole period of 7+ years leading up to the 2nd Coming of Christ, including much new revelation describing the judgments of God through His angels, His final witness to the world through the 2 witnesses and the 144,000, and the work of Satan through the antichrist, in controlling the world and persecuting God's people, through his final one-world Empire. It also describes how Christ ultimately triumphs over all His enemies and saves Israel at His 2nd Coming. Thus, it completes the Bible's revelation of the Tribulation.

Revelation confirms that the Day of the Lord (Tribulation) will start on the same day as the Rapture. In Revelation 4-5, after the Church Age in Revelation 2-3, the raptured Church is seen in Heaven, as represented by the 24 elders, who sing the praises of the Lamb, for redeeming them with His Blood from every tribe, tongue and nation. Then in Revelation 6, Christ immediately starts to break the first 6 Seals of the Scroll with 7 Seals (the Title Deed of the earth), which results in judgments being released from Heaven onto the earth. The result of His breaking of the first Seal is the release of the antichrist onto the world-stage, as he goes forth to conquer the world (v1,2). So again, we see that the Tribulation starts immediately after the Rapture, and its opening event on earth is the initial rise of the antichrist (see also 2Thessalonians 2:1-8). In addition, we will see that the judgments released in Revelation 6, under the first 6 Seals, right at the start of the Tribulation, which then continue throughout the Tribulation, correspond exactly to Jesus' description of the BIRTH PAINS of the Tribulation (Matthew 24:7-13). This shows that the Birth Pains of the Tribulation (the time of Travail) are also judgments, initiated from Heaven, showing that this is also the Day of the Lord, the special time in history when God moves in world-wide judgment, at the End of the Age (Matthew 13:39,40,49, 24:3). Thus, the Birth Pains, the Tribulation, the End of the Age and the Day of the Lord all refer to the same period of time, and that, from its beginning, it is not just a time of great evil, suffering and persecution (man's wrath and Satan's wrath), but also a time of Divine Judgment and Wrath, which is why Jesus promises to deliver His Church from it, because we are not appointed to wrath, because of the Blood of Christ (1Thessalonians 1:10, 5:8-10, Romans 5:9).

Those who try and separate the chronology of this time into 2 parts: (1) the Tribulation (a time of man's wrath and Satan's wrath), followed by (2) the Day of the Lord (the time of Divine Wrath), ignore the fact that God's Judgments in Revelation start by Christ breaking the first Seal, not the 7th Seal, or 7th Trumpet or the first Bowl of Wrath, or the 2nd Coming of Christ. In other words, Revelation makes it clear that the whole Tribulation is a time of Divine Judgment and Wrath, for it is Christ Himself, who initiates the Tribulation, by starting to release judgments from Heaven, at its very beginning, from the first Seal onwards (Revelation 6). Since the term 'the Day of the Lord' speaks of the special time in history of Divine Judgment climaxing in the Return of the Messiah to establish His Kingdom on earth, it follows that the whole Tribulation is also the Day of the Lord. For example, although some say the Wrath of God only begins with the Bowls of Wrath, Revelation 15:1 makes it clear these 7 Bowls of Wrath represent the completion, not the initiation of God's Wrath: **"Then I saw 7 angels having the 7 last plagues, for in them the WRATH of God is COMPLETE."**

Moreover, the very nature and structure of Revelation 4-19 confirm that the whole Tribulation is a time of Divine Wrath.   Not only is the Tribulation initiated on earth by Christ breaking the first 6 Seals in Heaven, releasing judgments on every part of the world-system (Revelation 6), the whole narrative is written in a way that demonstrates that what happens on earth is being controlled by God's actions from Heaven.   The scene constantly moves between Heaven and earth, revealing their interactions, with actions on earth provoking Divine judgments, and Divine judgments being manifested on earth. In particular, we see God's sovereign control being enforced through a countdown sequence of ever escalating judgments, consisting of 7 Seals, 7 Trumpets and 7 Bowls, all initiated by Christ from Heaven.   First, the first 6 Seals are opened in quick succession at the start of the Tribulation (Revelation 6). The judgments of these Seals, being the Birth Pains, continue and intensify throughout the Tribulation until the 2nd Coming, when the Messianic Kingdom is born, just as birth pains continue and intensify until the birth of the baby.   After the first 6 Seals are broken, there is a delay of unknown duration, before the 7th Seal is broken (Revelation 8), which in turn represents a major escalation, emphasised by the dramatic build up to it (8:1-6). The 7th Seal then releases the first 6 Trumpets (8:1-2,6), which then begin to be blown in succession, releasing increasingly terrible direct judgments upon the earth (Revelation 8-9). Then again there is a special build up to the 7th Trumpet (10:1 – 11:14), signifying that it marks a further escalation in the intensity of judgment, confirmed by Heaven's reaction when it is sounded (11:15-19). Moreover, the last 3 Trumpets are also called the 3 Woes (9:12, 11:14) signifying they are worse than the previous Trumpets.   The 7th Trumpet releases all the remaining judgments, leading up to the establishment of the Messianic Kingdom (11:15-18), including the 7 Bowls of Wrath (Revelation 15-18), which are even more terrible than the first 6 Trumpets, the 7th Bowl being especially devastating as it results in the total destruction of Babylon – antichrist's world empire (Revelation 18).   Soon after that, Christ personally brings this time of judgment to its climax by His 2nd Coming to defeat the armies of antichrist at Armageddon (Revelation 19). Thus, together the 7 Seals, 7 Trumpets and 7 Bowls form a unified interconnected structure that governs the whole chronological outworking of God's judgments during the whole Tribulation, creating a dramatic description of continual escalation in the severity of these judgments, until they reach their climax at the personal Coming of Christ in power and glory. We know that the 7th Seal contains the 7 Trumpets, and that the 7th Trumpet includes the 7 Bowls of Wrath, because in both cases, unlike with the other Seals and Trumpets, there's no description of any particular judgment associated with them. Thus, they must contain and release all the judgments that take place after them in the narrative.   This is especially clear in the case of the 7th Seal containing the 7 Trumpets (8:1-6). The way all these judgments, released from Heaven, dominate the description of the Tribulation, beginning from when it starts, and the way they form the main skeletal structure of Revelation 6-18, prove that the defining characteristic of the whole Tribulation is that it is a time of Diving Wrath and Judgment – even the Day of the Lord.

Overview of the Chronology of the Tribulation

By harmonizing Revelation 6-19 with Daniel 9:27 and Matthew 24, we are able to construct an accurate chronological framework for all the events of this time. I do this later in this book, so now I just give a quick summary.

Immediately after the Rapture, the Birth Pains of the Tribulation will suddenly begin on earth, initiated by Christ in Heaven, when He breaks the first 6 Seals in Revelation 6. The conditions in the Tribulation get continually worse, due to both the increased manifestation of evil and the increased severity of the Divine Judgments. In the end things will get so bad that unless those days (of the Tribulation) were brought to an end by the 2nd Coming of Christ, no flesh would survive (Matthew 24:22). When Christ breaks the 1st Seal, this immediately releases the antichrist into manifestation, as he suddenly bursts onto the world scene. There is an initial unknown interlude of time (months or years), during which he rises to power to the point where he is able to make a covenant with Israel. During this time the 144,000, who will spearhead the evangelism in the Tribulation, are being prepared by God, through their salvation and sealing (Revelation 7). This antichrist covenant initiates the final 7-year countdown to the 2nd Coming, called Daniel's 70th Week (Daniel 9:27). This covenant requires Israel to put her trust in the antichrist, and in return she is released to worship at her rebuilt Temple. This is the moment the 2 witnesses begin their ministry at the Temple, for 1260 days, the first half of the 70th Week (Revelation 11:1-6). Their ministry is integral to the 3rd Temple Ministry (Zechariah 4). This also marks the start of the ministry of the 144,000. God's immediate response to the antichrist covenant is an escalation of Divine Judgment, through the breaking of the 7th Seal (Revelation 8:1), which releases the first 6 Trumpets (Revelation 8-9). The 1st Trumpet is blown at once, on the first day of the 70th Week, announced in advance by the 2 witnesses. During their ministry they announce many judgments, including the first 6 Trumpets (Revelation 11:10).

The next major escalation of Divine Judgment happens in the middle of the 70th Week, in response to the actions of the antichrist against God and His people, Israel. He breaks the covenant, by invading Israel, and taking over the Temple, killing the 2 witnesses, once they have completed their 1,260 days of testimony (11:7). Their dead bodies are displayed to the world for 3.5 days, and then God raises them from the dead and they ascend to Heaven before the eyes of the nations (11:8-12), as a final Sign of Jonah to Israel that Jesus, whom they preached, is the true Messiah. The antichrist desecrates the Temple by erecting 'the Abomination that brings Desolation' there, an idol to himself (the image of the beast), and proclaims Himself to be 'god', instead of the true God (Daniel 9:27, Matthew 24:15-16, 2Thessalonians 2:4). This act of Temple desecration calls forth increased desolating Judgments from Heaven, which are released by the 7th Trumpet (11:15), and include the 7 Bowls of Wrath (Revelation 15-18). The Abomination of Desolation and the 7th Trumpet mark the start of the Great Tribulation (Matthew 24:21), which lasts 1290 days (Daniel 12:11), and is brought to an end by the 2nd Coming. Since the antichrist is allowed to be world dictator for 1260 days = 42 months = 3.5 Times (Daniel 7:25, 12:7, Revelation 11:2, 12:6, 14, 13:5), before he is destroyed by Christ at His Return (19:20), it follows that there is an initial period of 30 days before antichrist is able to establish his world dictatorship, during which believing Israel make her escape to Jordan (Revelation 12, Matthew 24:15-21), and the antichrist and false prophet, using satanic signs and wonders, convince the world as a whole to worship and follow the antichrist, and enforcing this new religion and establishing total control over them through the mark of the beast (Revelation 13, 2Thessalonians 2:9-10).

The 7th Trumpet releases war in the first heaven, resulting in Satan and his angels being cast down to the earth's surface (12:7-12), as well as all the other judgments of the Great Tribulation, including the 7 Bowls of Wrath. Finally, the Great Tribulation is brought to its end by the Coming of Christ in power and glory (Matthew 24:29-30), on the Great and Awesome Day of the Lord, and complete the judgment of His enemies at Armageddon (Revelation 19). This will take place on the final day of Daniel's 70th Week. Then He will throw Satan and his angels into the Abyss for 1,000 years (20:1-3), resurrect the rest of the saints who have died, and establish His Kingdom on earth for 1000 years, when we will reign with Him (20:4-6). He will also judge those still alive on earth, separating the sheep (believers) from the goats (unbelievers), to determine who will enter into the Millennial Kingdom with Him (Matthew 25:31-46). Only the believers, who have eternal life, will be allowed to live and inherit the Kingdom (v34,41,46).

In conclusion, both the Old and New Testaments agree that there will be a Time of Trouble and Divine Wrath, called 'the Day of the Lord', just before the 2nd Coming, when evil will be allowed to come to its fullness, but only for a short time, for God will move in judgement and destroy all evildoers, and then establish His Kingdom on earth. Jesus called this special time-period leading up to His Coming in power and glory 'the End of the Age' (Matthew 24:3), and 'the Tribulation' (Matthew 24:9,29). It commences immediately after the Church Age ends at the Rapture, and ends with Christ's Return in power and glory (Matthew 24:29-30). It will last for at least 7 years, because it includes Daniel's 70th Week (Daniel 9:27), which starts when Israel makes covenant with the antichrist and ends with the Return of Christ. Half-way through the 70th Week, the antichrist will desecrate the Temple in Jerusalem with the Abomination of Desolation (Daniel 9:27, Matthew 24:15). This will initiate the final 3.5 years of the Tribulation, described by Jesus as the Great Tribulation (Matthew 24:21). The Church must be raptured before the Tribulation, because the whole Tribulation (not just the 2nd Coming or the 7 Bowls of Wrath) is a time of Divine Wrath, and the Church has been promised deliverance from the Wrath of God (Romans 5:9, 1Thessalonians 1:10, 5:9), and from this time of world-wide Trial and Trouble (Revelation 3:10-11). What Bridegroom would keep His Bride in a city He was about to bombard in His wrath, when He has the power to extract her first?

The true Church will be raptured before the Tribulation, but the apostate Church will go into the Tribulation, and Jesus will then spew her out of his mouth as Jesus warned in Revelation 3:16. We also see the judgment of this false harlot church in Revelation 17. He also speaks of her in <u>Revelation 2:22</u>: **"I will cast her into a sickbed, and those who commit adultery with her into Great Tribulation, unless they repent of their deeds."** Many will be saved in the Tribulation, and there will be many martyrs, especially in the Great Tribulation, whom John sees as being in Heaven in <u>Revelation 7:14</u>: **"These are the ones who come out of the Great Tribulation, and washed their robes and made them white in the Blood of the Lamb."**

The 2 Phases of the Day of the Lord

The DAY of the LORD has a dual meaning in Scripture. There is the shorter DAY of the Lord of 7+ years, where He acts as the Judge (the Tribulation and 2nd Coming), and the longer DAY of the Lord, where He acts as King for 1000 years. Remember: **"one DAY to the Lord is as 1000 years to man"** (2Peter 3:8). Sometimes the Scriptures describe a Day (time) of darkness and judgment, and sometimes they describe the Golden Messianic Age. Mostly however, 'the Day of the Lord' is used to describe the time of Trouble leading up to the Return of Christ to establish His Kingdom, which we know as the Tribulation. Just as all 24-hour days (which biblically speaking start at sunset), begin with a time of darkness, followed by a time of light, so the DAY of the LORD (when He directly intervenes in human history) will start with a time of DARKNESS and divine judgment (the Tribulation), followed by a time of LIGHT, when Christ reigns in glory over the whole earth (the Millennium).

2Peter 3:10 describes the whole 'Day of the Lord', including both its shorter and longer parts, describing both its (1) START and (2) END: **"The DAY of the LORD will (1) come (begin) as a thief in the night** (the Rapture, initiating the Tribulation, see 1Thessalonians 5:2-3); (2) **in the which** (at its close) **the heavens shall pass away with a great noise, and the elements shall melt with fervent heat, the earth also and the works that are in it shall be burned up."** This describes the destruction of this present universe at the end of the Millennium. Then Christ hands the Kingdom to GOD, the Father (1Corinthians 15:28), which introduces a new eternal DAY, with a new heaven and earth (the Eternal State) called: 'The DAY of GOD.' This is what Peter describes next: **"looking for and hastening (towards) the Coming of the DAY of GOD, because of which the heavens will be dissolved, being on fire, and the elements will melt with fervent heat? Nevertheless we, according to His promise, look for new heavens and a new earth in which righteousness dwells"** (2Peter 3:12-13). Peter is using the picture of a runner looking to the fixed finishing line and speeding toward it with all his might. Likewise, the times of Christ's Return and the final end are fixed by the Father (Acts 1:7, Mark 13:32), and we are to run our race with all our might, keeping our eyes on the finishing-line, which is coming ever closer, motivated by the everlasting joy and reward set before us, when we cross that line into glory.

The Dispensational Status of the Tribulation

Although the Tribulation is distinct from the Church Age and the Millennium, it is not a separate Dispensation. Rather it is a transitional period joining 2 Ages or Dispensations. First, it is the Consummation of this present Age (Matthew 24:3), that began at the resurrection of Christ, bringing it to completion through divine judgments, which come to their climax at the 2nd Coming of Christ, ushering in the new Messianic Age on earth. Just as a 9-month pregnancy comes to its consummation in a time of birth pains, which climax in the birth of a baby, bringing in a new era for the parents, so this present Age will come to its consummation in a time of Birth Pains, which will climax in the birth of God's Kingdom, bringing in a new era for the earth. Thus, the Tribulation (the 'darkness' phase of the Day of the Lord) also heralds and prepares the way for the bringing forth (birth) of a new Age, a new Day - the Messianic Kingdom, the Millennium, the 'light' phase of the Day of the Lord, the Day of 1000 years, when the Lord Jesus Himself will reign on earth in His Glory. The fact that the main biblical name for 'the Tribulation' is 'the Day of the Lord', signifies its close connection with the Messianic Age to Come (the Day of the Lord), for it marks the transition into this new golden Age when Christ will reign on earth.

The transitional period of judgment between the present Age and the Messianic Kingdom Age corresponds perfectly with the time of Noah's Flood. We have previously seen that Jesus used the world-wide judgment of the Flood (which lasted about a year), as a type of the world-wide judgment of the Tribulation (Matthew 24:37-39). The Flood was a transitional year of judgment between 2 Dispensations (Genesis 7-8), bringing the previous Age to its close, and preparing the way for the new Dispensation, defined by the Noahic Covenant (Genesis 9). Likewise, the Tribulation is a transitional year of judgment between the present Dispensation and the next Dispensation (the Messianic Kingdom), which will be defined by the Kingdom Law

Chapter 4: Dual Imminence
in the Teaching of Jesus

Before we study the detailed unfolding of future events after the Rapture, I would like to demonstrate how the end-time teaching of Jesus is foundational to the teaching of the apostles on this subject (especially Paul, James, Peter and John), so that the apostolic teaching repeats and develops the teaching of Jesus, using similar imagery, creating one unified body of doctrine. The Lord Himself declared that His own teaching was foundational (Matthew 7:24-27), and He commanded the apostles to: **"Go and make disciples of all the nations...TEACHING them to observe ALL THINGS that I have COMMANDED you; and lo, I am with you always, even to the End of the Age."** Thus, Jesus made it clear that His teaching was to be authoritative and normative for the whole Church Age, and so His apostles were commanded to base their teaching on His own teaching. Although, God would bring them into further revelation after His death and resurrection, this would build upon and develop what Christ had already taught. Therefore, to fully understand New Testament doctrine, in an area such as Prophecy, it is necessary to start from the foundation of Christ's own teaching in the Gospels. This agrees with the Spirit-led programme outlined by Jesus to the apostles, just before His death, for the development of New Testament doctrine, to be built on the foundation of Christ's own teaching. First, the Holy Spirit would: **"teach you all things, and bring to your remembrance all things that I said to you"** (John 14:26). This is the teaching of Jesus recorded in the Gospels. Then: **"when the Spirit of truth, has come, He will guide you into all truth... and He will tell you things to come"** (John 16:13). Thus, the Spirit not only helped them understand the teaching of Jesus (14:26), but also gave them further revelation that further develops His teaching, especially in the area of Eschatology (16:13). So, for example before Paul gave His teaching on the Rapture in 1Thessalonians 4, he said: **"you know what commandments we gave you through the Lord Jesus"** (v2), and **"this we say to you by the Word of the Lord"** (v15), which could also be translated: **"this we say to you IN** (line with) **the Word of the Lord** (Jesus)."

My aim in the next 3 chapters is to reveal how all the New Testament teaching on the Rapture and Tribulation connect together to form an integrated whole. We will also see that the harmonisation of the apostolic teaching with the teaching of Jesus provides a major confirmation that Jesus taught the Rapture in the Olivet Discourse. The Rapture, as part of the Mystery (1Corinthians 15:51), was not revealed in the Old Testament (unlike the 2nd Coming), so Jesus was the first to reveal it, for all Pre-Tribulation believers agree that John 14:1-3 is His promise to the Church of the Rapture. However, what is not agreed by all is that

He also spoke about the Rapture, on the day before this, in the Olivet Discourse (Matthew 24:36-44, Luke 21:36), as well as earlier (Luke 12:35-48, 17:26-30, 34-36). If this is correct, He did not just give the promise of the Rapture in John 14, but He also laid down a detailed foundation of teaching on the Rapture, which we can reconstruct by putting all His teachings together, with which the disciples were obliged to align their own end-time teaching. We will see that this is indeed the case, for the apostles used the same key words and images as Jesus, to describe the Rapture and its relationship to the Tribulation, in such a way that their teaching harmonizes perfectly with His teaching, both in repeating and developing it, and giving similar emphases and applications.

The foundation for the New Testament teaching on eschatology was laid by Jesus, which then was taken up and developed by the apostles, Paul, Peter, James and John. We will see that, as well as describing His Coming in power and glory at the end of the Tribulation (in agreement with the Old Testament), Jesus also introduced a brand-new teaching, which describes His imminent Coming in the Rapture, to rescue His own, just before the Tribulation starts. The Rapture and 2nd Coming could be seen as 2 phases of His 2nd Coming. His 1st Coming consisted a sequence of events over 33.5 years, so there is no reason why His 2nd Coming would not happen in stages. However, generally, to avoid confusion, when I refer to the 2nd Coming, I am referring to His Coming in power and glory at the end of the Tribulation. Whereas His 2nd Coming is not imminent (as it comes at the end of the well-defined sequence of dramatic events and signs in the Tribulation), by way of contrast, His Coming in the Rapture before the Tribulation is consistently described as sign-less and imminent. In fact, this is its most emphasised and definitive quality. This clear difference between His Coming in the Rapture and His 2nd Coming makes it easy to identify which future Coming of Christ is intended in any particular Scripture.

IMMINENCE

In Part 2 of this Series of books, we saw the consistent teaching of the New Testament is that the Coming of Christ for His Church in the Rapture is imminent – that is, He could come at any time, and His Coming will be sudden and unexpected, without signs or warning, and that no predicted events have to necessarily come first. Thus, the timing of His Coming is totally unpredictable, because God has chosen to keep it as His secret. Therefore, no man can know in advance when He is coming. Thus, the nature of this teaching of imminence is man's lack of knowledge. God's purpose in not revealing this information is that this requires us to stay constantly ready, alert and watchful for His return, eagerly waiting for Him - it keeps us on our toes. If we knew, for example, that He was not coming for another 10 years then it would not be necessary to be ready right now, we could delay our readiness until the time was closer, but the New Testament urges us to live in a constant state of alertness and readiness for His Coming.

If you had an important visitor coming to your house, you would want your house to be prepared and ready for his arrival. But if you knew that he would not come for a significant time, you would not have to get your house ready now, you could wait until the time was closer. But if he kept his time of arrival a secret, then he could come at any time, which means you and your house would need to be kept in a constant state of readiness. This is the attitude that Jesus told us to have – to expect His return at any time, and therefore to live in a constant state of readiness.

Unlike teaching on the Day of the Lord (Tribulation) and His Coming at its close, which, as we have seen, is in both Old and New Testaments, the teaching of Christ's imminent Coming is brand new teaching, for it is not in the Old Testament. It is part of **"the Mystery hidden in God from the foundation of the world"** (Romans 16:26, Ephesians 3:9, Colossians 1:29, 1Corinthians 15:51), which has now been revealed in the New Testament. The foundation for this New Testament belief in Christ's imminent Coming is from the teaching of Jesus Himself, which is then taken up and confirmed by the apostles, Paul, Peter, James and John.

DUAL IMMINENCE

When we study the Scriptures which teach imminence, we find that sometimes they describe (1) His imminent Coming to deliver, rescue and bless His people, while others describe (2) His imminent Coming to bring the Day of the Lord judgments on the earth. Other Scriptures hold both ideas together by describing both aspects happening at the same time. So, there are 2 events that are imminent: (1) the Rapture of the Church and (2) the Start of the Day of the Lord, a time of judgment, otherwise known as the Tribulation and the End of the Age. This is what we mean by DUAL IMMINENCE. The reason why both of these events are IMMINENT, is that they are also SIMULTANEOUS. That is, when Christ comes for His Church, He also comes to initiate the Day of the Lord on the earth. Thus, His Coming has 2 purposes, which are accomplished at the same time: He will come suddenly to bring judgment upon the earth, and at the same time, He will rescue His people from that coming judgment. This means that the Tribulation must begin on the same day of the Rapture, confirming the Pre-Tribulation Rapture. Scriptural support for the doctrine of Dual Imminence can be accumulated from verses that teach (1) the Imminence of the Rapture, (2) the

Imminence of the Day of the Lord, and (3) the simultaneity of the Rapture and the Start of the Day of the Lord (Tribulation).

The TEACHING of JESUS

First, in this chapter, I will show that the LORD JESUS taught Dual Imminence in all His prophetic teachings, and then in the following 2 chapters, I will show that likewise His APOSTLES, followed His example and consistently taught this same truth. Thus, Dual Imminence should be understood as a doctrine that lies at the very heart of all New Testament teaching on Bible Prophecy, a golden thread running throughout, holding it all together in unity.

LUKE 12

In Jesus' chronologically first teaching on the end-times in Luke 12, He describes a future Coming of His, through 2 analogies (1) the MASTER returning and knocking on the DOOR, and (2) the coming of a THIEF in the night.

*(1) The MASTER returning to His SERVANTS

Luke 12:35-38: **"Let your waist be girded and your lamps burning and you yourselves be like men who WAIT for their MASTER** (Lord)**, when he will RETURN from the wedding, that when he comes and knocks, they may open to him immediately. BLESSED are those SERVANTS whom the MASTER, when he comes, will find WATCHING. Assuredly, I say to you that he will gird himself and have them sit down to eat, and will come and serve** (minister to) **them. And if he should come in the 2nd watch, or come in the 3rd watch, and find them so** (ready)**, BLESSED are those** (believing, faithful) **SERVANTS."**

Here we see that Christ instructs His servants to be constantly ready, waiting and watching for His arrival, because He could come at any time. He is the Lord and Master, who has gone away to Heaven, and who has promised to return to His House (the Church), and He expects to find us ready and waiting for Him. Now, you only WAIT for someone if they might arrive at any time. If, for example, you know they will not come for at least another 7 years, or until certain events have to happen first, then it would be pointless watching and waiting for them. Therefore, this speaks of an IMMINENT Coming of Christ, which is quite different from the 2nd Coming, which is preceded by all the signs and events of the Tribulation. The servants in this Parable have no idea when the Master will come or not come, so they have to stay in a state of preparedness. This is confirmed by Luke 12:40: **"Therefore, you also be READY, for the SON of MAN is COMING at an hour you do NOT EXPECT."** Therefore, this speaks of an imminent Coming of Christ, that is different from His signposted Coming in power and glory at the end of the Tribulation, previously revealed in the Old Testament. This is a new revelation, brought forth by Jesus, the Prophet. It is part of the Mystery, hidden in God from the foundation of the world, but now revealed through Christ and His apostles. In fact, this is the first mention of His imminent Return. Later, He developed this teaching in other passages, as did the New Testament apostles.

In particular, we will see the apostles pick up and use His terminology of WATCHING, WAITING and LOOKING for Christ, to describe the appropriate spiritual posture that believers should have in living in the light of His imminent Return in the Rapture. These words describe walking in fellowship with the Lord, keeping our eyes on Him, looking to Him as our continual Source of grace and leadership (wisdom, instructions and guidance) for our lives, and waiting in hope (confident expectation) for His promised manifestations in our lives, especially waiting for and living in the light of His imminent Return for us in the Rapture, when all His promises to us will be fulfilled. If this is the way we live as believers, then He will surely find us READY when He comes for us. The word for WATCHING in Luke 12:37 is *gregoreo* (to watch, be alert, be awake), and is used 22 times in the New Testament. In every case, it is used in connection with an imminent event, which is why constant alertness was required (for example Matthew 26:38.40.41,45). 12 of these uses are in prophetic contexts, all in relation to watching for Christ's Coming. Therefore, we should expect a unified use of this word in all 12 prophetic passages, do describe the response Christ expects from us in the light of His imminent Coming. 10 of these are spoken by Jesus, 7 recorded in the Gospels and 3 in Revelation (3:2,3;16:15). In addition, Paul uses *gregoreo* twice (1Thessalonians 5:6,10). This is good evidence that Paul borrowed the prophetic use of this word from the Lord, and used it in the same way as Him. Since Paul applied it in the context of the imminent Pre-Tribulation Rapture, then surely it follows that Christ did also, in these prophetic passages (Luke 12:35-38, Matthew 24:42-43, 25:13, Mark 13:33-37).

This passage reveals that in this Coming, He will come to His House (the Church), and will BLESS His faithful servants, who believe His instructions and stay ready for His Coming, watchfully living their lives in the awareness of His imminent Return. As Jesus and His apostles develop this teaching, we will see that this Parable is an initial description (in seed form) of His imminent Coming for the Church in the Rapture, when He will bless His faithful servants, rewarding them generously at His Judgment Seat, when they will receive His eternal rewards.

*(2) The sudden COMING of a THIEF

Having described His imminent Coming to bless His faithful servants, He then changes the imagery in a surprising way, introducing a theme that is repeated by Paul, Peter and John – the COMING of the SON of MAN is compared to the COMING of a THIEF in Luke 12:39-40: **"But know this, that if the master of the house had known what hour the THIEF would COME, he would have WATCHED and not allowed his house to be broken into. Therefore, you also be READY, for the SON of MAN is COMING at an hour you do NOT EXPECT."**

By comparing His COMING with the coming of a THIEF, Jesus is confirming that His COMING is IMMINENT. A thief does not announce the time of his arrival, nor does he give any warning signs, but rather he comes suddenly, without warning, when you do not expect him. Likewise, the Son of Man, like a thief, will come suddenly: **"at an hour you do not expect."**

Luke 12:39-40 is clearly talking about the same Coming as v35-38. This now tells us that His Coming will not be a blessing for all, but for those unbelievers, who are not expecting and watching for His Return, they will experience His Coming as a THIEF. Now, a thief does not come to bless, but rather to bring loss. A thief is not welcome, but rather breaks in by force, and the result of his visit is loss of property. Thus, the primary application of Jesus coming like a thief is His imminent Coming to bring judgment (the Day of the Lord) upon the earth. Unbelievers will suffer loss, because they will not be prepared and ready for His Return (for they are still in their sins). Thus, for faithful believers His Coming is imminent, and results in immediate blessing, but for unbelievers His Coming is imminent, and results in immediate loss and judgement – for they will immediately be overtaken by the events of the Tribulation.

Thus, another reason to be ready for His Coming, is that if you are not ready, you will experience His Coming as the coming of a THIEF – that is, you will be overtaken by His sudden judgment, and you will suffer loss as a result. Notice that this description of Jesus COMING like a THIEF does not fit with His 2nd Coming, because (1) the 2nd Coming is not imminent, but is heralded by a sequence of signs lasting at least 7 years, and also (2) a thief does not come to kill or remove the occupants from the house, in order to totally take over the house himself (which is what Jesus does at His 2nd Coming, when He removes all the wicked from the earth by death).

Thus, Jesus gives a 2-fold description of His Coming (a 2-sided Parable) to describe 2 aspects of His Coming, as it will be experienced: (1) by His faithful servants (v35-38), and (2) by unbelievers (v39). The truth of IMMINENCE applies to both pictures: (1) His Coming to His faithful servants, and (2) His Coming as a thief to the unbelieving world - which is to be expected, because in both cases it is the same Coming. This is confirmed by the fact that Jesus' conclusion in Luke 12:40 is a clear statement of imminence, applying to both groups of people:

"Therefore, you also be READY, for the SON of MAN is COMING at an hour you do NOT EXPECT."

Therefore, there are 2 reasons to make sure you are READY for Jesus' RETURN: (1) if He finds you ready, then you will be blessed, but (2) if you are not ready you will experience His Coming as a thief, and you will experience loss. In conclusion, (1) for faithful believers, His Coming is imminent and results in immediate blessing (v35-38), but (2) for unbelievers His Coming is also imminent, and results in immediate loss and judgement (v39-40), for they will be immediately overtaken by the events of the Tribulation. Since both aspects take place at His Coming, they will happen at the same time. Thus, this passage teaches Dual Imminence.

Dual Imminence is actually encoded in the analogy of Christ's Coming as a THIEF, because He is experienced in 2 different ways, depending on the observer: (1) The coming of a thief is a negative experience to the occupants of the house, but (2) for the precious things that He removes from the house, they experience a change of location. The one who seems to act like a thief takes that which is valuable to be with himself – this is the essential thing that makes him a thief. Therefore, if Jesus is coming like a thief, it follows that He is coming in order to take some things from the house (of the earth), which He considers precious and valuable. This of course, speaks of the Rapture of the Church. When Jesus returns, He will remove all His believers from the earth, so they can be with Him forever. Now we know, of course, that He is not actually a thief, because He is only coming to take what belongs to Him, His precious saints, who He has purchased with His Blood and who have surrendered their lives to Him. But as far as the rest of the world is concerned, their experience will be that a THIEF has suddenly come and surprised them by removing a billion people, and then immediately after that the world will be plunged into a time of Divine Judgment – the Day of the Lord. However, for His own, they do not experience His coming as a judgment, but as a blessing – we are taken from the house (the earth) to be with our Lord Jesus forever. For the world, they will experience His Coming as a thief in the night, but for His own, we will experience His Coming as a Bridegroom coming for His Bride. Therefore, the THIEF analogy in itself encodes Dual Imminence.

Jesus also compared His Coming to the sudden surprise coming of a thief in the Olivet Discourse (Matthew 24:43) and in Revelation 3:3 and 16:15. In each case, it describes how unbelievers will experience His sudden Coming. Likewise, the apostles describe the Day of the Lord suddenly coming upon and overtaking unbelievers as a thief (1Thessalonians 5:2,4, 2Peter 3:10). Thus, both His Coming and the Start of the Day of the Lord are compared to the sudden arrival of a thief. This indicates that when Christ comes to rescue us in the Rapture, He will also come upon the unbelieving world as a thief, and will immediately initiate the Day of the Lord, and as a result the world will suffer great loss. Therefore, both the Rapture and the Start of the Tribulation are imminent, because they are simultaneous. We know Jesus originated the thief imagery, as it does not appear in the Old Testament or any extrabiblical Jewish literature. He used this new imagery to describe the new revelation of His imminent Coming, which was part of the mystery hidden in God. It follows that the apostles borrowed this imagery from Jesus, as they could not have got it from anywhere else. Therefore, consistent interpretation requires that all the mentions of His Coming as a THIEF refer to the same event – His imminent Coming before the Tribulation. Since this is clearly the case in 1Thessalonians 5, it follows that when Jesus used the thief imagery in Luke 12 and Matthew 24, He was talking about the same event.

So, the whole Parable of the imminent Coming of Christ (Luke 12:35-40) applies to both believers and unbelievers, and it shows that they will experience His Coming in 2 very different ways. For BELIEVERS, His imminent Coming will initiate a time of great BLESSING, but for UNBELIEVERS His same Coming will initiate a time of great destruction and LOSS. This is Dual Imminence. (1) For His own, His Coming to rescue and bless them is imminent, and (2) for the world (outside of Christ), His Coming to bring them into a time of judgment is imminent. These are clearly 2 aspects of the same Coming. Both (1) His Coming to His own to BLESS, and (2) His Coming as a thief to those who do not know Him, bringing sudden JUDGMENT, are IMMINENT, because it is the same Coming of Christ. Thus, at the same time that (1) Christ comes for His Church in the Rapture, He will also (2) initiate a time of world-wide Judgment, called the Day of the Lord or the Tribulation, which will come to its climax in the Great and Awesome Day of the Lord (the 2nd Coming), when He will be manifested in power and glory to the whole world. This Dual Imminence is only possible with a Pre-Tribulation Rapture, and it also means the Tribulation must begin on the Day of the Rapture.

v41: "Then Peter said to Him: "Lord, do You speak this PARABLE only to US (believers), or to ALL PEOPLE (both believers and unbelievers)?" Notice that Peter realises Luke 12:35-40 is one (2-sided) Parable revealing His imminent Coming, the 2 aspects being united by the single exhortation, in v40, to be ready, based on the imminence of His Return. Thus, he understands that the parables of the imminent return of a master to his house, and the imminent coming of a thief to a house, actually form 2 aspects of one Parable, since in both cases they describe the imminent Coming of Christ.   However, Peter asks for further clarification, because although Jesus has described how His imminent Coming will affect people in 2 different ways, he was not sure if He was talking about the impact of His Coming on 2 groups within the Church, or whether He had the whole world in view, with the 2 groups being the believers and the unbelievers. Thus, he is asking whether these events just affect believers, or whether they affect unbelievers also. In other words, were those who suffer loss at the hands of the thief, the unfaithful believers or the unbelievers? Also, if the answer is 'the unbelievers', the question then arises, 'what happens to unfaithful believers?' I have previously interpreted the Coming of Christ as a THIEF (v39), as describing the loss that UNBELIEVERS will experience, after Christ comes to remove His Church. This is clear from the change of imagery from Christ coming to His own House – the Church (v35-38), to Christ coming to someone else's house, as a thief (v39). This must apply to the world of unbelievers, who do not belong to Him in the way that believers do. In other words, the correct answer to Peter's question is: 'ALL PEOPLE'.

To confirm that this Parable of His imminent Coming applies to ALL PEOPLE, and to describe what happens to unfaithful servants in His House (who have not yet been discussed), Jesus next develops and expands His picture of the Master returning suddenly to His Household, describing 3 kinds of servant. He does this by describing 3 KINDS of SERVANT in His House: (1) the FAITHFUL BELIEVER, (2) the UNBELIEVER, who nevertheless is in God's House (the Church), and (3) the UNFAITHFUL BELIEVER.

*(1) The FAITHFUL BELIEVER is described in Luke 12:42-44: **"And the Lord said: "Who then is that faithful and wise STEWARD** (we are all stewards or managers of God's resources. We do not own anything, even ourselves - everything we have belongs to God), **whom his master will make RULER over his household, to give them their portion of food in due season? BLESSED is that SERVANT, whom his MASTER will find so DOING, when he COMES. Truly, I say to you that he will make him RULER over all that he has."**

This is an expansion of v35-38, which makes the important point that being ready, watching and waiting for His Coming is not a passive spiritual posture, but rather, looking for His Coming motivates us to faithful obedient service to God and people, as we live in the light of His imminent Coming. Moreover, Jesus now shares more about the BLESSING the faithful servant will receive at His Coming. Not only will He give them His approval (Matthew 25:21,23), and minister His grace to them in a special way (v37), He will give them greater authority and opportunity to serve Him in the future (v43-44). This reveals that at His Coming, He will judge His servants for rewards, based on how faithful they have been as stewards of His resources (time, money, gifts). This speaks of the Judgment Seat of Christ, which He develops in more detail in the Parables of the Talents and the Minas (Matthew 25:14-30, Luke 19:11-27). Since God is our Owner and the Owner of everything we have, one day when Jesus returns, we will have to give an account to Him, for how we have used His resources, that He has given us to steward. So, after Jesus comes in the Rapture, we will stand before Him, and He will judge us as His servants and stewards.

*(2) The UNBELIEVER in God's House is described in Luke 12:45-46: **"But if that servant says in his heart: 'My Master is DELAYING his COMING,' and begins to beat the male and female servants, and to eat and drink and be drunk, the Master** (Lord) **of that servant will come on a day, when he is not looking for him, and at an hour when he is not aware, and will cut him in 2, and appoint him his portion** (place) **with the UNBELIEVERS."**

Although this wicked servant is in the Master's House (the visible Church of Christ) and calls Jesus his Master (Lord), his lawless actions reveal his unregenerate heart (cf. Matthew 7:21-23). Although he has a profession of faith, in his heart, he is not submitted to Christ as Lord. He shows himself to be an UNBELIEVER by his abusive actions, and so Christ deals with him as an UNBELIEVER. This means he will be judged as an unbeliever, and appointed to go to the same place of Judgment, as all the other unbelievers (those who were not part of the Church). He will be cut off and cast out of His House and His Presence. In the light of later Scriptures, which teach that Christ's imminent Coming initiates the Day of the Lord, a time of judgment on unbelievers, I believe that the judgment on this unbelieving servant will initially be that he will go into the Tribulation, to face the judgments of the Day of the Lord, along with all the other unbelievers (see also Matthew 24:48-51). Thus, at His Coming, all unbelievers (whether or not they call themselves Christians) will find themselves under the severe judgments of the Tribulation. This means he (like the rest of the unbelievers) will still have a short time to repent, before it is too late. But if he does not repent in the Tribulation; when he dies, either during the Tribulation, or at its close when Christ returns to remove all the wicked from the earth, he will then face his final judgment of being eternally cut off from God's goodness.

One manifestation of his lack of faith is his denial of the Lord's teaching that His Coming is imminent, saying instead that: 'He delays His Coming' – a direct contradiction of imminence. Jesus described this denial of imminence as a key factor leading to his unrestrained behaviour. This illustrates the positive power of the teaching of imminence, for it motivates us to get right with God, overcome the flesh and live holy lives, knowing that at any moment Jesus might return, and then we will have to stand before Him and give an account for our lives. The denial of imminence opens the door to the flesh, deceiving us into thinking we can repent at leisure. Notice that just as His Coming to bless His faithful servants is described as imminent (v35-38), so His Coming to judge unbelievers is also described as imminent (v45-46), for the unbeliever's disbelief in imminence was shown to be false. Again, we see the teaching of Dual Imminence.

Although in Luke 12:45-46 Jesus only directly discussed the result of His Coming on unbelievers in His House (Church), in so doing, He also revealed the fact that the rest of the unbelievers will suffer the same fate as this wicked servant. In this way, Jesus revealed that His imminent Coming will initiate a time of judgment on all unbelievers, which answered Peter's question in v41 about whether His Parable described the effect of His imminent Coming on unbelievers, as well as on believers. In this amplification in v45-46, He confirms His teaching in v39, that His imminent Coming will affect ALL PEOPLE, for He is coming both (1) to bless His own (in the Rapture), and (2) to bring judgment on all unbelievers (by initiating the Day of the Lord on the earth). It now remains for Him to describe what will happen to unfaithful servants, who are nevertheless born-again believers.

*(3) The UNFAITHFUL BELIEVER is described in Luke 12:47-48: **"And that servant who KNEW his Master's WILL, and did NOT PREPARE himself or DO according to his WILL, shall be beaten with MANY STRIPES. But he who did NOT KNOW** (his Master's WILL)**, yet committed things deserving of stripes, shall be beaten with FEW. For everyone to whom much is given, from him much will be required; and to whom much has been committed, of him they will ask the more."**

This describes a different kind of servant. Again, he is unfaithful, but his sin is omission rather than commission – he does not abuse others, but he is lazy and does not do what the master called him to do. He is not cast out of the House, like the other servant (the unbeliever), but he does suffer temporary pain in being corrected for his laziness (rather than rejection and permanent condemnation). This speaks of the Judgment Seat of Christ, where we must all give an account for our life as God's servants. This does not result in permanent condemnation and casting out of God's Kingdom, but for many it will involve a painful correction, as their lives are reviewed and compared to what they should have done. The lashes speak of the corrective revelation and words of Jesus, which will sting (also 1Corinthians 3:13-15), before He wipes away all the tears from their eyes (Revelation 21:4). However, the unfaithful servants will suffer loss of eternal rewards. Thus, after the Rapture, all believers will stand before His Judgment

Seat, where we must all give an account for our life as God's servants (Romans 14:10, 2 Corinthians 5:10), and receive our eternal rewards.

In conclusion, the Parables of Luke 12:35-48 reveal DUAL IMMINENCE, namely that His Coming is imminent, both (1) to bless her in the Rapture and judge her for rewards at His Judgment Seat, and at the same time (2) to render judgment to the unbelievers by casting them into the Tribulation. Dual Imminence means His Coming will affect all people - for believers it will mean eternal blessing, but for the rest it will mean entering into the judgments of the Day of the Lord. The 2 parables of (1) the master's imminent return to his house, and (2) the thief's imminent coming to a house, form one dual Parable, for both describe Christ's imminent Coming of. The coming of the master to bless His servants, who are watching for His Return (v35-38), describes the experience of believers, but the coming of the thief, to bring loss (v39), describes the experience of unbelievers at Christ's Return. In both cases, His Coming is imminent (v40).

LUKE 17

The next prophetic teaching of Jesus is in <u>Luke 17:22-37</u>, where He describes both the Rapture and the 2nd Coming, and events in the Tribulation. Since, in Luke 17, Jesus does not always follow a strict chronological order, it will be occasionally necessary to compare these verses with their parallel verses in Matthew 24, to gain clarity on their exact timing.

<u>Luke 17:22</u>: **"Then He said to the disciples, "The days will come when you will desire to see ONE of the DAYS of the Son of Man, and you will not see it."** This shows that there are more than one DAY when Christ will return. The 2 DAYS of Christ's RETURN are (1) the RAPTURE, when He comes to the air for His Church, and (2) the 2nd COMING to the earth.

<u>Luke 17:23-24</u>: **"And they will say to you: 'Look here!' or 'Look there!' Do not go after them or follow them. For as the lightning that flashes out of one part under heaven shines to the other part under heaven, so also the Son of Man will be in His DAY** (of the 2nd Coming)." This describes the 2nd Coming at the end of the Tribulation (Matthew 24:27,30).

Having described the 2nd Coming in power and glory, in <u>Luke 17:25</u>, Jesus then went back in time to the START of the CHURCH AGE: **"But FIRST, He** (the Son of Man) **must suffer many things and be rejected by this generation** (of Israel)."

Then in <u>Luke 17:26-27</u>, Jesus goes forward in time to the END of the CHURCH AGE, comparing it to the DAYS of NOAH before the FLOOD: **"And as it was in the DAYS of NOAH, so it will be also in the DAYS of the SON of MAN** (leading up to His Coming). **They ate, they drank, they married wives, they were**

given in marriage, until the DAY that Noah entered the Ark, and the FLOOD came and destroyed them all" (also Matthew 24:37-39).

The FLOOD was a world-wide JUDGMENT of God, that came upon all UNBELIEVERS. As such, it is a type of the TRIBULATION, which all UNBELIEVERS will have to endure. In this passage the Flood is described as coming suddenly, when life was going on as normal on the earth, with no warning signs, taking the world by surprise. Jesus said it will be like that in the days leading up to the initial phase of His Coming – life will be going on as normal and then suddenly the Tribulation-Flood will overtake them, and all unbelievers will be destroyed by the end of the Tribulation (however, they will have a final chance to repent in the Tribulation, and become believers and so be saved). So, first of all, Luke 17:26-27 tells us that onset of the end-time worldwide judgment (the Day of the Lord) is imminent - it will suddenly overtake the world, without any signs coming first, just as the Flood suddenly overtook them in the days of Noah.

In the parallel passage in Matthew 24:37-39, the sudden unexpected coming of the FLOOD is related to the imminent COMING of Christ: **"As the days of Noah were, so also will the COMING of the SON of MAN be. For as in the days before the FLOOD, they were eating and drinking, marrying and giving in marriage, until the day that Noah entered the Ark, and did not know until the FLOOD came and took them all away, so also will the COMING of the SON of MAN be."** Compare Luke 17:26: **"As it was in the DAYS of NOAH, so it will be also in the DAYS of the SON of MAN"** and Matthew 24:37: **"As the DAYS of NOAH were, so also will the COMING of the SON of MAN be."** Comparing these passages reveals that the world-wide judgment of the Day of the Lord (the Tribulation-Flood) is initiated by a Coming of the Lord. This cannot be the same as the Coming of the Lord at the end of the Tribulation to bring this time of worldwide judgment to its climax and close. Thus, the Coming of Christ to initiate the worldwide Tribulation-Flood is imminent; it will happen suddenly, without preceding signs or any special warning, while normal life is going on in the world.

Jesus is comparing the world-wide judgment of the FLOOD to the whole TRIBULATION, NOT merely to the judgments at the 2nd COMING of CHRIST (at the end of the Tribulation). In other words, the DAY of the LORD is the whole TRIBULATION, not just the 2nd Coming. Those who limit the time of Divine judgment and wrath (the Day of the Lord) to the 2nd Coming, ignore the fact that the whole Tribulation is a time of judgment (Revelation 6-19).

The FLOOD was an extended period of world-wide judgment over 40 days, 150 days, or a year, depending on how you measure it. It was not limited to a single day, when the rain began to fall. Likewise, the whole TRIBULATION is an extended period of world-wide judgment, lasting at least 7 years, and concluding with the 2nd Coming. This is made perfectly clear by John in Revelation 6-19. The 2nd Coming of Christ, the Great and Awesome Day of the Lord (Revelation 19) brings this extended time of worldwide judgment, the Day of the Lord, to its close (Revelation 6-18), whereas Matthew 24:37-39 speaks of a Coming of Christ, which initiates this time of end-time worldwide judgment, corresponding to the Flood. Thus, this cannot be talking about the 2nd Coming. So, there's a Coming of Christ to initiate the Tribulation, as well as a Coming of Christ to end it. We could summarise this by saying there are 2 phases to the 2nd Coming. First, Christ comes to the air to rescue His Church in the Rapture (1Thessalonians 4:16-17), and then after a time of world-wide judgment, He comes to the earth in power and glory to establish His Kingdom here (Zechariah 14).

Ignoring the distinction between His Coming to initiate the judgments of the Tribulation, and His Coming in power and glory at its close, results in contradictions, impossible to reconcile.

*(1) His 2nd Coming will be signposted by the events of the Tribulation, as Jesus outlined in Matthew 24:7-31, and moreover it will be knowable (predictable) in terms of its timing. In the context of events directly leading up to the 2nd Coming, Jesus gave the Sign of the Abomination of Desolation, pointing us to Daniel for further understanding (Matthew 24:15), who tells us that this will happen in the middle of the final 7 years (Daniel 9:27). Daniel 12 gives even more exact information: **"How long shall the fulfilment of these wonders be?"** (Daniel 12:6). The answer given was: **"From the time the Abomination of Desolation is set up** (in the Temple)**, there shall be 1,290 days"** (v11). Therefore, the 2nd Coming is NOT IMMINENT, whereas the Coming of Christ, that Jesus described in Luke 17:26-27 and Matthew 24:36-44, which initiates the final period of world-wide judgment, corresponding to Noah's Flood, is IMMINENT. Whereas the 2nd Coming will be preceded by many signs, and will be knowable for those living at that time, Jesus introduced a revelation, not revealed before, about a Coming of Christ, before this time of judgment, that will have no signs, but will be unknowable, and therefore imminent. This distinction is consistently upheld in later Scriptures, which describe His imminent Coming in the Rapture for (to rescue) His Church, before releasing His wrath, for we are not appointed to wrath, but salvation through our Lord Jesus Christ (1Thessalonians 5:9).

*(2) The situation on earth, described by Jesus in Luke 17:26-30 and Matthew 24:37-39, before the sudden outpouring of the end-time world-wide judgment, initiated by His Coming, and symbolised by the Flood, is totally

different from the situation on earth leading up to the 2nd Coming (Matthew 24:7-31, Revelation 6-18). Before this flood of judgment is poured out, life will be going on as normal, but before the 2nd Coming, life is anything but not going on as normal, with the 7 Seals, the 7 Trumpets, and the 7 Bowls of Wrath poured out, followed by Armageddon. Jesus even said mankind will be on the brink of extinction (Matthew 24:22).

So, the first truth revealed by Luke 17:26-27 and Matthew 24:37-39 is the imminence of His Coming to initiate the world-wide judgment of the Day of the Lord. The second truth is that just before He initiates this judgment, He will rescue His own by removing them from the scene of judgment. He points out that on the very same day as the Flood, immediately before it fell, all the believers were removed from the scene of judgment into the safety of the Ark (Genesis 7:11-13), above the waters of judgment, and then the Flood was released upon the earth. He then said: **"so also will the COMING of the SON of MAN be"** (Matthew 24:37,39). Thus, He connects both the rescue of the righteous and the release of wrath on the unrighteous with an imminent Coming of Christ. Therefore, Jesus will come to rescue His own from the world, and to release His wrath upon the world. So, this is a picture of the Church being taken from the scene of judgment (the earth) into Christ (our Ark of Salvation), who will return to the air (above the earth), to receive us to Himself in the Rapture, just before He releases the judgments of the Tribulation upon the earth, on the very same day. Thus, again we see Dual Imminence in these verses, for both (1) His Coming to remove His own from the earth in the Rapture, and (2) His Coming to release the judgments of the Day of the Lord on the earth, are imminent, because they essentially happen at the same time – the Tribulation will start on the same day as the Rapture, just as the Flood started on the same day that Noah entered into the Ark.

So, the TRIBULATION will start suddenly, just like the FLOOD, initiated by Christ's COMING, when He will simultaneously RESCUE His own from the scene of judgment (in the RAPTURE), just as Noah's family were rescued by going into the Ark at the same time the Flood fell. This is Dual Imminence. We will see that Peter, in his epistles, uses this analogy of the Flood, introduced by Jesus, as the main focus of his end-time teaching, and confirms this new revelation introduced by Jesus, of His imminent Coming to rescue us before the Day of the Lord.

Jesus then reinforced the fact that the Day of the Lord is imminent and that all believers will be removed from the earth (the scene of judgment), just before the Tribulation judgments fall from Heaven in Luke 17:28-30: **"Likewise, as it was also in the DAYS of LOT: They ate, they drank, they bought, they sold,**

they planted, they built; but on the (same) **DAY that LOT WENT OUT of Sodom it rained Fire and Brimstone from Heaven and destroyed them all. Even so, will it be in the DAY when the SON of MAN is REVEALED** (comes).**"** Thus, the events surrounding His Revelation (Coming) will be parallel to what happened in the days of Lot, just as they were parallel to what happened in the days of Noah.

The analogy of Lot's escape from judgment reinforces the same lessons as Noah's rescue from the Flood, and they complement each other perfectly. The type of Noah's Flood tells us that the Day of the Lord is a world-wide judgment, whereas the type of Lot's escape from Sodom before God's wrath fell upon Sodom, makes it clear that God will provide an escape for His own by removing them from the scene of judgment (the earth), before He releases His wrath on the whole world (rather than keeping the righteous in the world, and protecting them from this wrath). The analogy of Lot also provides other details that correspond to the Rapture. Just as the Lord (Christ) came with His angels and appeared to Abraham (Genesis 18:1), and rescued Lot from Sodom, before releasing judgment on Sodom (Genesis 18-19), so likewise He will appear to His own, coming with His angels to rescue us from this world, before the Tribulation starts (1Thessalonians 1:10, 4:14-17). This confirms what we saw in Matthew 24:37,39, that the rescue of God's people, immediately followed by the release from God's wrath, happens in connection with an Appearance (Coming) of the Lord, which indicates that one of the purposes of this Coming is to rescue His own. Jesus affirmed this truth explicitly, when He said: **"even so, will it be in the day when the SON of MAN is REVEALED"** (v30). Moreover, Genesis 18 provides the theological basis why Lot had to be rescued from the scene of judgment before God's wrath fell, which also explains why the Rapture must come before the Tribulation, for Abraham pleaded with God: **"Far be it from You to do such a thing as this, to slay the righteous with the wicked, so that the righteous should be as the wicked; far be it from You! Shall not the Judge of all the earth do right?"** (v25). As Abraham pointed out in his prayer, it would be unrighteous of God to pour out His judgment on the righteous, along with the wicked, and God agreed with him, and so answered his prayer by arranging Lot's rescue (19:29). Likewise, it would be unrighteous for God to pour out His wrath on His Church, who are justified by faith and delivered from the wrath of God (Romans 5:9), and so He will arrange a rescue for us, by sending His Son with His angels to rescue us, before the Tribulation judgments fall, for we are not appointed to wrath (1Thessalonians 1:10, 4:14-17, 5:9), just as in the days of Lot.

Notice that Jesus again emphasised the sudden and unexpected nature of the judgment on Sodom. Life was going on as normal; there were no warning signs, until they were taken totally by surprise by the fiery judgment that suddenly fell from above, so that they could not escape. Also, as with Noah, He pointed to the fact that God provided a rescue for the believers, by removing them from the scene of judgment, immediately before He released His wrath, so that the rescue and the initiation of His judgment took place on the same day. In fact, as soon as Lot was clear from the judgment zone, God released His wrath upon Sodom (Genesis 19:22-25), as what happened to Lot's wife makes clear (v26). So again, we see Dual Imminence, that as in the days of Lot, both the rescue in the Rapture and the wrath of the Day of the Lord take place on the same day, and in such a way that they are both imminent.

In making His prophetic application, He declared: **"As it was also in the DAYS of LOT … even so, will it be in the DAY, when the SON of MAN is REVEALED"** (Luke 17:28,30). Notice in this analogy, He connects the imminent outpouring of Divine Wrath and the simultaneous Divine Rescue with a Revelation or Appearance of Himself to His own.   This agrees with the corresponding statement: **"so also will the COMING of the SON of MAN be"** (Matthew 24:37,39) in Noahic analogy. Thus, the Tribulation will be initiated by a COMING of Christ, when He will REVEAL Himself to His own (but not to the world) and RESCUE them, by removing them from the scene of judgment. So, the very same day when Jesus COMES to rescue us in the Rapture, He will release His Tribulation judgments on the earth, and both events are imminent – they will suddenly happen without warning, while normal life is going on.

Then, in Luke 17:34-36, Jesus described this RESCUE of the righteous at His COMING, who will be TAKEN from the scene of judgment (the earth), just like Lot: **"I tell you, in that night there will be 2 men in one bed: the one will be TAKEN** (to safety) **and the other will be LEFT** (to go through the Tribulation). **2 women will be grinding together: the one will be TAKEN and the other LEFT. 2 men will be in the field: the one will be TAKEN and the other LEFT."** This is a dramatic description of the RAPTURE of the saints. When we study the parallel verses in Matthew 24:40-41, I will give further justification why those 'taken' are the believers in the Rapture. This is another picture of IMMINENCE, showing that people will be going about their normal lives, totally unaware of what is about to happen, when suddenly the believers will be rescued (taken) by the Rapture, leaving the rest to go into the Day of the Lord.

Luke 17:31-33 are parenthetical verses, which describe the escape of Israel at Mid-Tribulation, which is made clear by the parallel verses in Matthew 24:15-21. We are justified in connecting Luke 17:34-36 with Luke 17:26-30, as both describing events at the same time (His Coming at the Start of the Tribulation), by comparison with the parallel passage in Matthew 24:37-41, where Matthew 24:37-39 corresponds to Luke 17:26-30, and Matthew 24:40-41 corresponds to Luke 17:34-36. Matthew 24:40 makes it clear that the event of Matthew 24:40-41 takes place on the same day as the event described in Matthew 24:37-39, through the use of the word 'THEN': **"THEN 2 men will be in the field: one will be taken and the other left."** It follows that Luke 17:34-36 takes place on the same day as Luke 17:26-30. Thus, having revealed the simultaneous rescue of the saints and release of wrath at His Coming (v26-30), He described what this rescue will look like in v34-36, as Christ suddenly removes all the living saints from the earth in the Rapture. Christ's description of the Rapture here is the basis for Paul's description in 1Thessalonians 4:15-17 (which is why Paul says what He is revealing is in accordance with the Word (teaching) of the Lord Jesus in v15). Both Jesus and Paul describe the same event - the sudden Coming of Christ to receive His people to Himself. Whereas Jesus described it as it will be seen by an outside observer, Paul described from the viewpoint and experience of the believer. Jesus also described this escape from earth into the Presence of Christ, just before the Start of the Tribulation in Luke 21:34-36.

Jesus' prophetic talk concludes with Luke 17:37: **"And they answered and said to Him, "WHERE, Lord?" So, He said to them: "WHEREVER the body** (carcass) **is, there the vultures will be gathered together."** This enigmatic saying creates much speculation. To interpret it correctly, we must compare it to its parallel verse in Matthew 24:28, which tells us that its timing is the 2nd Coming at the end of the Tribulation (v27): **"As the lightning comes from the east and flashes to the west, so also will the Coming of the Son of Man be. For WHEREVER the carcass is, there the vultures will be gathered together"** (Matthew 24:27-28). Therefore, it describes the location of the 2nd Coming. Matthew 24:27-28 tells us that the question and answer in Luke 17:37 is connected to Luke 17:24: **"As the lightning that flashes out of one part under heaven shines to the other part under heaven, so also the Son of Man will be in His day"**, which was His original description of the 2nd Coming at the start of the talk.

So, in v37 the disciples changed the subject from the Pre-Tribulation Rapture to the 2nd Coming, by asking a question about the great event Jesus described at the start of this talk in v24. This question was: *"WHERE will Christ return to earth at His 2nd Coming?"* But, in giving His answer, why does He talk about the vultures descending on a carcass? What is the meaning of this imagery, and how does relate to the 2nd Coming? Now, we know the answer to this question is Israel (Zechariah 14:2-4, Revelation 16:16), because Christ comes to save His elect nation (Matthew 24:22), as she calls on Him to return as her Messiah-King (Matthew 23:37-39), and deliver her from imminent destruction in the Battle of Armageddon, when all the armies of the world will be gathered by antichrist to destroy Israel (Revelation 16:12-16). It follows that the carcass is Israel and the vultures are the armies of antichrist, gathered to consume her. So, this is necessarily where Jesus will return to destroy these armies and deliver His elect nation. This is the initial revelation of Armageddon, which is revealed more fully in Revelation. When the vultures (antichrist's armies) gather to eat the carcass (Israel), which is on the point of death, this requires Jesus to return to Israel to save her from the vultures (Revelation 14:18-20, 19:11-21).

So now, we can understand the overall structure of Luke 17:22-37. In describing the days of the Son of Man (v22), Jesus started with what they were particularly interested in, and what they already understood from the Old Testament - His Coming in power and glory to establish His Kingdom on earth (v23-24). Then He went back in time to describe the sequence of events leading up to the 2nd Coming, starting with His 1st Coming and the start of the Church Age (v25), then the end of the Church Age, Rapture and Tribulation (v26-36), until finally returning to the 2nd Coming, in response to His disciples' question: **"WHERE, Lord?"** (v37) - referring to His 2nd Coming (v24), the climactic event of His talk. In order to explain the location of the 2nd Coming, He connects it to the War of Armageddon, which will threaten Israel's existence (v37).

The OLIVET DISCOURSE (Matthew 24, Luke 21, Mark 13)

Later Jesus reinforced His end-time teaching in the Olivet Discourse. Matthew 24:1-3 tells us the setting: **"Then Jesus went out and departed from the Temple, and His disciples came up to show Him the buildings of the Temple. And Jesus said to them: "Do you not see all these things? Assuredly, I say to you, not one stone shall be left here upon another, that shall not be thrown down." Now as He sat on the Mount of Olives, the disciples came to Him privately, saying: "Tell us, (1) when will these things** (the destruction of the Temple) **be, and what will be the SIGN (2) of Your COMING, and (3) of the END** (suntelia - consummation) **of the AGE** (the Tribulation)**?"**

The Olivet Discourse is Christ's answer to these 3 Questions. Matthew does not record His answer to the first Question concerning the destruction of the Temple, but Luke does. Luke 21:7 gives the full question: **"Teacher, when will these things be? And what SIGN will there be when these things are about to take place?"** Then Luke 21:20-24 records Christ's answer.

Questions 2 and 3 are two different questions, but they are phrased grammatically to express the fact that they can be seen as one compound question. In other words, the disciples understood there was a close relationship between the two events in question – His Coming and the End of the Age (the Day of the Lord). As we have seen, they knew from the Old Testament that leading up to the Coming of the Messiah in power and glory, there would be a time of Divine Judgment and Trouble (Tribulation), also described as the Birth Pains of Messiah, and the End *(suntelia)* of the Age. So, the answer to Question 2, the SIGNS of His 2nd Coming, is the events of the End of the Age. Then Question 3, which is about the SIGN of 'the End of the Age' is a different question, requiring a different answer.

The term 'the END of the AGE' is generally misunderstood. The word translated 'end' is *sun-telia*, which means the closing period or consummation, rather than the final end *(telos)*. *Sun-telia* literally means *'with the end'* – the period associated with the final end. This naturally points to the Tribulation, whose end *(telos)* is the 2nd Coming. This is confirmed by its origins in the Old Testament, where the Tribulation is described in detail from Daniel 11:35b – 12:11, and the name used most for this time is 'the Time of the End' (Daniel 11:35,40, 12:1,4,9). In fact, the way God signifies that the prophecy is moving from describing events before Christ, which have now been fulfilled (11:1-35a), to describing the future Tribulation (especially the activity of the antichrist) is by saying: **"The Time of the End - because it is still for the appointed time"** (v35b). In the Septuagint (the translation into Greek), the word used for 'end' in all these verses is *suntelia*, signifying the closing period of the Age, leading up to Messiah's Return. Therefore, when Jesus talked about 'the End of the Age' (Matthew 24:3), the disciples knew He was talking about the Tribulation. This is confirmed perfectly by Jesus' previous description of 'the End of the Age' in the Parable of the Wheat and the Tares (Matthew 13:39-40,49), where He distinguishes 'the End of the Age' from the Church Age. Whereas the Church Age would not be the time when the Tares (unbelievers) are judged (v28-29), the End of the Age would be like the harvest-time (v30), a time of Divine Judgement, especially through His angels, by the end of which all the tares would be thrown into His fire: **"the Harvest is the End of the Age, and the reapers are the angels. Therefore, as the tares are gathered and burned in the fire, so it will be at the End of this Age"** (v39-40). This description of Divine Judgment through angels perfectly agrees with Revelation's account of the Tribulation. Thus, the End of the Age is the same period of time as the Tribulation and the Day of the Lord (the time of judgment).

Christ's Answer to Question 2 – The Signs of His 2nd Coming (Matthew 24:7-35)

In answering Question 2, in Matthew 24:3, Jesus first described the sequence of events of the END or CONSUMMATION of the AGE (the Tribulation), which will lead up to His COMING in power and glory (v7-31). In so doing, He confirmed that this Coming is not imminent, but signposted. He compared this period of time (the End of the Age) to the BIRTH PAINS suffered by a woman about to give birth: **"Nation will rise against nation, and kingdom against kingdom** (a Hebrew idiom for world-war). **And there will be famines, pestilences, and earthquakes in various places** (world-wide). **All these are the BEGINNING of SORROWS** (literally: BIRTH PAINS)" (v7-8). There will be a time of BIRTH PAINS leading up to the BIRTH (the MANIFESTATION of CHRIST and His KINGDOM on earth at His 2nd Coming. It is clear that Jesus equates this time of world-wide BIRTH PAINS leading up to the 2nd Coming, when the Kingdom of God is BORN (manifested) on the earth, with the END of the AGE – the Consummation or final Period of the Age. Comparing this time to birth pains at the end (consummation) of a pregnancy paints the picture of a succession of painful events (judgments), that not only continue, but increase in intensity and come closer and closer together, until the end when the Kingdom of God is manifested on the earth. As a woman must endure the whole period of labour before giving birth, so Israel and the nations must endure the whole Tribulation until Christ returns. There is no escape. Jesus' description of the Tribulation paints the very same picture. First, by using the phrase: **"All these are the BEGINNING of BIRTH PAINS"** (v8), Jesus was indicating that the events at the start and in the first half of the Tribulation are merely the 'beginning', with the expectation of greater birth pangs in the 2nd half of the Tribulation (which He called 'the Great Tribulation' - v21). Thus, the whole Tribulation is like Birth Pains. As there are 2 phases of Birth Pains (the beginning labour and then the full labour), so the Tribulation is divided between the less severe and the more severe expressions of Divine Wrath.

Jesus also described this time as a special time of TRIBULATION, that would increasingly get worse and ultimately turn into the GREAT TRIBULATION: **"Then they will deliver you up to TRIBULATION and kill you, and you will be hated by all nations for My Name's sake... For then there will be GREAT TRIBULATION, such as has not been since the beginning of the world until this time, no, nor ever shall be"** (v9,21). The Olivet Discourse (Matthew 24) describes the continual worsening conditions as the Tribulation progresses, so that mankind will even be in danger of extinction (v22). Finally, the Great Tribulation will be brought to an end by the Return of Christ. So just as natural birth pains intensify, until they are brought to an end by the delivery (manifestation) of the baby, the Tribulation will wax increasingly worse, until it is brought to an end by the glorious manifestation of Christ, delivering the world from its birth pains: **"Immediately after** (or: 'at the close of') **the TRIBULATION of those days the sun will be darkened, and the moon will not give its light... Then the sign of the Son**

of Man will appear in Heaven, and then all the tribes of the earth will mourn, and they will see the Son of Man coming on the clouds of Heaven with power and great glory" (v29-30). At His RETURN, He will be manifested in glory and personally establish His KINGDOM on earth, which corresponds to the BIRTH.

Our word 'tribulation' translates the Greek word *thlipsis*, which is used to describe the anguish of childbirth. It was used that way by Jesus Himself in <u>John 16:21</u>: **"A woman, when she is in LABOUR** (Birth Pains), **has sorrow because her hour has come; but as soon as she has given birth to the child, she no longer remembers the ANGUISH** (*thlipsis* - tribulation), **for joy that a human being has been born into the world."** Thus, the 2 phrases used by Jesus to describe this time: TRIBULATION (*thlipsis*) and 'LABOUR PAINS' are related. Thus, we could call (1) the Tribulation, and (2) the Great Tribulation, (1) the Travail (the beginning of birth pains), and (2) the Great Travail (the time of being in full labour). Thus, we see Jesus' teaching is consistent with the Old Testament, based on which, the Jews refer to this time as the Birth Pains of the Messiah. This same continual escalation of judgments over time until the 2nd Coming is described in Revelation 6-19, with the 7th Trumpet initiating the Great Tribulation.

Paul agrees with Jesus. In <u>1Thessalonians 5:2-3</u>, he equated this unique time of BIRTH PAINS, when destruction suddenly comes upon the whole earth, with the DAY of the LORD, showing the Day of the Lord is NOT limited to the 2nd Coming of Christ, but describes the whole period of worldwide judgment leading up to the 2nd Coming: **"The DAY of the LORD so comes as a THIEF in the night. For when they** (unbelievers) **say: "Peace and safety!", then SUDDEN DESTRUCTION** (ruin) **comes upon them** (unbelievers), **as LABOUR PAINS on a pregnant woman. And they shall not escape."** The impossibility of escape reveals it is a worldwide judgment. Sudden ruin will overtake the world, when the Day of the Lord suddenly comes upon them like a thief. This beginning of the DAY of the LORD is compared to the sudden onset of LABOUR PAINS, the same description used elsewhere in the Bible for the unique time of Tribulation that comes immediately before Messiah's Manifestation in glory.

Therefore, the DAY of the LORD (the time of Divine Wrath) is the same as the time of BIRTH PAINS at the END of the AGE, the time-period known as the TRIBULATION. This is further confirmed by Revelation. After promising the true Church deliverance **"from the HOUR of TRIAL** (Tribulation), **which shall come upon the whole world, to test those who dwell on the earth"** (3:10), it then describes in great detail this future unique time of the Tribulation in Revelation 6-19. It is clearly a time of Divine Judgment, because Christ initiates it from Heaven, by breaking the first 6 Seals in quick succession (Revelation 6). As this time-period continues the judgments from Heaven continue and intensify through the 7 Trumpets and 7 Bowls, until the glorious manifestation of Messiah and His Kingdom at the 2nd Coming (Revelation 19), just as normal birth pains continue and intensify until the birth (manifestation) of the baby.

Thus Revelation 6-19 describe the DAY of the LORD. Moreover, the results released upon the earth by the first 6 SEALS, which are opened at the Start of the Tribulation, correspond exactly to Jesus' description of the BIRTH PAINS of the Tribulation (Matthew 24:7-13). This confirms that the time of Birth Pains or Travail, the Tribulation, is also the Day of the Lord, when God moves in judgment. Therefore, this is not just a time of great evil, suffering and persecution, but a time of Divine Judgment and Wrath. It is this aspect of Divine Judgment, which primarily differentiates the Tribulation from the Church Age. Thus, the Bible's terminology and teaching on the Day of the Lord, Tribulation, End of the Age, and Birth Pains is fully consistent.

In Matthew 24:7-30, Christ described the events of the Tribulation, leading up to His 2nd Coming (v30), which together constitute the signs of the 2nd Coming, in answer to Question 2. Then in v31, He completed His description of the 2nd Coming by describing what He will do once He has returned to Jerusalem – He will regather all Israel from the ends of the earth by blowing a Great Trumpet in fulfilment of Isaiah 27:12-13.

The Parable of the Fig Tree and all the Trees

Then Luke 21:28-33 and Matthew 24:32-35 give His concluding comments about the SIGNS leading up to His 2nd COMING. Luke 21:28: **"Now when these THINGS BEGIN to HAPPEN, look up and lift up your heads, because your REDEMPTION** (the salvation of the elect, Israel, at the Return of Christ) **draws NEAR."** These must be signs of the 2nd Coming, not the Rapture, because the Rapture has no signs – it is ever imminent. There is a deliberate ambiguity here. These THINGS must refer to all the conditions in the TRIBULATION that He had just been describing. When these things BEGIN to happen could either refer to (1) their beginning at the Start of the Tribulation, or to (2) their beginning (origin) in events that take place BEFORE the Tribulation, which help to set the stage for the End of the Age. In this case, certain world-conditions will arise before the Tribulation, which will come to their fullness in the Tribulation, and so these are end-time signs (before the Tribulation) of the approach of the 2nd Coming. A classic example of one of these signs (or world-conditions) is the regathering and rebirth of Israel as a nation in her land (the Fig Tree putting forth its leaves – v29), which is necessary to set the stage for the Tribulation prophecies to be fulfilled. Now, living as we do in the end-times near the End of the Age, we know that the

Sign of the Fig Tree has appeared (in 1948), as well as other end-time signs, and yet the Tribulation has not yet begun. Therefore, we now know that the BEGINNING (origin) of the THINGS (world conditions) in the Tribulation came forth in the time before the Tribulation. However, it did not have to happen that way. For example, Israel's Rebirth could have happened after the Rapture (I show later in this book that the Tribulation is not necessarily limited to Daniel's 70th Week, which is just its last 7 years – thus the length of the time between the Rapture and 2nd Coming is unknown). Had Christ revealed clearly that certain Signs, such as the Sign of the Fig Tree (Israel), must take place before the Rapture and Start of the Tribulation, then these would no longer be imminent, which in turn would contradict many other Scriptures. Therefore, the reason for the ambiguity was to preserve the imminence of the Rapture, which means it could happen at any time, independent of world-conditions, as it is a sign-less event.

Then, Jesus compared these SIGNS (these THINGS) to TREES, and used them to set a time-limit for when He would return to establish His Kingdom on earth. Luke 21:29-33: **"Then He spoke to them a Parable: "Look at the FIG TREE, and ALL the TREES. When they are already BUDDING, you see and know for yourselves that SUMMER is now NEAR. So, you also, when you see THESE THINGS happening, know that the KINGDOM of GOD** (established at the 2nd Coming) **is NEAR. Assuredly, I say to you, this generation** (that see these signs) **will by no means pass away till ALL THINGS** (the events of the Tribulation) **take place. Heaven and earth will pass away, but My words will by no means pass away."**

Matthew's version is similar, but puts particular emphasis on one SIGN of special importance – the FIG TREE: **"Now learn the Parable of the FIG TREE: When its branch has already become tender and puts forth leaves** (in SPRING)**, you know that SUMMER is NEAR. So, you also, when you see all THESE THINGS** (beginning to happen)**, know that it** (the Kingdom of God) **is NEAR—at the doors! Assuredly, I say to you, this generation** (that see these signs) **will by no means pass away till ALL THESE THINGS take place. Heaven and earth will pass away, but My words will by no means pass away"** (Matthew 24:32-35).

By comparing these SIGNS to TREES, He is making it clear that He's referring to WORLD-CONDITIONS, which develop over time, rather than to one-off events. (This explains why Jesus said: **"when these things BEGIN to HAPPEN"** – Luke 21:28). He is saying that these world-conditions function as signs, in the same way as trees function as signs. They put forth their leaves and bud in the Spring, and then bear fruit in the Summer (the Tribulation), which then are harvested, when they are ripe (which corresponds to the 2nd Coming, at the end of the Tribulation). In this way, the putting forth of leaves in the Spring is a sign of the soon-coming Summer and the time of fruit harvest. Moreover, just as we know, from the budding of trees in Spring, roughly how long it will be until the fruit harvest, so we can know from the appearance of certain world-conditions something about the timing of the 2nd Coming of Christ.

The classic example of this is the main sign that Jesus focuses on - Israel, the Fig Tree (see Luke 13:6-9, where Jesus gives the first part of the Parable of the Fig Tree, and identifies it as Israel). In Matthew 24:32 and Luke 21:29, He completes the Parable of the Fig Tree, and predicts that in the end-times, the Fig Tree that was cut down (as a nation) and removed from her land in first century, for not bearing the fruit of faith (Luke 13:6-9), will be planted again and initially put forth leaves, but not fruit. This agrees with many prophecies about the initial Regathering of Israel to her land in unbelief in the last days. Having witnessed its fulfilment in 1948, we now know that the beginning of this Sign of the Fig Tree took place before the Tribulation. In other words, we are living in the springtime of this Parable – the last days of the Church Age before the Tribulation. It follows that the next season (summer) must represent the Tribulation (a time of great heat). Indeed, we know from Scripture, that Israel will come to faith (start to bear fruit) in the Tribulation, and by the end of the Tribulation this fruit will be fully ripe ("all Israel will be saved" – Romans 11:26), and ready for ingathering at Christ's 2nd Coming. In this way, the appearance of the Fig Tree in 1948, putting forth its leaves, is the major Sign that we are living near the end of the Church Age (in Spring), with the start of the Tribulation (Summer) drawing near, which is also confirmed by the appearance of a number of other Signs (Trees) – see Part 1 for more detail. So, we are in Spring, the season immediately before the Summer (Tribulation).

The fact that the Trees represent world-conditions which develop over a significant time (compared to seasons of the year), and the fact that there is a continuity of history (conditions normally change gradually over time, rather than all at once), make it very reasonable that the beginning of all these Trees would take place in the time before the Tribulation. In this way, we can understand the signs of our times, in terms of world-history moving toward the Tribulation. What has happened over the last century or so has been preparing the way and setting the stage for what is will take place in the Tribulation. For example, the rapid unprecedented development of scientific knowledge has prepared the way for the very advanced technology revealed in the Tribulation prophecies. Another example is the great increase in moral evil during our time, as seen in the violence on a greater scale than ever before, as seen in the world-wars and holocaust, the growth of sexual immorality in various forms, the industrialised murder of babies through abortion, and the increase of godlessness, secular humanism and materialism in many parts of the world, to name only a few cases in point. As in the days of Noah and Lot, the increase of human evil will make it necessary for God to move in judgment, which He will do when He initiates the Tribulation. Thus, the Day of the Lord will be God's response to the Tree of unparalleled human evil, which started to grow in the time leading up to it. Thus, this Tree of evil prepares the way for the Tribulation, not only in terms of bringing world-conditions into line with what they will be like in the Tribulation, when evil will come to its fullness, but also because it will call forth God's world-wide Judgment. Thus, as we see this Tree growing today, it is one of the Signs of the approaching Tribulation, when its fruit of evil will be in full manifestation, as revealed in the Tribulation prophecies in the Bible.

Thus, Jesus' Parable of the Fig Tree and all the Trees is very relevant for us, now that we know that all these Trees have now appeared and are budding (in other words, that these things have begun to happen – Luke 21:28). According to Jesus, the 2nd Coming, when all these things will have taken place, is NEAR, and if the 2nd Coming is near, that means the Rapture and the Start of the Tribulation is even nearer (by at least 7 years). We are surely living near the end of the Church Age. Notice, that although we now know these things (like the Rebirth of Israel) took place before the Tribulation, that does not contradict imminence, for from our present point of view, the Rapture can still take place at any time. If anything, the appearance and growth of these Trees only increases our expectancy of an imminent Rapture. Although imminence has always applied throughout the Church Age, we have more reason in our generation than ever before to watch for His Coming, because of these end-time Signs. Jesus' Parable tells us that in the time in which we live (Spring), we are to expect world conditions to get closer and closer to what the Bible describes they will be in the Tribulation (Summer), just as the heat of Spring gets closer to the heat of Summer, and as Spring approaches Summer, the Trees get closer in appearance to what they will look like in the Summer. This is indeed coming to pass. Those who read Revelation hundreds of years ago would have struggled to imagine it all coming literally to pass, but for us, living much closer to its fulfilment (in the Spring, rather than in the Winter), it is much easier, for we can see how things are rapidly moving closer to their climax in the Tribulation.

Finally, the Parable of the Fig Tree sets an upper time limit for the 2nd Coming, saying that the generation that see this Sign appear (at its beginning) will not all pass away before ALL THESE THINGS (all the events of the Tribulation, that He just described in Matthew 24:7-31) take place. In other words, the 2nd Coming must be within a man's lifetime (120 years at most) from the initial appearance of the end-time Trees, and the Fig Tree in particular (Genesis 6:3).

This passage giving the Parable of the Trees is still part of Jesus' answer to Question 2, because He uses the imagery of Trees to symbolise the Signs of the 2nd Coming. We see this, because the endpoint to which all the Signs are pointing is (1) 'the Kingdom of God' (Luke 21:31), which Christ will establish on earth at His 2nd Coming, and (2) when 'all these things' (the events of the Tribulation, Matthew 24:7-31) will have taken place (Matthew 24:34). Moreover, these Trees cannot be Signs of His Coming in the Rapture, because it is sign-less and imminent. This parable provides a perfect conclusion to His answer to Question 2, because it takes all the Signs together, and by using the analogy of Trees, He shows how they all function together as Signs of His 2nd Coming at the end of the Tribulation, for those living within a man's lifetime of the end (like us). Thus, these verses complete His answer to Question 2.

The Answer to Question 3: The Sign of the End of the Age

Having described all the signs leading up to the 2nd Coming (v7-35), Jesus then indicated that He was now changing subject, by the use of 'PERI DE', translated 'BUT' in v36 (used also in the parallel passage in Mark 13:32). A better translation would be 'now concerning.' Matthew 24:36: **"BUT of** ('now concerning') **that day and hour no one knows, not even the angels of Heaven, but My Father only."** It is well established that when 'peri de' stands at the start of a sentence it marks a new section of thought. It is a frequent device for introducing a change from one phase of a subject to another phase of the same subject or from one subject to another subject (Matthew 22:31; Mark 12:26; 13:32; Acts 21:25; 1 Corinthians 7:1; 7:25; 8:1; 12:1; 16:1,12; 1 Thessalonians 4:9,13). A good example is in 1Thessalonians 5:1, where the thought moves from the Rapture to the timing of the Rapture and the Day of the Lord. Although there is a shift in thought, it is still the same general subject. Likewise, in Matthew 24:36 marks a transition in thought, but the general subject is still the events at the closing of the Age. Paul used of 'peri de' in 1Corinthians (see above) to move from one of the questions (issues) raised by his correspondents to another. In each case it is a rhetorical formula for a new beginning. By analogy this indicates that Jesus used this phrase here to mark the transition from His answer to Question 2 (the Signs of the 2nd Coming) to His answer to Question 3 (the Signs of the End of the Age).

Thus, 'peri de' in v36 functions as a structural marker indicating a transition to Question 3. This is confirmed by the total contrast between v36-50, and the previous verses which describe the many Signs leading up to His Coming in power to reign over the earth. But suddenly from v36 onwards Christ's main emphasis is the imminence of His Coming, that there are NO SIGNS. Before v36 the emphasis is on how His disciples can KNOW by the Signs that His Coming is near (see v32-33), but in v36 and after the emphasis is on how the disciples CANNOT KNOW when He will come (v36,39,42,43,44,50. Clearly, Christ is talking about a different Coming of His, or better, a different aspect or phase of His Coming. Since Jesus introduced the imminence of His Coming by the use of 'peri de', Paul used the same words to introduce His description of the imminence of His Coming, when he stated that they knew perfectly well that the time of the Lord's Coming was unknown in 1Thessalonians 5:1-2: **"But** (peri de') **concerning the times and the seasons, brethren, you have no need that I should write to you. For you yourselves know perfectly that the day of the Lord so comes as a thief in the night"** (1Thessalonians 5:11-is parallel to Matthew 24:36-44).

Thus, at v36 Jesus moved from giving the Signs of His 2nd Coming (v7-35), to giving the Signs, or rather the lack of Signs, for the Start of the End of the Age (Tribulation), which He also related to His Coming to rescue His believers in the Rapture, a repeating emphasis in v37-44). In other words, Jesus is transitioning from describing events leading up to the climax of the Day of the Lord, to the subject of the inception of the Day of the Lord (and the accompanying Pre-Tribulation Rapture), and immediately declares how its timing cannot be known, and that there are no Signs that might signal its beginning.

So, we can now track the overall flow of Christ's thought. His disciples had asked about the Signs of His Coming to establish His Kingdom, and the Signs of the End of the Age (the time of Birth Pains) that would herald His Coming. So firstly, He confirmed and expanded their knowledge from the Old Testament of the events of the End of the Age leading up to His Coming, confirming that this time of Tribulation includes Daniel's 70th Week, by pointing to the Abomination of Desolation (v15, Daniel 9:27), as a major Sign in the events immediately leading up to His Coming (v15-30), marking the start of the Great Tribulation, a time of trouble **"such as has not been since the beginning of the world until this time, no, nor ever shall be"** (v21), a reference to Daniel 12:1, set in the End of the Age, and by which Sign it will be possible to know the exact day of Christ's Return (Daniel 12:11). But when He came to answer Question 3 about the start of the End of the Age, He gave new revelation that was not in the Old Testament (v36-50), namely that (1) the Start of the Day of the Lord has no preceding signs and is imminent, and (2) it would be initiated by His Coming to rescue the righteous from this time of judgment. In other words, He uses the term 'Coming' (*Parousia*) to describe 2 distinct events, one being the climax of the Tribulation and the other being the initiating event of the Tribulation. He logically starts with the Coming with which they are familiar, before introducing His initial Coming before that, in order to deepen their understanding. For example, imagine an evangelist, who is going to come to a big city to do a Crusade, and he is asked: 'when will you come'? He would first say: "I am coming on 10th October to preach the Gospel, and this public event is for everyone", but if he also planned to come some-time before the Crusade to meet with all the local believers involved in putting it on, he would then add something like: "but I am also coming before that, to meet privately, with those who are invited." Thus, His coming to the city is in 2 stages, the first time just for the believers and the 2nd time for everyone. The reason Jesus used the same word *Parousia* for both the Rapture and the 2nd Coming was to emphasise the close connection between these 2 phases of His Coming. We see a similar use of language to describe the Trinity. The initial emphasis is that God is one, but then this is clarified by the revelation that there are 3 who are God – God the Father, God the Son, and God the Holy Spirit.

Understanding this transition is vital to interpret Matthew 24:36-44 correctly as describing the imminent Rapture rather than the 2nd Coming. The main reason that many Pre-Tribulation believers deny that the Rapture is in view in these verses is their proximity to Christ's description of the 2nd Coming (v29-30), so they assume that they must describe the 2nd Coming. This in turn forces them to deny any interpretation of these verses that includes the Rapture, since they know (rightly) from Paul that the Rapture is before the Tribulation, not at the 2nd Coming. They then buttress this conclusion by unjustified assertions such as only Paul revealed the Rapture (when all agree Jesus revealed it the very next day in John 14:1-3), and that the Olivet Discourse only has to do with Israel and not at all with the Church (when in fact, His disciples represent the Church, and knew about the Church, as well as Israel – Matthew 16:18, 18:17, 28:18-20). This way of thinking leads to massive inconsistencies, because all Pre-Tribulation believers agree that the primary basis for distinguishing the Rapture from the Tribulation is that the Rapture is imminent, whereas the 2nd Coming is clearly signposted. However, the Coming of Christ described in Matthew 24:36-44 is clearly imminent. In fact, of all the passages that describe the imminence of Christ's Coming, this one is the strongest and clearest. Therefore, if this actually describes the 2nd Coming, this would automatically invalidate all other arguments for the Pre-Tribulation Rapture based on imminence from other scriptures. Moreover, we will see the great harmony between this passage in its terminology and thought and 1Thessalonians 5:1-11, showing how Paul derived his prophetic teaching from Christ, as he himself claimed (4:1,2,15). Since all agree that Paul taught the Pre-Tribulation Rapture here, then consistency demands that Jesus was speaking of the same events in Matthew 24:36-44. The original reason for rejecting His Coming in the Rapture, as the correct interpretation of these verses, can be seen to be without basis, once the significance of 'peri de' is appreciated. Once this is understood, we can see that Christ is answering 2 different Questions, and therefore describing 2 different phases of His Coming in v7-35 and v36-44. This in turn removes the inconsistencies that arise, not only within the Olivet Discourse, but between Matthew 24:36-44 and 1Thessalonians 5, when v36-44 are interpreted as the 2nd Coming. Now we can see how the teaching of Jesus has a perfect internal harmony, as well as harmonising with Paul's teaching, as we would expect.

The Imminent Coming of Christ (Matthew 24:36-51)

<u>Matthew 24:36</u>: **"BUT** ('peri de') **of THAT DAY and HOUR** (of the Start of the End of the Age) **NO ONE KNOWS, not even the angels of Heaven, but My Father only."** We have established that having answered the 2nd Question in v3, in this verse Jesus starts His answer to Question 3 about the Signs of the Start of the End of the Age. He immediately declares that the timing of the Start of the Tribulation is UNKNOWABLE and therefore it has no warning Signs. No one knows when it will start except God Himself (it is God's secret). This confirms that He has moved on from talking about His signposted 2nd Coming in power and glory, and by way of contrast He is now talking about the imminent Start of the Tribulation. As confirmation that 'that DAY and HOUR' refer to the Start of the Tribulation, it should be noted that 'that DAY' is used in Scripture to denote 'the DAY of the LORD' (Zephaniah 1:7-15, Ezekiel 30:3). The word *hemera* (day) can speak of an extended period, and Paul uses the word *hemera* for the imminent Day of the Lord in 1Thessalonians 5:4. It is likely Paul's use of *hemera* connects to v36. Likewise, the word *hora* (hour) can be used the same way, as in Revelation 3:10, where the Tribulation is described as 'the HOUR of Testing.' Thus, the phrase 'that Day and Hour' that no one knows, signifies the sudden and unexpected start of the Day of the Lord, the Hour of Testing, for all who dwell on the earth. Therefore, v36 is a statement of the imminence (unknowability) of the Start of the Tribulation, which stands in total contrast with the knowability of the timing of the 2nd Coming for those alive in the Tribulation. So, the use of 'BUT' to translate 'peri de' is appropriate: **"BUT** by way of contrast) **of that day and hour** (of the Start of the End of the Age) **NO ONE KNOWS, not even the angels of Heaven, but My Father only"** (Matthew 24:36).

Then, again and again in the following verses, Christ reinforces the imminence of His Coming to initiate the Tribulation. In <u>Matthew 24:37-39</u>, Jesus develops the thought of v36 of the unexpected sudden coming of the worldwide judgment of the DAY of the LORD, by comparing it to the unexpected sudden unexpected coming of the worldwide judgment of Noah's FLOOD: **"But as the days of Noah were, so also will the COMING of the Son of Man be. For as in the days before the FLOOD, they were eating and drinking, marrying and giving in marriage, until the DAY that Noah entered the Ark, and did not know until the FLOOD came and took** (*airo*) **them all away** (in a world-wide judgment)**, so also will the COMING of the Son of Man be."** But He also adds another thought, by twice directly relating His COMING to the sudden coming of the worldwide judgment of the FLOOD. This can only mean that His COMING is imminent, and that at this COMING, He will initiate a world-wide judgment corresponding to the FLOOD, namely the DAY of the LORD (the Tribulation-Flood). Thus, just like the FLOOD, the TRIBULATION will start suddenly, initiated by Christ's imminent COMING. Thus, this teaches that both His Coming and the Start of the Tribulation are imminent, for they are simultaneous. Moreover, this analogy reveals what He will do for believers at this same time. He said what will happen at His Coming will correspond to what took place in the days of Noah, and specifically pointed out that all the believers were rescued by being physically removed from the earth (where judgment was about to be released) into the safety of the Ark, and then on the very same day He released the world-wide Flood. Therefore, at His Coming, Christ will RESCUE all His believers, by removing them from the earth to a place of safety (even into Himself – for He is our Ark of Salvation), and then on the same day, He will release the Tribulation-Flood of judgment upon the whole world. In other words, at His COMING, He will rescue His own in the RAPTURE, by removing them from the scene of judgment, and simultaneously initiate the DAY of the LORD upon the rest of humanity, who are left on the earth. Moreover, He emphasises the IMMINENCE of these events, by emphasising that in the days of Noah normal life was going on, until the day all the believers entered the safety of the Ark, and then on that very same day, the Flood suddenly fell and took them by surprise (they "did not know" until it happened). Therefore, in the same way, Christ will suddenly come while normal life is going on, and receive His own to Himself, and immediately start to release the worldwide judgments of the Tribulation. Therefore, v37-39 teach Dual Imminence.

In summary, Jesus compared His imminent Coming to initiate the worldwide judgment of the Tribulation, to the previous worldwide judgment of the Flood. Just as the Flood came without warning and took the world by surprise, so will be His Coming. Just as in the days of Noah, before the Flood fell, life in the godless world will be going on as normal, until a key event takes place (the removal of all the believers), which immediately triggers a worldwide judgment, from which no one can escape. Thus, the Day of the Lord will suddenly fall and take the whole world by surprise. Thus, the Rapture is likened to Noah's family entering the Ark. In the days of Noah, once all believers were removed to the safety of the Ark, God was free to release His judgment, and so it then fell immediately. It follows that a similar sequence of events will happen when the Lord comes; He will remove all believers from the earth in the Rapture, and then He will immediately initiate the judgments of the Tribulation. So, the Lord will come to call His own to Himself in the Rapture, just as He called Noah and his family into the Ark (a type of Christ). Then, immediately worldwide judgment will fall, which no one will be able to escape.

<u>Jesus draws out 3 points of comparison with what happened in the days of Noah</u>:

*(1) Life before God's judgment fell was going on as normal, so when it suddenly fell from above it was a total surprise to the godless world - **"so also will the Coming of the Son of Man be."** So, likewise, just before the Tribulation, life will be carrying on normally, with no signs of Divine Judgment about to fall, and they will even be saying: "peace and safety" (1Thessalonians 5:2-3), so when it falls it will be totally unexpected.

It is clear from these verses that Jesus links His Coming with a worldwide judgment corresponding to the Flood. Some say this is His 2nd Coming at the end of the Tribulation, but this is impossible for 3 reasons. (1) Christ describes this Coming to save His people and initiate judgment as IMMINENT, which the 2nd Coming is certainly not. (2) If worldwide judgment is only initiated by Christ at His 2nd Coming (that is, it is the 2nd Coming that corresponds to the Flood), then it follows that the time before the 2nd Coming is not a time of Divine Judgment on earth, but this is contradicted by the Book of Revelation, which makes it clear that the whole Tribulation is a time of worldwide Divine Judgment initiated by Christ from Heaven. (3) In the days of Noah before the Flood, normal life was going on. They had no idea or signs from world-conditions that judgment was about to fall from heaven, even though Noah had warned them. If the Flood represents God's judgment at the 2nd Coming, then it follows that Jesus is teaching here that in the days leading up to the 2nd Coming, normal life will be going on, but nothing could be further from the truth. This is the Great Tribulation, the worst time ever in all history (v21), so that if Jesus does not cut it short by His Return, all flesh would be destroyed (v22). It is described in detail in Revelation. So, Christ cannot be talking here about His 2nd Coming! Therefore, the Flood is a type of the whole Tribulation, and not just of the 2nd Coming,

*(2) The final event just before judgment falls was the disappearance of all believers into the Ark, when God removed them from the scene of judgement and lifted them above it. Likewise, the final event just before the Tribulation-Flood falls upon the world will be the disappearance of all believers into Christ at

the Rapture. Jesus will come for us in the Rapture, to remove us from the earth, and gather us into Him. This is confirmed by the next verses, when Jesus described the Rapture of believers that happens in conjunction with His Coming: **"THEN 2 men will be in the field: one will be TAKEN** (to be with Christ) **and the other LEFT** (to go through the Tribulation). **2 women will be grinding at the mill: one TAKEN and the other LEFT. Watch therefore, for you do not know what hour your Lord is COMING"** (v40-42). According to the pattern set by what took place in the days of Noah, God will remove His true Church from the earth, by lifting us above the scene of judgment, gathering us all to meet Christ in the air (1Thessalonians 4:16-17), before pouring out His Tribulation judgments.

*(3) Immediately after the believers entered the Ark, the worldwide judgment of the Flood suddenly fell, in which all unbelievers were killed. Likewise, immediately after the Rapture, the worldwide Judgment of the Tribulation will suddenly fall upon the whole earth, so that there will be no escape. Moreover, once all the judgments are completed no unbelievers will be left alive on earth, so that only believers will be left alive on earth to inherit the Messianic Kingdom as its initial population (Matthew 25:34). However, because these judgments are graciously spread over at least 7 years, many unbelievers will be saved during the Tribulation.

So, just as in the days of Noah, life on earth will be going on as normal, and then suddenly the worldwide Tribulation-Flood will fall upon the whole earth. Thus, the Day of the Lord is imminent. At the same time all the believers will be rescued to safety into Christ, the Ark of our Salvation – the Rapture. This imminent rescue of the believers will come suddenly, without warning, while people are going about their normal lives, which is the message of the next verses: **"Then 2 men will be in the field: one will be TAKEN** (*para-lambano*) **and the other LEFT** (*aphiemi*). **2 women will be grinding at the mill: one will be TAKEN and the other LEFT"** (v40-41). The right interpretation of these verses depends on correctly identifying those who are TAKEN, and those who are LEFT. Pre-Tribulation believers, who (wrongly) assume that this passage describes events at the 2nd Coming, deny it is speaking of the Rapture, as that would mean a Post-Tribulation Rapture, which must be rejected based on other clear passages. Those who deny these verses describe the Rapture say that those who are TAKEN are unbelievers TAKEN in judgment at the end of the Tribulation, whereas it is the believers who are LEFT on earth to enter the Messianic Kingdom. To justify this, they point to the previous verse that says: **"the Flood came and TOOK** (*airo*) **them all away"** (v39). They argue that since v39 speaks of a 'taking' in judgment, it follows that those 'taken' in v40-41 are also taken in judgment. However, 2 different Greek words are used for the action of taking, *airo* (v39) and *para-lambano* (v40,41), so Jesus is not making that connection. On the contrary, if He meant to say that those taken in v40-41 are the same as those taken in judgment in v39, He would have used the same word in both cases. Instead, He used a different word for 'taken' (*para-lambano*), which He used again the next day to describe the Rapture of believers, where it is translated as 'receive': **"I will come again and will RECEIVE you to Myself"** (John 14:3). The apostles would naturally have associated the 2 expressions. In light of this, the change from *airo* to *para-lambano* indicates a change in meaning, with *airo* describing judgment (v39) and *para-lambano* the rapture (v40-41).

This is confirmed by the literal meaning of *para-lambano* and its primary usage. It literally means 'to take to oneself' or 'take to be with oneself' (*para* = alongside, *lambano* = take). The thought is always one of accompaniment, often for close fellowship. For example, it is used when a man 'takes' a woman to be his wife, for example, when Joseph 'took' Mary to be his wife (Matthew 1:20). We saw a similar example in John 14:2-3, when Jesus our heavenly Bridegroom promised His Bride, that He will **"come again and RECEIVE (take) us to Himself, that where I am, there you may be also."** So, it is generally used in a positive sense, not in a negative way (to describe a judgment), and it is a perfect word to use to describe the RAPTURE in Matthew 24:40-41: **"Then 2 men will be in the field: one will be TAKEN** (*para-lambano*) **and the other LEFT** (*aphiemi*). **Two women will be grinding at the mill: one will be TAKEN** (*para-lambano*) **and the other LEFT** (*aphiemi*)**."** This agrees with Paul's description of the purpose of the Rapture: **"We who are alive and remain shall be caught up together with them in the clouds to meet the Lord in the air. And thus, we shall always be with the Lord."** (1Thessalonians 4:17). Therefore, those who are TAKEN are the believers taken by Christ in the Rapture at His Coming, which means those who are LEFT are the unbelievers, who are left behind on earth to go through the Day of the Lord. This is further confirmed by the fact *aphiemi* ('to leave') takes on the meaning of 'abandon', whenever it's a person who has been 'left' (Matthew 4:11, 22; 8:15; 13:36; 19:29; 22:22,25; 26:56), for example, a spouse abandoning (leaving) their partner (1Corinthians 7:11–13), and the Good Shepherd not abandoning His sheep (John 10:12), and how the Father has certainly not abandoned His Son (John 8:29). Thus, *aphiemi* is the perfect word to use to describe God leaving unbelievers behind to go through the Tribulation. No passages in the New Testament use *aphiemi* to express what the Lord will do to believers. In fact, just 2 days later, Jesus used *aphiemi* to affirm what He would not do to His disciples: **"I will not leave** (*aphiemi*) **you as orphans; I will come to you"** (John 14:18). Moreover, Jesus used *aphiemi* is used to describe a judgment, as in <u>Matthew 23:38</u>: **"See! Your House** (the Temple) **is LEFT to you desolate."** Likewise, unbelievers will be left to face the Day of the Lord.

Thus, <u>Matthew 24:40-41</u> should be interpreted as: **"Then 2 men will be in the field: one** (the believer) **will be TAKEN** (suddenly from the earth by Christ in the Rapture) **and the other** (the unbeliever) **LEFT** (abandoned to judgment). **2 women will be grinding at the mill: one will be TAKEN** (to be with Christ) **and the other LEFT** (on earth to go through the Day of the Lord)**."** Thus, having said that at His Coming, He would provide a physical salvation for believers from the worldwide judgment, that He was about to release, just as He did in the days of Noah (v37-39), He then described what this rescue would look like (v40-41). As in v38, the people in v40-41 will be going about their normal lives, and then suddenly, without warning, the believers will be taken from the earth to be with Christ. At the same time, as in the days of Noah, the rest will be left behind to face the worldwide judgment which will quickly overtake them. Thus, v40-41 confirms the Dual Imminence of the rescue of believers in the Rapture and the simultaneous assignment of the rest for judgment, which will start at once, as in the days of Noah.

Having described His imminent COMING to rapture His saints and initiate judgment on earth, Jesus makes an urgent application to our lives: **"WATCH** (*gregoreo*, be alert)**, therefore, for you do not know what hour YOUR LORD is COMING"** (Matthew 24:42). This is another strong statement of imminence. As we have seen the call to WATCH (*gregoreo*) is always in relation to an event that can happen at any time, which requires a constant state of alertness and vigilance. If one knows that His Coming is at least a number of years away, then the appeal to be alert and ready for His arrival is not applicable. The explanation that we cannot know the hour of His Coming, repeats the thought of v36, which confirms that He is still talking of the same event. This lack of knowledge is the essence of imminence, for since we do not know, from our point of view, He could come at any time. Notice also, that it is not just unbelievers, who are in the dark concerning the timing of His Coming, but believers also, for in this verse He is talking specifically to believers: **"you do not know what hour YOUR LORD is coming."** The fact that He addresses believers here, shows that He is talking about His imminent COMING for His own, to rapture and reward them (as we saw in v40-41), and therefore they need to be watchful, spiritually awake and ready, serving Him, so that when He comes for them, He will be pleased with them, and reward them accordingly. We saw in v36-39 that this unknown time relates to the imminent Start of the DAY of the LORD, whereas in v42 it relates to His imminent COMING for His saints (v40-41). This can only mean that at His imminent Coming, He will simultaneously rescue and reward His saints and initiate the Day of the Lord on earth (Dual Imminence).

In the next 2 verses, it is clear that Christ is still describing the same imminent event, whose timing is unknown, and He continues His emphasis on the need for watchfulness: **"But know this, that IF the master of the house had KNOWN what hour the THIEF would COME, he would have WATCHED** (*gregoreo*, 'been on the alert'), **and not allowed his house to be broken into. Therefore, you also be READY, for the Son of Man is COMING at an hour you do not expect"** (v43-44). In v43, Christ's description of His COMING takes a surprising twist, as He compares it to the COMING of a THIEF. The reason for the change is that He is moving from the viewpoint of believers, for whom Christ is their Lord and Master (v42), to unbelievers, who are the master of their own house (life). Note the contrast between the Parables of His imminent Coming, when the Lord returns to His own House to be greeted by His own servants (Mark 13:32-37), with the Parable of the Thief, who breaks into someone else's house. Although He is the rightful Owner of all men, unbelievers don't accept His claim on them, and so from their viewpoint His intervention in their lives in judgment is like the action of a thief.

Like believers, these unbelievers do not know the timing of His Coming. Indeed, they do not even believe that He will return, and therefore, unlike believers, they do not watch for His Coming, and so are totally unprepared. Unlike believers, who will experience rescue and blessing at His Coming, unbelievers will experience His Coming as the coming of a THIEF. The analogy of a thief gives further emphasis on imminence, for a thief comes suddenly, without warning. Moreover, a thief breaks into a house uninvited, and the result of his coming is LOSS. Thus, Christ's Coming as a thief speaks of His sudden Coming to bring JUDGMENT upon the unbelieving world, in agreement with v36-39. It speaks of a godless world going about its normal life, totally unexpectant and unprepared for Christ to suddenly break into human history to initiate the Day of the Lord, which will bring great loss to all earth-dwellers. Moreover, a successful thief is not seen by the members of the household, but they certainly experience the aftereffects of his coming. By definition, a thief comes suddenly, without warning, to remove the precious things from the house. Likewise, Jesus is coming to take His own from the world, to be with Him forever (He values us as most precious for He created us and redeemed us with His Blood). Of course, He is not really a thief, for He will only take what belongs to Him (those who have given their hearts to Him), but for the world, which will suddenly discover a billion people missing after the Rapture, it will appear as if a thief had come. The initial LOSS that the world will immediately experience will be the multitudes of believers (His true Church), who contribute much goodness, value and blessing to the world, through their prayers, works, and the way God uses them to restrain the spread of evil. As well as experiencing the loss of God's Presence in the world, through the removal of the Church, as time goes on, the world will increasingly discover and experience the great loss resulting from the Coming of the Thief to initiate the Day of the Lord. So, to the world, Christ will come (in judgment) as a Thief, but for us, He will come as the Bridegroom for His Bride, to rescue us from danger, before waging war on the world-system, under the power of the evil one.

The picture of His Coming as a THIEF encodes Dual Imminence, because it speaks of His imminent Coming to TAKE His own from the godless world, that denies His Ownership and Lordship, and to bring about LOSS (judgment) upon the world, and all who dwell in it. The fact that the Thief comes to suddenly TAKE His own from the world (v43), harmonises perfectly with the description of the RAPTURE in v40-41, where the believers are suddenly TAKEN from the world. Jesus originated the image of the THIEF (Matthew 24:43, Luke 12:39), and it is clear that the apostles understood it and used it in their teaching also (1 Thessalonians 5:2,4, 2 Peter 3:10, Revelation 3:3, 16:15). So, it follows that they used it to describe the same Coming, as Christ Himself. Since Paul clearly used this image (1 Thessalonians 5:2,4), in connection with Christ's Coming in the Rapture (1 Thessalonians 4:13-18) and the Start of the Tribulation (1 Thessalonians 5:2-4), we know that he was referring to the Coming of Christ to initiate the Tribulation; and so, consistency demands that Christ must have also been talking about the Rapture in Matthew 24:43, otherwise Paul would be guilty of misapplying the teaching of Christ. The descriptions of His sudden Coming as a Thief, cannot possibly describe His Coming at the end of the Tribulation in power and glory, for this event is not imminent, but clearly signposted, by all the predicted events of the Tribulation, with clear timings, so it will be possible for anyone in the Tribulation to know exactly when He will return. Moreover, His actions at the 2nd Coming in no way correspond to the actions of a thief. At that time, He does not come and go unseen, having removed the valuable, but rather He claims ownership of the house and takes it over by force and establishes His control over it forever.

Some of the prophetic references to the coming of a THIEF say that CHRIST Himself will COME (*erchomai*) as a THIEF (Matthew 24:43, Luke 12:39, Revelation 3:3, 16:15), whereas others give another side to this event, namely that the DAY of the LORD (Tribulation) will COME (*erchomai*) as a THIEF (1Thessalonians 5:2,4, also 2Peter 3:10). The connection between these 2 descriptions is strengthened by the fact that Paul uses the word for COME (*erchomai*) to describe the Start of the Day of the Lord, the same word used by

Jesus for His Coming as a thief. Along with the fact that it comes 'as a THIEF' indicates this time of judgment is initiated by the sudden COMING of a PERSON. Harmonising these 2 statements tells us that when Jesus comes suddenly, like a thief (to take His own), He will also initiate the Day of the Lord on the earth. So, the same time that He comes to receive His Church in the Rapture, He also comes to initiate the Tribulation, and both events are imminent. So again, we see Dual Imminence.

Throughout this passage (v36-43), Jesus teaches His imminent Coming to (1) rescue His Church in the Rapture, and (2) to release the Tribulation-Flood (the Day of the Lord) on the earth, and both will happen suddenly without warning, on the very same day. So, this proves He is COMING before the worldwide judgments of the Tribulation are released upon the earth. He described the Day of the Lord as 'that Day', a time of worldwide judgment, which will suddenly fall upon the whole world, from which there will be no escape, like Noah's Flood (v37-39), which will be initiated by the Rapture (v40-41), the Coming of the Lord as a Thief (v42-44).

Then He concludes this section of Scripture by emphasising again the imminence of this Coming in the strongest possible way, and then giving the application of this truth to all people: **"Therefore, you also be READY, for the Son of Man is COMING at an hour you do not expect"** (v44). This statement of imminence complements and completes v36. Not only do we not know when He will come (v36), neither do we not know when He will not come (v44), even if we think we do, for He will come when we do not expect Him. In other words, He says here that we can have no idea when He will come. This statement is designed to humble us, by confounding all our reasonings as to why He cannot return yet, and all speculations as to when He might come. It is in particular a warning to believers, who believe the Church must go through part or all of the Tribulation, that they are liable to be caught unprepared, because they do not expect Him to come now, because all certain events have not yet taken place. Jesus says He is coming, when they do not expect Him to come. This statement can only be true in the case of a Pre-Tribulation Rapture. If He only comes at the end of the end of the Tribulation, then He will come He is expected to come in contradiction to v44. The application Jesus makes from His imminent Coming is that we should be alert and ready for Him to come at any time, because the consequences of our state of readiness at His Coming will be great, both good and bad. For unbelievers, who are not ready for Christ, they will be plunged into the Day of the Lord, a time of darkness and judgment. For believers, who are awake, watching for His Return, they will receive His commendation, blessing and great eternal rewards at His Judgment Seat, but lax believers, who will be found asleep at His Coming, not living in fellowship with God, will not do so well at His Judgment Seat.

In Matthew 24:45-51, Jesus continues His description of His imminent Coming, by describing the total contrast between what will happen to (1) faithful believers and (2) unbelievers, even if they live in His House (church-goers): **"(1) Who then is a faithful and wise servant, whom his master made ruler over his household, to give them food in due season? BLESSED is that servant whom his master, WHEN he COMES, will find so DOING. Assuredly, I say to you that he will make him ruler over all his goods** (eternal rewards). **(2) But if that evil servant says in his heart: 'My MASTER is DELAYING his COMING,' and begins to beat his fellow servants, and to eat and drink with the drunkards, the master of that servant will come on a day when he is not looking for him and at an hour that he is not aware of, and will cut him in two and appoint him his portion with the HYPOCRITE. There shall be weeping and gnashing of teeth."**

This unbeliever, who is in the House of the Lord (the Church) is called a hypocrite, because he professes to be a believer, and that Jesus is his Lord, but his actions reveal his true heart and nature. These religious unbelievers are cast out of His House, into a place of judgment (the Day of the Lord). I have commented on this Parable already, as it is also in Luke 12:42-46. Its context in Matthew 24 is the imminent Coming of Christ, for which we need to be ever ready. That this Parable is speaking of the same imminent event is confirmed by the fact that it warns us to not be like the evil servant, who denied of the imminence of His Coming, saying: 'My MASTER is DELAYING his COMING.' This denial set him free to full express his sin-nature. This shows the power of Imminence to inspire us to the highest standards. By contrast we can assume that the faithful servants were motivated by their belief in imminence and their readiness for their Master's Return was manifested in faithful service. Finally, this Parable also confirms Dual Imminence, for when the Master comes to His House, He deals with the believers and unbelievers at THE SAME TIME. That is when He comes, He (1) and blesses and rewards the faithful servants (the Rapture and Judgment Seat of Christ), and (2) He judges the hypocrites (by sending them into the Day of the Lord).

Mark 13:32-37

In Mark's version of the Olivet Discourse, Mark adds an additional Parable, which he places right after Mark 13:32: **"But** (peri de) **of that day and hour no one knows, not even the angels in Heaven, nor the Son, but only the Father."** This corresponds to Matthew 24:36, which as we saw, was the introductory verse to Christ's teaching on His imminent Coming, to rapture and rescue His own from the Day of the Lord, and simultaneously initiate the Day of the Lord. When Christ originally gave His Discourse, it is most probable that He gave the Parable recorded by Mark (and omitted by Matthew) before His teaching on the days of Noah (Matthew 24:37-39). So, as we saw, the immediate context for this Parable is His statement that no one can know the time of the Start of the End of the Age (Tribulation). He then reaffirmed this in v33: **"Take heed, WATCH** (be alert) **and PRAY; for you do not know when the time is."** Again, he emphasises the imminence of the event, which calls for constant watchfulness.

Mark 13:34-37: **"It is like a man going to a far country, who left his house and gave authority to his servants, and to each his work, and commanded the doorkeeper to WATCH** *(gregoreo)***. WATCH** *(gregoreo)* **therefore, for you do NOT KNOW when the MASTER of the house is COMING—in the evening, at midnight, at the crowing of the rooster, or in the morning— lest, coming suddenly, he finds you sleeping. And what I say to you, I SAY to ALL: WATCH** *(gregoreo)***!"**

In this Parable, He again emphasises imminence by repeating that fact that even His servants do NOT KNOW when He is COMING, so that they must stay WATCHFUL. This emphasis is increased by His triple use of *gregoreo* (watch), which we have seen is always used in connection with imminent events. Moreover, He declares that His command to WATCH for His COMING applies to ALL in the Church Age, because He could come at ANY TIME, irrespective of any signs. This would all make no sense, if He was speaking of His Post-Tribulation Coming, because watching would be a futile activity, if His Coming was years away, because the Tribulation has not even begun yet. Finally, we can again see Dual Imminence in this Parable. The context tells us that the unknown time is the Start of the Day of the Lord, but the Parable itself tells us that this is also the unknown time of His Coming. Therefore, He is speaking about His imminent Coming to initiate the Day of the Lord (as confirmed by the parallel passage - Matthew 24:36-39). In addition, the Parable is about the Master returning to His House (the Church), where His servants live. So, it primarily focuses on His imminent Coming to His servants, and it is designed to motivate them to be watchful, so He will be pleased with them when He returns, so that He might reward them. Thus, Christ has gone to a far country (Heaven), but He might return at any time, and when He does, He will come for His servants, and also at the same time He will initiate the Day of the Lord on earth.

Luke 21:34-36

Finally, Luke 21:34-36 gives Christ's closing remarks at the end of this part of the Olivet Discourse (he omits the material in Matthew 24:36-51). The context is all the events of the Tribulation (Luke 21:10-11,25-33), summarised as "all these things" (v12,32) or "these things" (v28,31). Then Jesus said: **"But take heed to yourselves, lest your hearts be weighed down with carousing** (dissipation, wasting your life, indulging the flesh), **drunkenness, and cares of this life, and that DAY** (the Day of the Lord) **come on you UNEXPECTEDLY** (suddenly). **For it** (the Tribulation) **will come as a SNARE** (suddenly snapping tight) **on all those who dwell on the face of the whole earth** (it will be a worldwide judgment). **Watch** (be alert) **therefore, and pray always, that you may be COUNTED WORTHY** (or 'have the strength') **to ESCAPE** (in the Rapture) **ALL THESE THINGS that will come to pass** (in the Tribulation)**, and to stand before the Son of Man."** This is a clear statement of the Pre-Tribulation Rapture.

Again, (1) we see the imminence of the Day of the Lord, which will suddenly overtake the whole world. (2) At the same time, God will provide an ESCAPE for His people from ALL these THINGS (all the events of the Tribulation, previously described). Since the events of the Tribulation will come upon ALL who dwell on the earth, the only way to escape ALL these things (all the events of the Tribulation) is to be removed from the earth itself, BEFORE the Tribulation even starts, and this is exactly what Jesus will do for His people, when He comes for them in the Rapture. They will be lifted up from the earth and find themselves standing before the Son of Man in their glorified bodies. Since the Day of the Lord is imminent, the Rapture of the saints must also be imminent, since it must either take place before the Start of the Day of the Lord or at the very same time. But if the Rapture takes place sometime before the Day of the Lord, then the Day of the Lord would no longer be imminent. Therefore, the Rapture takes place at the same time as the Start of the Day of the Lord. In other words, Christ's Coming to rescue His saints in the Rapture and the Start of the Day of the Lord are both imminent events, because they are simultaneous. Thus, when Christ suddenly comes for His Church in the Rapture, He will also initiate the day of the Lord at the same time (Dual Imminence).

Those who qualify to escape the Tribulation in the Rapture are described as those counted who are: "COUNTED WORTHY to escape", or according to other manuscripts, those who "have the STRENGTH to escape" (v36). Now no one could be worthy enough in themselves or have the necessary strength in themselves to escape the earth in the Rapture. We know from other Scriptures, that we can only be COUNTED WORTHY to stand before God through receiving Christ as our Lord and Saviour, for then His righteousness (worthiness) is put to our account. We are forgiven of our sins and clothed in His righteousness. Moreover, Therefore, we can only have the strength (power) to escape in the Rapture, through the indwelling Holy Spirit, who will transform our mortal bodies into immortal bodies. Therefore, those who will be raptured will be those who are justified by faith in Christ, and possess the indwelling Spirit of God. These true believers are characterised by a lifestyle of walking in fellowship with God (spiritually awake) and praying (v36); in this way they demonstrate the genuineness of their faith. On the other hand, Christ warns those who are living a sinful lifestyle, rather than trusting in God (living under sin rather than under Christ's Lordship), that the judgments of the DAY of the LORD will suddenly come down upon them (v34), and they will be forced to go through the Tribulation (v35), but the true believers will escape in the Rapture (v36). Thus, there is an unknown day coming, when Christ will rescue His own from the godless world, and at the same time initiate the Tribulation.

John 14:1-3

The next day, Jesus completed His teaching on the Rapture in John 14:1-4: **"Let not your heart be troubled; you believe in God, believe also in Me. In My Father's House** (Heaven) **are many mansions; if it were not so, I would have told you. I go to prepare a place for you** (in Heaven). **And if I go and prepare a place for you** (in Heaven), **I will COME again and RECEIVE** (para-lambano) **you to Myself; that where I am** (Heaven), **there you may be also. And where I go** (to the Father in Heaven) **you know, and the way you know."**

On the day after the Olivet Discourse, Jesus spoke these words to His disciples at the Last Supper to prepare them for His death on the following day. He assured them that He was going to His Father in Heaven (see also v6). The Father's House is Heaven, as many scriptures confirm (Matthew 5:16,45,48, 6:1,9, 7:11,21, 10:32,33, 12:50,16:17, 18:10,14,19, 23:9, Mark 11:25,26, Luke 11:2). Then, He gave them (as representatives of the Church) the promise that He would not forget them, but rather He will COME again and RECEIVE them to Himself. These are the tender words of the Bridegroom to His newly betrothed Bride, promising that He will go away and prepare a dwelling place for her, where they will live together forever: **"that where I am, there you may be also."** This is the promise of the RAPTURE. According to the Jewish wedding customs, the bridegroom goes to his father's house to prepare the place where the couple will live and prepare for the wedding day, and when his father releases him, the bridegroom returns to fetch his bride and bring her back to his father's house, where the wedding takes place and she becomes his wife. Thus, these verses describe the fulfilment of the Divine Romance. This clearly speaks of a COMING of CHRIST exclusively for His true Church (His Bride), to take us back to Heaven, to be with Him there. This is very different from His 2nd Coming at the end of the Tribulation, when He will manifest Himself to the whole world, and remain on earth to establish His Kingdom here. These verses refute the Post-Tribulation Rapture, because in that theory, when Christ raptures His believers, they will rise to meet Him in the air and then do a U-turn, and return with Him to the earth, for the establishment of His Kingdom here. Thus, if the Rapture coincides with the 2nd Coming, Christ cannot fulfil His precious promise in John 14:1-3 to come for us and take us to be with Him in Heaven. On the other hand, John 14:1-3 agrees perfectly with the Pre-Tribulation Rapture, when Christ will come before the Tribulation to receive us to Himself and take us to Heaven with Him, where the Marriage will take place, and from where we will return with Him at His 2nd Coming. This also agrees with Revelation 19:7-8,11-14, where the Wife of the Lamb (the glorified Church) is already seen in Heaven BEFORE the 2nd Coming, having received the promise of John 14:1-3 some time before the end of the Tribulation, and then she returns with Him to the earth in the 2nd Coming (v14).

It is significant that Jesus used *para-lambano* (translated RECEIVE in v3), to describe the Rapture, which literally means He will TAKE us to be WITH Him, just as a bridegroom takes his bride to be with him. This is the very same word, He used to describe the Rapture in Matthew 24:40-41, when He said: **"Then 2 men will be in the field: one will be TAKEN** (*para-lambano)* **and the other left. 2 women will be grinding at the mill: one will be TAKEN** (*para-lambano*) **and the other left."** This indicates He is talking about the same event here as in John 14:1-3. In Matthew 24:40-41, He describes His imminent COMING to TAKE His own from the world, before releasing the judgments of the Day of the Lord (see v37-39). Likewise, John 14:3 teaches the imminence of the Rapture, by using the futuristic use of present tense for the verb 'to come', when He said: **"I will COME again and RECEIVE you to Myself."** A more literal translation would be: **"I AM COMING and WILL RECEIVE you to Myself."** The combination of the present tense ('I am coming') and the future tense ('I will receive you') is clearly a futuristic use of the present tense, which strongly implies imminence. The meaning is: *"I am on my way and I may arrive at any moment."* Thus John 14:3 harmonises perfectly with Matthew 24:40-41, and since all Pre-Tribulation believers agree John 14:3 describes the Rapture, then Matthew 24:40-41 must do also. In that case, we can see how Paul based His description of the imminent Rapture in 1Thessalonians 4:13-18 on the Lord's teaching, just as he claimed (v15). In John 14, Jesus focused on His imminent Coming to fetch His Bride, giving us additional revelation that at this time He will personally come and receive her to Himself and take her with Himself to Heaven. He does not mention anything about the Tribulation coming upon the world, because here He is just speaking to His Bride, reassuring her that although He is going away, they will not be separated forever, but He will return at any time, and so she should stay ready for His Return.

This brings our review of the extensive prophetic teaching of Christ to a close. We have seen He was the one who initiated the teaching of His imminent Coming to both (1) judge the world and (2) deliver the faithful, in contrast to the non-imminent 2nd Coming at the end of the Tribulation. Next, we show how the apostles Paul, James Peter and John, developed this teaching of Dual Imminence, basing their teaching on the words of Jesus. In particular, they repeated His use of the pictures of (1) a master who may return at any time to his house, (2) the surprise arrival of a thief, and (3) the rescue of believers and worldwide Flood judgment in the days of Noah.

Chapter 5: Dual Imminence
in the Teaching of Paul

In this chapter, I demonstrate how the prophetic teaching of Paul agrees perfectly with the teaching of Jesus, especially the Dual Imminence of the Rapture and the Day of the Lord.

1Thessalonians 1:9-10

1Thessalonians 1:9-10: **"You turned to God from idols to serve the living and true God, and to WAIT for His Son from Heaven, whom He raised from the dead, even Jesus who DELIVERS** (rescues) **us from the WRATH to COME."** Believers are characterised as those who WAIT for Christ's Coming from Heaven. To WAIT for Christ speaks of us waiting and watching for His Imminent Return, for you only wait for someone, who could come at any moment. If you know they are not arriving for some time, then you do not wait for their arrival. We can recognise that the origin of this requirement to WAIT for Christ's Return is the regular commands in the teaching of Jesus to WATCH, in the light of His imminent Return.

We see this same language of WAITING for the Imminent Coming of the Lord in other letters of Paul. In each case, we see different aspects of what He will do at His Coming. In 1Thessalonians 1:10, Christ comes to rescue believers from the coming wrath of the Day of the Lord. In Philippians 3, Paul tells us that at this Coming, He will complete our salvation by giving us glorified bodies, just like His resurrected body: **"Our citizenship is in Heaven, from which we also eagerly WAIT for the SAVIOUR, the Lord Jesus Christ, who will TRANSFORM our lowly BODY that it may be conformed to His GLORIOUS BODY according to the working by which He is able even to subdue all things to Himself"** (v20-21). Likewise, 1Corinthians 1:7-8 says: **"Eagerly WAITING for the REVELATION of our Lord Jesus Christ, who will also confirm you to the end, that you may be blameless in the day of our Lord Jesus Christ."** In Titus 2:13, he uses the parallel terminology of LOOKING, to describe our spiritual attitude in the light of His imminent Return to save us: **"We should live soberly, righteously, and godly in the present age, LOOKING for the BLESSED HOPE and glorious APPEARING of our great GOD and SAVIOUR Jesus Christ."**

Hebrews 9:28: **"To those who eagerly WAIT for Him** (Christ), **He will APPEAR a second time, apart from sin, for SALVATION."** Notice that in this imminent Coming, Christ will only APPEAR to His true Bride, who consists of those who eagerly WAIT for Him, whereas at His 2nd Coming, He will APPEAR in His glory to the whole world. So, this is speaking of a different event, the Rapture, when

He only APPEARS to His Bride, who is looking expectantly for His any-moment Return. The purpose of His Coming for His Bride is to complete her SALVATION, by giving us immortal bodies and glorifying us.

The language of WATCHING, WAITING, and LOOKING for His Coming only makes sense if its imminent, and its origin is the teaching of Jesus. The reason we need to always watch, wait, look and be alert for His Coming is that we cannot rely on any warning signs coming first, that will alert us to the need to get ready and prepare for Him.

All of the above verses focus on His imminent Coming in relation to the Rapture of the Church, but 1Thessalonians 1:10 is of special interest, because it also relates His imminent Coming to the coming of the Day of the Lord Wrath upon the earth, so let us take another look at this verse: **"to WAIT for His Son** (to come) **from Heaven, whom He raised from the dead, even Jesus who DELIVERS** (rescues) **US from the WRATH to COME."** This Coming to RESCUE His own, who are WAITING for Him, must be His Coming in the RAPTURE, which He describes in more detail in 1Thessalonians 4:13-18. This is confirmed by the phrase: **"whom He raised from the dead"**, for it is on the basis of Christ's resurrection that we receive the transformation of our body at our rapture or resurrection. This must be the reason Paul mentions this truth at this point. So, the RAPTURE is described as a RESCUE from the WRATH to come. This must refer to the WRATH of the eschatological DAY of the LORD on the earth (rather than the wrath Hell), because the RESCUE is directly connected to Jesus' imminent RETURN from Heaven to earth. It is an intervention of Christ into human history that rescues us from a time of wrath that is about to come on the earth. This is of course the Day of the Lord, and because it is a time of Divine Wrath upon all earth-dwellers, it is not possible that His Bride should be present to endure His wrath: **"Much more then, having now been justified by His Blood, we shall be SAVED from WRATH through Him"** (Romans 5:9). Later in 1Thessalonians 5, in the context of teaching about the DAY of the LORD (v2), Paul declares the same truth: **"For God did NOT APPOINT us to WRATH, but to obtain SALVATION through our Lord Jesus Christ** (salvation of our bodies in the Rapture, and deliverance from the wrath of the Tribulation)**"** (v9).

The strength of emphasis on Dual Imminence in 1Thessalonians 1:10 is somewhat lost in translation, because when Paul says Jesus 'delivers us', he uses a present participle (literally: 'He is delivering us' – something that is a potential present reality. This futuristic use of the present tense speaks of the imminence of a rescue that could happen at any time. Moreover, 'the wrath to come' is literally 'the coming wrath', where 'coming' is again a futuristic use of a present participle, meaning its breaking on the scene is imminent, it could happen at any moment. So, it a better translation is: **"to WAIT for His Son from Heaven, even Jesus who** (by His coming to us) **is DELIVERING us from the COMING WRATH** (the wrath that is already on its way and is about to come upon the earth)." Thus, both the Coming of Jesus to rescue us from the coming wrath, and the coming of the wrath of the Day of the Lord itself are imminent events, so again we see Dual Imminence. This can only be the case if both events are simultaneous, or 2 aspects of the same event, because the rescue must happen before the wrath begins, but if the wrath began sometime after the Rapture, then it would not be imminent, but signposted by the Rapture. So, when Jesus comes to rescue His Church in the Rapture, He is also coming to initiate the Day of the Lord upon the earth. In this way, the glorious Rapture of the Church, when we receive the salvation of our bodies, is also a deliverance from the wrath of the Tribulation. This Dual Imminence confirms the Pre-Tribulation Rapture, and the fact that the Tribulation starts on the same day as the Rapture, as this is the only position (viewpoint) that is consistent with and explains the Dual Imminence of the Rapture and the Day of the Lord.

1Thessalonians 4 and 5

Paul's classic description of the Rapture is in <u>1Thessalonians 4:13-18</u>. After introducing the subject in <u>v13-14</u>: **"I do not want you to be ignorant, brethren, concerning those who have fallen asleep** (believers who have already died), **lest you sorrow as others who have no hope. For if we believe that Jesus died and rose again, even so God will bring with Him** (from Heaven the spirits of) **those who sleep in Jesus."** He then said: **"This we say to you by the WORD of the LORD..."** (v15a). Here he declares that his teaching on the Rapture was according to the Lord's own teaching, for, as we have seen, the revelation of the Rapture originates from Jesus (especially Matthew 24:37-44 and John 14:1-3).

He continues by saying in <u>v15-18</u>: **"that WE who are ALIVE and REMAIN until the COMING of the Lord will by no means precede those who are asleep. For the Lord Himself will descend from Heaven with a shout, with the voice of an archangel, and with the Trumpet of God. And the dead in Christ will rise first. Then WE who are ALIVE and REMAIN shall be CAUGHT UP together with them in the clouds to meet the Lord in the air. And thus, WE shall always be with the Lord. Therefore comfort one another with these words."** Paul has already described Christ's Coming for His Church as imminent in 1Thessalonians 1:10. The imminence of the Rapture is further emphasised in these verses in a few ways. (1) Paul described those who would be ALIVE at the time of the Rapture as WE, showing that he lived in the expectancy that he would be raptured rather than resurrected from the dead. In other words, the Rapture was for him an imminent hope, something that could happen at any time. (2) The whole dramatic nature of the passage speaks of Christ suddenly breaking into history, taking everyone by surprise. (3) The key word that describes the Rapture is *harpazo*, translated 'caught up', means 'to seize and transport away suddenly, to snatch away' (Acts 8:39), including from earth to heaven (2Corinthians 12:2,4, Revelation 12:5). This speaks of an event that happens suddenly, without warning.

This imminence is further confirmed by Paul's parallel description of the Rapture a few years later in 1Corinthians 15:51-52: **"Behold, I tell you a MYSTERY: WE shall not all sleep, but WE shall all be changed—in a MOMENT, in the twinkling of an eye, at the last Trumpet. For the trumpet will sound, and the dead will be raised incorruptible, and WE shall be changed."** Not only does he show his belief in imminence by saying: **"WE shall not all sleep, but WE shall all be changed"**, but also by emphasising the sudden nature of this event, in that it takes place **"in a MOMENT"** (*atomos* – an atomic second, the shortest possible length of time), **"in the twinkling of an eye."** There will be no signs or warnings. It will suddenly happen and take us all by surprise, and it will all be over as soon as it starts. Before people know what is happening, it will be over. Paul's use of the term MYSTERY speaks of a revelation that is not in the Old Testament (that was hidden in God, but now revealed), but introduced for the first time by Jesus and His apostles, confirming that this is not the 2nd Coming.

1Thessalonians 4:13-18 resonates with the teachings of Jesus on the Rapture: (1) It describes how all the believers will suddenly be snatched and taken to meet Jesus in the air, which corresponds exactly to Matthew 24:40-41. (2) The result from the world's point of view will be as if a THIEF had come and taken a multitude of believers (Matthew 24:43, Luke 12:39). (3) The outcome and purpose of this event is that: **"we shall always be with the Lord"** (v17), which is a source of comfort while we wait (v18). This agrees perfectly with Jesus' description of the purpose of His Return for us: **"that where I am, there you may be also"** (John 14:3).

In 1Thessalonians 1:10, Paul linked the Rapture with the Start of the Day of the Lord, implying that these 2 events are simultaneous. As we move now from 1Thessalonians 4 to 5, we will see that he takes this connection for granted. Despite the chapter break, 1Thessalonians 4:13 - 5:11 forms a single connected passage, and it is important to bear this in mind. This is clear from the consistency of content in discussing end-time events, and the parallel verses 4:18 and 5:11, which describe the common purpose of imparting comfort to God's people through this revelation. Having described the Rapture in 1Thessalonians 4:13-18, he then transitions to discuss the TIMING of this event, that he has just been describing (the Rapture), and its relation to the next SEASON of world history, in 5:1: **"But** (*peri de*) **concerning the TIMES and the SEASONS, brethren, you have no need that I should write to you."** The reason why Paul said he did not need to write to them on this issue is that they already knew the answer, but nevertheless Paul gave it to them: **"For YOU yourselves know perfectly that the DAY of the LORD so COMES** (begins) **as a THIEF in the night"** (v2). Notice that continuity with the previous section (1Thessalonians 4:13-18) tells us that the question he was addressing was the TIMING of the RAPTURE, but he gave his answer in terms of the START of the DAY of the LORD. In other words, in his mind these 2 events are simultaneous, 2 sides of the same coin. Thus, for Paul, the RAPTURE is the initiating event of the DAY of the LORD, as in 1:10. His answer to the TIMING of the Rapture and Start of the Day of the Lord is that it is unknown, it could happen at any time, because it comes as a THIEF. A thief comes suddenly and at a time that cannot be predetermined, when people are not expecting. The coming of a thief satisfies all the requirements of imminence: (1) suddenness, (2) unexpectedness, (3) unpredictability, (4) the lack of any warning signs, and (5) the possibility of occurrence at any moment. His answer to the question, as to what new SEASON this special event of the RAPTURE will inaugurate, is clearly that it will initiate the DAY of the LORD. Thus, the imminent sudden arrival of the Day of the Lord as a thief (5:2) is directly connected (simultaneous) with the imminent Coming of the Lord in the Rapture (4:13-18). This is Dual Imminence.

Paul takes the image of a THIEF from the teaching of Jesus (Matthew 24:43, Luke 12:39), and we can see how the teaching of Paul and Christ harmonise. The only difference is that Jesus said HE is coming as a THIEF, whereas Paul said the DAY of the LORD is coming as a THIEF. They must both be speaking of the same imminent event. Thus, the Day of the Lord is coming as a thief, because when Jesus comes as a thief, He will immediately initiate the Day of the Lord. Moreover, the Coming of Christ as a thief must be the very Coming of 4:15-18, His Coming to rapture the Church. Thus, this Coming in the Rapture is to rescue us from the DAY of the LORD, which He initiates at the same time. The reason why this rescue is necessary is that this DAY is a time of Divine WRATH, as Paul confirmed in 5:9: **"God did not appoint us to WRATH, but to obtain SALVATION through** (the Coming of) **our Lord Jesus Christ** (in the Rapture)." The context of this verse is his discussion of the exemption of the believers from the Day of the Lord (see 5:2-5), therefore he is referring to the WRATH of the DAY of the LORD. Therefore, God did not appoint us (believers) to go through the Day of the Lord on earth, but instead to receive the salvation of our bodies and deliverance from this time of wrath in the Rapture at the Coming of our Lord Jesus

Christ. Thus 5:9 confirms our previous conclusion that Christ is coming in the Rapture to save us from the Day of the Lord, just before His wrath is released.

Thus, Paul's teaching here is in full agreement with the teaching of Jesus, that the DAY of the LORD will start suddenly, without warning, as the COMING of a THIEF – this being the COMING of the LORD Himself to receive His own to Himself in the Rapture (4:13-18), and to initiate the Day of the Lord on earth (5:2). As a THIEF, He comes to take the precious things (His Church) from the house (world), and to bring loss (judgment) to the house. So, this confirms the teaching of Jesus, that when He comes in the Rapture as a THIEF to remove His people from the earth, at the same time He initiates the DAY of the LORD (judgment) upon the earth. In this way both JESUS comes as a THIEF (Matthew 24:43-44) and "the DAY of the LORD comes as a THIEF" (1Thessalonians 5:2). Since the coming of a thief is imminent, it follows that the Rapture and the Start of the Tribulation are both imminent events (Dual Imminence). Thus, in 1Thessalonians 5:2, Paul addressed the issue of the timing of the Rapture and the Start of the Tribulation, using the same terminology and coming to the same conclusion as the Lord Jesus. Since we agree Paul was discussing the imminent Pre-Tribulation Rapture in 1Thessalonians 4:13 - 5:11, it follows that Christ was also discussing the same events in Matthew 24:26-44.

1Thessalonians 5:3: **"For when THEY** (the unbelievers) **say: "Peace and safety!" then SUDDEN DESTRUCTION comes upon THEM** (the unbelievers)**, as LABOUR PAINS upon a pregnant woman. And THEY** (unbelievers) **shall not escape** (it's a worldwide judgment)**."** Having mentioned the coming of the DAY of the LORD (v2), in v3 he (1) gives more detail about its START, and (2) defines what he means by 'the DAY of the LORD.'

*(1) The main that he makes about the START of the Day of the Lord is its IMMINENCE, which is emphasised in a number of ways. The Day of the Lord comes suddenly upon the whole world: **"The DAY of the LORD comes as a THIEF in the night"** (v2). Just before it happens, the world is saying 'peace and safety.' This indicates that normal life is going on, and there are no signs indicating that judgment is about to fall (just as Jesus described in Matthew 24:37-39). This is in stark contrast to the time before the 2nd Coming, which will be the time of Great Tribulation worse than any other time in history, with the Bowls of Wrath being poured out, and Armageddon under way, so bad, in fact that Jesus said unless He cuts this time short by His Return, no flesh would survive (Matthew 24:22). While life in the world is carrying on normally, out of nowhere: **"SUDDEN DESTRUCTION comes UPON THEM"** (v3). This describes the sudden destruction that will overtake the world, when the Day of the Lord suddenly comes upon them like a

THIEF. The word for 'destruction' does not mean the end of existence, but would best be translated as 'ruin'. Thus, the Day of the Lord will be a time when the world suddenly falls into a state of RUIN, and this will happen SUDDENLY, when Christ comes as THIEF to initiate the Day of the Lord, a world-wide judgment from which no one on earth will escape. So, the Tribulation is initiated by the Coming of the Lord as a Thief to take His own in the Rapture.

*(2) The definition of the DAY of the LORD is essential to get right, as many wrongly say it is the day of His 2nd Coming. This issue is settled by this verse, which confirms it refers to the whole TRIBULATION, not just the 2nd Coming. This beginning of the DAY of the LORD, bringing sudden destruction on the earth, is compared to the sudden onset of LABOUR PAINS, which then continue and intensify until the Birth (at the 2nd Coming). This is the description used elsewhere for the unique time of TRIBULATION that comes immediately before Messiah's manifestation in glory. The Jews refer to this time as the Birth Pains of the Messiah. In particular, Paul is expounding the teaching of Jesus in Matthew 24:7-30, where He describes the End of the Age (the Tribulation) as the time of worldwide BIRTH PAINS (v8), which lead up to the 2nd Coming, when God's Kingdom is manifested (born) on the earth. So, Paul equates this unique time of BIRTH PAINS, when the whole earth suddenly begins to fall into ruin, with the DAY of the LORD, proving that the Day of the Lord describes the whole period of judgment leading up to the 2nd Coming. The impossibility of escape shows its worldwide nature. Thus, the DAY of the LORD is the time of worldwide LABOUR PAINS. This proves the DAY of the LORD is the whole TRIBULATION, not just the 2nd Coming. It also shows the New Testament, is consistent with the Old in its use of language, in describing the Day of the Lord. This meaning of the Day of the Lord is vital to understand, in correctly interpreting 2Thessalonians 2:2-3.

In 1Thessalonians 5:2-11, Paul consistently contrasts the experience of believers (referred to as YOU and US) and unbelievers (referred to as THEY and THEM) in relation to the Day of the Lord: **"YOU yourselves know perfectly that the Day of the Lord so comes as a THIEF in the night. For when THEY** (unbelievers) **say: "Peace and safety!" then sudden destruction comes upon THEM** (unbelievers)**, as labour pains upon a pregnant woman. And THEY** (unbelievers) **shall not escape** (the Day of the Lord). **BUT YOU brethren, are not in** (the kingdom of) **darkness, so that this DAY** (of the Lord) **should overtake YOU as a THIEF"** (v2-4). He specifically says that the sudden destruction of the Day of the Lord (the Birth Pains) will come on THEM, and they will not escape, because they are in the kingdom of darkness, and therefore subject to Divine Judgment. Thus, the Day of the Lord will suddenly come upon and overtake THEM like a Thief, and they will not escape its judgments. BUT, in contrast to the godless world, this will not be the experience of true believers in Christ, who are not in satan's kingdom, and therefore who are not subject to Divine Judgment, including the Day of the Lord. Therefore, we will not be overtaken by the Day of the Lord, and neither will we experience it as the coming of a thief. So, we will not have to go through this time of worldwide judgement, because Christ will rescue us from it by the Rapture (1:10, 4:15-18).   The world will experience the Rapture as if a thief has come, after a billion people are suddenly taken from the earth. On the other hand, the true Church will not experience the Rapture as the coming of a thief, but as an escape from the darkness of the Tribulation, being rescued by our Bridegroom.

So, it is the Lord who initiates the time of worldwide judgement called the Day of the Lord, by coming as a Thief to remove the Spirit-filled Church from the earth, and in so doing He will remove the restraining force on the antichrist and evil generally (2Thessalonians 2:6-8). This results in the Birth Pains of the Tribulation starting suddenly, causing great destruction all around the world, and intensifying until Christ returns in power and glory. Thus, the Tribulation is initiated by the Coming of the Lord as a Thief to take His own in the Rapture. Moreover, both the Coming of Christ to rapture His saints and His Coming to initiate the Day of the Lord are imminent, because they are simultaneous, as he previously asserted in 1:10 (Dual Imminence).

1Thessalonians 5:5-7: **"YOU are all sons of light and sons of the day** (members of the Kingdom of light). **WE are not of the night nor of** (the kingdom of) **darkness. Therefore, let US not sleep, as others do, but let US WATCH** *(gregoreo)* **and be sober. For those who sleep, sleep at night, and those who get drunk are drunk at night."** Here Paul applies the truth of Christ's imminent Return to call believers to wake up from their sleep and walk in the light, in fellowship with God, so that they WATCH for His imminent Return for them (Paul's emphasis on WATCHING to describe the right response to the imminent Rapture, derives from the teaching of Jesus, which is another confirmation that when Jesus said 'WATCH' in prophetic passages, He was speaking of the Rapture). Since we belong to the kingdom of light, we should be spiritually awake, and living in the light of God. We are not in the kingdom of darkness, so we should not be living like the sons of darkness, as if we are living in darkness, being spiritually asleep (out of fellowship with God), just as they are, drunk with the lusts and cares of life. The judgment of the Day of the Lord is about to come upon all those in the kingdom of darkness, so it is totally inappropriate for sons of light to be living in the darkness, just like the people of this world. So instead of sleeping we should watch, and instead of being drunk, we should be sober.

1Thessalonians 5:8: **"But let US who are of the day** (the Kingdom of God's light) **be sober, putting on the breastplate of faith and love, and as a HELMET the HOPE** (confident expectation) **of** (future) **SALVATION."** Hope relates to the future, so this helmet over our head, signifies that our thoughts should be focused on our future salvation, which in the context of this passage, must be a reference to the SALVATION that we will receive at the RAPTURE, (1) the SALVATION of our BODY, and (2) our SALVATION from the DAY of the LORD (the Tribulation). Thus, this is a command parallel to the command to watch (v6). Therefore, we are told to WATCH for the Coming of the Lord (v7), in expectant HOPE that He will SAVE us (v8). Therefore, we are to WATCH for His imminent COMING in the RAPTURE to save (transform) our lowly bodies, as well as to deliver us from the WRATH, about to come upon the earth (v9).

1Thessalonians 5:9: **"For God did not appoint us to WRATH, but to obtain SALVATION through** (the Coming of) **our Lord Jesus Christ."** In the context, this WRATH is the WRATH of the DAY of the LORD (v2,4), not the wrath of Hell. This confirms that the Day of the Lord is a time of Divine Wrath. Moreover, the SALVATION in v9 must be the same as the future SALVATION of v8, that is, the SALVATION that we will receive through the Coming of the Lord in the Rapture. So, Paul has been saying that the Day of the Lord (Tribulation) is coming as a thief upon the whole godless world (v2-3), but believers will not go through it (v4), because we belong to the Kingdom of God (v5). Therefore, we should WATCH for Christ's imminent Coming for us (v6), rather than sleeping and living in spiritual darkness (v7). We have the blessed HOPE of imminent SALVATION through the RAPTURE, when our body will be saved, and we will be delivered from the Day of the Lord (v8). We can set our hope on our imminent SALVATION in the Rapture, rather than having to fear the coming imminent WRATH of the Day of the Lord, because God has not appointed us to WRATH, but instead to obtain SALVATION through the Coming of the Lord (v9). Thus, although the wrath of the Day of the Lord is imminent, we do not have to fear it, but rather we can look forward to our imminent rescue in the Rapture, before any part of the Day of the Lord begins. Therefore, the only way that the Start of the Day of the Lord can be imminent, as well as the Rapture is if both events are simultaneous. This agrees perfectly with the parallel verse of 1Thessalonians 1:10.

The fact that the SALVATION of v8 and v9 is what we will receive at the RAPTURE is confirmed by 1Thessalonians 5:10-11: **"who DIED for us, that whether we WAKE** (*gregoreo* - live and stay watchful) **or SLEEP** (die), **we should LIVE together with Him. Therefore, COMFORT each other and edify one another, just as you also are doing."** These concluding verses of Paul's teaching in 1Thessalonians 5:1-11 contain a number of parallelisms with his teaching on the Rapture in 1Thessalonians 4:13-18. (1) The completion of our salvation (our bodily transformation and resurrection) in the Rapture and our deliverance from God's wrath was accomplished on the basis of Christ's death and resurrection (5:10, compare 4:14). (2) Paul divides the Church into 2 groups, those who are ASLEEP and those who are AWAKE at His Coming (5:10), which corresponds to those who are ASLEEP, the dead in Christ (4:13,14,15,16), and those who are ALIVE and REMAIN (v15,17) at His Coming. (3) The result of the Rapture is that we will all: "live together with Him" (v10), which corresponds with: "thus we shall always be with the Lord" (4:17). (4) The effect of the teaching in 1Thessalonians 5 is to COMFORT believers (5:11), just as the effect of the teaching of the Rapture in 1Thessalonians 4 is to COMFORT believers (4:18). These similarities with the classic Rapture passage in the previous chapter, show the Rapture is still central to the thought of 1Thessalonians 5:1-11, confirming that when we are told to look expectantly for the future SALVATION, that will come through our Lord (5:8,9), this is referring to our CATCHING up from the earth to meet Jesus in the air (4:17) in the RAPTURE, by which action of God's grace and mighty power, we will be rescued from the Tribulation (5:2-5,9), and physically changed and glorified (1Corinthians 15:50-57).

Finally, it is worth noting that the believers, who are still ALIVE at the Rapture, are described as those who are AWAKE, in contrast to those who are ASLEEP in death (v10). Paul used the word *gregoreo*, normally translated 'WATCH', to describe those believers who will be alive at the Rapture. Jesus often used this word to describe the spiritual state of expectancy and alertness, that He expects us to have, as we live in the light of His imminent Return. Likewise, Paul had just used the same word in v6 with this very same meaning, exhorting us all to WATCH. This word is not normally used as a synonym for those who are physically alive, so by using it he is saying more than that. Of course, only those who are ALIVE will be WATCHING for His rescue in the Rapture from the Day of the Lord (v2-4), so it does refer to believers still alive at the Rapture. Having commanded us to WATCH in faith (v6), Paul now conveys his expectation that believers will be those who are WATCHING for His Return. This is a defining characteristic of a true believer (see also 1Thessalonians 1:10, Hebrews 9:28, Titus 2:13, Philippians 3:20). This is not to say that there will not be some believers who will be out of fellowship, when Jesus returns, but Paul does not consider them worthy of discussion. (This is similar to Jesus' lack of mention of unbaptised believers in Mark 16:16). They will deeply regret their unfaithfulness, when they stand before Christ at His Judgment Seat to give an account of their service to Him.

To summarise, 1Thessalonians 5:1-11 confirms the teaching of Jesus about 'the Day of the Lord' (v2), being a time of Birth Pains and Destruction, which will suddenly come upon the whole world, and intensify until the Birth (2nd Coming), and there will be no escape (v3). This Day of the Lord is initiated by the Rapture (4:13-18), when the Lord comes as a Thief in the night (v2), in agreement with Matthew 24:42-44. The true Church will not go through the Day of the Lord, but will be saved from it by the Rapture (v4-10), for it is a time of Divine Wrath and we are not appointed for wrath (v9). In the Rapture, Jesus will come from Heaven to deliver us from this wrath to come (1:10). Thus, this passage teaches Dual Imminence.

2Thessalonians 1:4-10

In writing to the Thessalonians saints, Paul starts by saying he boasts in their patience and faith in enduring all the persecutions and tribulations that they are facing (2Thessalonians 1:4-5). Then he goes on to assure them that God's righteous judgment will ultimately prevail: **"Since it is a righteous thing with God to (1) repay with tribulation** (thlipsis) **those who trouble** (thlibo) **you, and to (2) give you who are troubled** (thlibo) **rest** (anesis) **with us, when the LORD JESUS is REVEALED from Heaven, (1) with His mighty angels in flaming fire taking vengeance on those who do not know God, and on those who do not obey the Gospel of our Lord Jesus Christ, who shall be punished with everlasting destruction** (separated) **from the Presence of the Lord and from the glory of His power, when He COMES, in that DAY, (2) to be glorified in His saints and to be admired among all those who believe, because our testimony among you was believed"** (v6-10).

This complex sentence is a challenge to interpret for those who distinguish between Christ's Coming in the Rapture and His 2nd Coming. Twice Paul describes a Coming of the Lord (as His Revelation from Heaven and as His Coming) and twice he describes the two-fold result of this Coming: (1) to bring tribulation and judgment upon the unrighteous, and (2) to give rest and glory to the believers. There is an interesting alternating structure moving between (1) His judgment upon unbelievers, and (2) His blessing upon believers (rest and glory), both of which are accomplished by His Coming.

The key question is whether He is describing the Rapture before the Tribulation or the 2nd Coming at the end of the Tribulation. At first sight, some phrases seem to fit better with the Rapture and others with the 2nd Coming, so perhaps Paul is somehow combining both events into one description? For me, this idea seems to be over complex, whereas the natural reading of this passage is that it is describing a single dramatic intervention of Christ into history, with dramatically different results for the just and the unjust. In other words, His Coming simultaneously brings rest and glory to the just, and affliction and judgment upon the unjust. Because of the strong judgment imagery, it is commonly assumed that this must describe the 2nd Coming, because many minimise the Divine Judgment aspect of the whole Tribulation, blinding them to the possibility that it might refer to the judgments of the Tribulation. Even those who believe in a Pre-Tribulation Rapture often think that the real judgments of God only happen at or just before the 2nd Coming. Moreover, they generally think of the Rapture, as just being about Christ coming for His saints, and not relating it directly to the Tribulation. If one's idea of the Rapture is disconnected from the Day of the Lord (judgment), then one would naturally assume these verses describe the 2nd Coming. This is the way I thought, until I began to see the truth of Dual Imminence and how it runs throughout and connects together all the New Testament prophetic scriptures (as I am demonstrating), so that they cannot be fully understood without it. This truth is that when Christ comes for His Church, at the same time He also comes to initiate the Day of the Lord (judgment) on earth. We saw from 1Thessalonians 1 and 4-5 that this concept was intrinsic to Paul's whole way of thinking. Once I renewed my mind to think in line with Dual Imminence, this difficult passage suddenly made sense, and I saw that it perfectly fits with the classic Rapture-Tribulation pattern, that we see throughout the New Testament. In particular, Dual Imminence accounts for the combination of blessing and judgment in this passage. I aim to prove that when read through the eyes of Dual Imminence, it gives a detailed description of the results of Christ's Coming in the Rapture for both believers and unbelievers. In other words, this passage is a classic example and proof of Dual Imminence, because it provides the way to harmonise all of its aspects within a Pre-Tribulation framework.

Let us look at each phrase at a time, starting with: **"it is a righteous thing with God to repay with tribulation** *(thlipsis)* **those who trouble** *(thlibo)* **you"** (v6). This is something God will do: **"when the Lord Jesus is revealed from Heaven"** (v7a). This is looking forward to a future event (a Coming of Christ), when He will justly punish those who had brought tribulation upon the saints, by causing them to experience what they had been inflicting on believers, namely ongoing tribulation over a period of time: **"your patience and faith in all your persecutions and tribulations** *(thlipsis)* **that you endure"** (v4). The use of *thlipsis* (v6) does not speak of their immediate death, so it cannot refer to what happens at the 2nd Coming. Paul clearly chose this word to correspond to the *thlipsis* the Thessalonians were presently experiencing (see v4,6). So, in the context, to use *thlipsis* to describe the suffering that will come upon the wicked at the 2nd Coming would be inappropriate and misleading. This word, especially in this context, carries the idea of ongoing continuous pressure and suffering over a period of time, rather than a final climactic judgment. Whereas the use of *thlipsis* is not a good fit with the experience of the ungodly at the Revelation of Christ at His 2nd Coming, it perfectly describes their continuous suffering throughout the Tribulation, that is initiated by the Revelation of Christ at His Rapture. This is confirmed by the fact that the word Paul used to describe this time (*thlipsis*) is the very same word Jesus used as His name for the special time of trouble leading up to the 2nd Coming, namely, 'the Tribulation (*thlipsis*)' (Matthew 24:9,21,29). As we have seen, Paul built his prophetic teaching on the foundation of Christ's teaching, so by using *thlipsis* to describe a future time of judgment on unbelievers, he is making an obvious association with the Tribulation at the End of the Age that Jesus described. Thus, the natural reading of v6 is that God will repay those who oppose and persecute the Church, by causing them to go through a future period of time, during which they will suffer affliction and tribulation, in other words the Tribulation! This perfectly describes what will happen immediately after the Rapture, when Christ will come from Heaven and reveal Himself to His Church (but not to the world), as we rise to meet Him in the air (1Thessalonians 4:15-17). At that same time, He will initiate the Tribulation, which will come upon those who remain. Thus 2Thessalonians 1:6-7a tells us that Christ's Coming in the Rapture will immediately initiate the Tribulation, which agrees perfectly with Dual Imminence.

At the same time that Christ will bring the Tribulation upon the unjust (v6), He will also, **"give you** (believers) **who are troubled REST** *(anesis)* **with us, when the LORD JESUS is REVEALED from Heaven with His mighty angels"** (v7). The word translated 'rest' speaks of the release and relief of believers from the affliction, tension, stress, strain and suffering brought about by their persecutors (see v4,5). This general relief from tribulation for living believers takes place when the Lord comes from Heaven. Clearly this refers to the Rapture (not the 2nd Coming), assuming a Pre-Tribulation Rapture. This also agrees with the final phrase, because when Jesus comes in the Rapture, He comes with an army of His angels, under the command of an archangel (1Thessalonians 4:16). The fact that Paul includes himself in this event reflects his expectancy to be alive at the Rapture, based on imminence, which he expressed elsewhere (1Thessalonians 4:15,17, 1Corinthians 15:51). Thus 2 things will happen at the same time when Jesus comes from Heaven: (1) unbelievers will enter into Tribulation and (2) believers will enter into rest. Both of these must refer to what happens at the Rapture, not the 2nd Coming. So, again, v6-7 is a direct statement of Dual Imminence.

Some argue Paul is thinking of the Tribulation saints, who will suffer great persecution, and only enter into rest at the 2nd Coming. Based on this, they say the 2nd Coming is in view here. However, this is inconsistent with a Pre-Tribulation Rapture, as Paul is clear to which believers he is giving this promise of rest at Christ's Coming. It is the Thessalonian believers ('you') and Paul's team ('us') – all of whom are Church Age believers. Therefore, this is specifically a promise to believers in the Church Age, and it will be fulfilled at the Rapture. Now, due to Paul's belief in imminence, he spoke as if he (and the Thessalonians) will be alive at the Rapture, as in 1Thessalonians 4:15,17, even though they have now all died, and so will not experience the Rapture of the living, as he had hoped and desired. However, that does not invalidate the promise of believers receiving rest at the Rapture (2Thessalonians 1:7), for it will be fulfilled for all who those who are still alive when He comes, in the very same way that the rapture-promise of 1Thessalonians 4:15,17 will be fulfilled for all those who are still alive when He comes.

In the next part of the sentence, Paul expands on the judgments that will be released on the wicked at this time: **"when the Lord Jesus is revealed from Heaven, with His mighty angels in flaming fire taking vengeance** (executing righteous judgments) **on those who do not know God, and on those who do not obey the Gospel of our Lord Jesus Christ, who shall be punished with everlasting destruction** (separated) **from the Presence of the Lord and from the glory of His power"** (v7b-9).

These are the verses that cause people to think that Paul is referring to the 2nd Coming, because they assume that angels only execute judgments at the 2nd Coming, but a closer examination shows otherwise. In the 2nd Coming, it is Jesus Himself who personally and directly judges His enemies (Revelation 19:11-15), whereas during the Tribulation He is the Judge, but He uses the angels as His instruments of judgment. Jesus made this clear in the Parable of the Wheat and the Tares, where He describes the time of judgment (reaping the harvest) as 'the End of the Age'. In chapter 1, we established that this refers to the Tribulation. During this time, it is the angels that carry out their Master's judgments on the tares (Matthew 13:39-42): **"The Son of Man will send out His angels"** (v41). His judgments through angels on the tares come before the wheat are gathered into the barn at the 2nd Coming (v30). The tares are uprooted (suffer physical death) and then thrown into a furnace of fire, where they will suffer everlasting punishment (first in the fire of Hades, and then later in the Lake of Fire). Moreover, the description of v7-9 fits Revelation 6-18 very well, with angels being Christ's main instruments of judgment throughout the Tribulation. As well as the high-ranking angels administering the 7 Trumpets and 7 Bowls from Heaven, there are the angelic host that cast Satan and his angels from their positions in the 1st heaven (the atmosphere), ruling over the darkness of this world (Ephesians 6:12). Since the angelic host already operate in the earth (2Kings 6:16-17, 7:6), surely their earthly activity will be far greater in the Tribulation. Thus 2 Thessalonians 1 does not describe the completion of judgment on the day of the 2nd Coming, but the Coming of Christ in the Rapture to initiate a time of judgment, which continues until its climax at the 2nd Coming.

The key issue in deciding whether these verses (v7b-9) refer to (1) the 2nd Coming or (2) to the Rapture, is whether they describe Christ (1) exercising the judgments directly Himself, or (2) through His angels. In other words, is it (1) the Lord Jesus 'in flaming fire' taking vengeance on the God-rejectors, or is it (2) the angels 'in flaming fire' who are Christ's instruments of vengeance at this time? I submit that the evidence is strongly in favour of the latter. First of all, the angels are described as 'mighty angels' indicating that they will exercise great power at this time. This phrase should have been translated literally as: 'the angels of His power', which makes it clear that they are the instruments of His power (judgment) at this time. Thus, He is revealed from Heaven with the angels of His power, who will immediately start executing judgments on the ungodly. Secondly, this is confirmed by the word order in the Greek, for 'in flaming fire' is placed right after 'the mighty angels' not 'the Lord Jesus.' Thirdly, angels are described in this exact same way in Hebrews 1:7: **"And of the angels He says: "Who makes His angels spirits, and His ministers a flame of fire"** (see Psalm 104:4). In conclusion, this describes a Coming of Christ from Heaven with the fiery angels of His power, who then start to exercise His vengeance (literally: His righteous punishment) on the ungodly ('taking vengeance' is in the present tense indicating ongoing action over a period of time). This is an accurate description of what happens throughout the Tribulation. The objects of this judgment are all unbelievers, who are guilty of suppressing the truth of God revealed through Creation and conscience (Romans 1:18-23), and of rejecting the Gospel of Christ for their salvation. This is confirmed by the closest parallel verse: **"For the Son of Man will come in the glory of His Father with His angels, and then He will reward** (repay) **each according to his works"** (Matthew 16:27, also Luke 9:26). Although this can be applied to both the Rapture and the 2nd Coming, the primary meaning must be the Rapture, because He is motivating His disciples, who will live in the Church Age (not the Tribulation) to be ready for His Coming, when He will repay everyone according to their works. We know the Judgment Seat of Christ, when the saints of the Church Age will be judged for their reward, takes place at the Rapture, not the 2nd Coming. This verse also implies that at this same Coming He will also repay the ungodly by means of judgment, another example of Dual

Imminence. Of course, this verse also describes what He will do in His 2nd Coming to those who are in the Tribulation.

So 2Thessalonians 1:7b-8 describe the 2 aspects of His Coming at the Rapture, as it applies to: (1) His people, and (2) the world, namely: (1) His personal revelation to His Church, and (2) His release of the angels of His power to administrate judgments to the world. In the Day of the Lord: **"When (1) the Lord Jesus is REVEALED** *(apokalypsei)* **from Heaven** (to His Church), **(2) with His mighty angels in flaming fire taking vengeance** (executing righteous judgments) **on those who do not know God, and on those who do not obey the Gospel of our Lord Jesus Christ."** Other Scriptures, where the terminology of REVELATION *(apokalypse)* is used to describe the RAPTURE, that is, Christ's REVELATION to His Church, are 1Corinthians 1:7, 1Peter 1:7, 1:13 and 4:13. There is nothing in these verses that directly implies that Christ will reveal Himself in His glory to the whole world at this time, simply that He will initiate judgments.

The role of the mighty angels in the Tribulation will be to exercise temporal judgments upon the ungodly, up to and including physical death, but next Paul points out that this temporal judgment is just the prelude to their everlasting judgment, which begins after death for all unbelievers: **"who shall be punished with everlasting destruction** *(olethros)* **from the Presence of the Lord and from the glory of His power"** (v9). *'Olethros'* in the Bible never refers to annihilation, which cannot be everlasting. Instead, it describes the state of being separated from God, and the loss of everything worthwhile in life. A good translation would be 'ruin.' The nature of this permanent destruction is described in the next phrase, which reinforces the idea of separation from God: **"from** *(apo* – 'separated from') **the Presence** (face) **of the Lord and from the glory of His power."** Separation from the Lord's loving, life-giving, peace producing Presence is the essence of eternal punishment, resulting in the loss of everything that brings meaning and blessedness to life. Everlasting banishment from God's Presence is how Jesus described the punishment of the lost (Matthew 7:23, 8:12, 22:13, 25:30, Luke 13:27). This is the opposite of what is promised to believers, that: **"we will be with the Lord forever"** (1Thessalonians 4:17). Being in His Presence and experiencing His Glory is what makes Heaven heaven. Now the preposition 'apo', translated here as 'from', is capable of 2 possible interpretations: (1) it can carry a causal force, signifying 'proceeding from', in which case Paul is describing the destruction proceeding from the Lord's Presence. It is this way of reading it that causes some to identify this as taking place at the 2nd Coming. However, most scholars prefer the alternative reading that (2) it carries a spatial force, signifying 'away from', 'separation from' or 'alienation from.' This is reflected in many English translations that use phrases like: "banished from the "Presence of the Lord", "they will be kept far from the Presence of our Lord", "they will suffer the punishment of eternal destruction, away from the Presence of the Lord" (ESV), "separated from the Presence of the Lord", "excluded from the Presence of the Lord", "shut out from the Presence of the Lord" (NIV). This way of reading this verse fits better with the context, and keeps it from being a mere repetition of the idea in v7-8. Moreover, it gives a fuller picture of the abiding nature of this everlasting punishment. Whereas the causal meaning just describes the initiation of this punishment in time, the spatial meaning describes the ongoing nature of this everlasting punishment. Since Paul moves from the temporal judgments on the unsaved in v7-8 (ultimately resulting in death), to their everlasting judgment (ruin) in v9, which begins at death, it is surely better to interpret his meaning as describing the nature of this everlasting punishment, rather than simply describing its source. Understood properly therefore, v9 is not a description of the 2nd Coming, but of the everlasting punishment of all unbelievers at death, in particular those who are killed in the judgments by angels in the Day of the Lord.

To summarise, 2Thessalonians 1:7b-9 reveals 2 stages of judgment upon the lost. First, (1) the temporal judgment of an early death inflicted by Christ and His angels on unbelievers throughout the Tribulation (including the 2nd Coming) – verse 8, followed immediately in each case by (2) their everlasting judgment of everlasting separation from the Presence (goodness) of God, that begins for unbelievers immediately after their death (first in Hades, then later in the Lake of Fire) - verse 9: **"When the Lord Jesus is revealed from Heaven, (1) with His mighty angels in flaming fire taking vengeance on those who do not know God, and on those who do not obey the Gospel of our Lord Jesus Christ, who shall be punished with everlasting destruction** (separated) **from the Presence of the Lord and from the glory of His power."**

So far in v6-9 we have seen Paul describe what happens, when the Lord Jesus is revealed from Heaven: (1) He will initiate a time of Tribulation, which will come upon the ungodly, but not upon the believers, for at this very same time, (2) He will cause His own to enter into perfect   rest from tribulation (through the Rapture). This is Dual Imminence. Then He gave more detail about the Tribulation judgments He will initiate at this time upon those who reject the Gospel, emphasising the role of angels, and the fact that as a result many will be killed. He then made it clear their judgment will not end at death, for they will then experience everlasting separation from God. This also implies it will then be too late for them to repent for their fate will be sealed. Paul then concludes this sentence by saying: **"when He COMES, in that DAY, to be glorified in His saints and to be admired among all those who believe, because our testimony among**

you was believed" (v10). In the Greek, Paul puts 'in that DAY' emphatically at the end of the whole sentence, so it should be translated: **"when He COMES to be glorified in His saints and to be admired among all those who believe, because our testimony among you was believed - in that DAY."** In other words, His Revelation from Heaven, when He rescues His people from all tribulation, and releases a time of judgment on the rest, will take place when He COMES to be glorified in His saints – a clear reference to the Rapture, when we will receive our new perfect bodies and be glorified. His glory will be fully manifested in us, and as a result He will receive all the glory for the total transformation He has worked in us, for all the saints will marvel at what He has accomplished in them by His grace and glory, and they will see Christ and be awestruck at His Glory, and at what He has done for all His people. Interpreted within a Pre-Tribulation framework, and remembering Paul is specifically writing to Church Age saints to encourage them there is a day coming when Christ will personally intervene in history and bring them relief from tribulation and glorify them, then this must be speaking of the Rapture, not the 2nd Coming, for the 2nd Coming is not when He comes to be glorified in the Church Age saints.

It remains to note how Paul ended this long sentence with: **"in that DAY."** Surely this signifies that everything he has just described takes place on ONE very special DAY, the day of the Coming and Revelation of Christ from Heaven, when He will (1) start to release tribulation and judgment upon His enemies, and (2) when He will give His own rest from trouble and glory. The key question is whether this DAY is the day of the Rapture or the day of the 2nd Coming. From the Pre-Tribulation viewpoint (previously established by 1Thessalonians), it is clear that the description of what Christ will do for His people on this day, requires that this is the day of the Rapture. If this is correct then it also follows that Christ will initiate the judgments of the Day of the Lord on the same day as the Rapture. That is, the Rapture initiates the Tribulation. This is the same conclusion (Dual Imminence) that we have previously seen again and again in all the prophetic teaching of Jesus and Paul, and which we will see again in all the prophetic teaching of James, Peter, and John. In particular, we saw Dual Imminence in 1Thessalonians - that Christ's Coming is imminent, when He will rescue His Church from the Wrath of God that is about to come on the earth (1:10), indicating that this Wrath starts on the same day as the Rapture. Then having described the Coming of Christ in the Rapture (4:15-18), Paul immediately compares this Coming of Christ to the coming of a thief in the night, bringing loss (judgment) to an unsuspecting world, through initiating the Day of the Lord, a time of ruin that will suddenly overtake the whole world, like Birth Pains (5:1-3), this also being a time of Divine Wrath (5:9). Both the Rapture and the Start of the Day of the Lord are described as imminent, because they take place on the same day. It follows that this interpretation of 2Thessalonians 1:6-10 (above) agrees perfectly with what Paul had already established in 1Thessalonians, that on the same day that He raptures His Church, Christ will initiate the judgments of the Day of the Lord on earth. This confirms that 2Thessalonians 1:6-10 describes events on the Day of the Rapture, and thus it constitutes a strong and detailed statement of the truth we are establishing in this chapter.

Thus, this interpretation of 2Thessalonians 1:6-10 harmonises perfectly with the previous context (the pattern of thought established in 1Thessalonians). Moreover, it harmonises with and makes better sense of what immediately follows in 2Thessalonians 2:1-3, which directly flows from 2Thessalonians 1:6-12 (v11-12 is a prayer based on v6-10). 2Thessalonians 2 starts with the Rapture: **"Now concerning the Coming of our Lord Jesus Christ and our gathering together to Him"** (v1). 'Now concerning' indicates a transition of thought, but the basic subject matter is the same – the events related to the future Coming of Christ at the End of the Age. Also remember that originally there were no chapter breaks, so we should expect a continuity of thought from chapter 1. Consistency requires that the Coming of the Lord to give the saints rest and glory in (1:6-10) is the same Coming as in 2:1 (the Rapture). If Paul describes the 2nd Coming in 1:6-10, but then shifts to describing the Rapture in 2:1, that would be an unnatural break of thought. Yes, the start of 2Thessalonians 2 marks a transition, but only in so far as Paul is now applying the truth that he established concerning the Rapture to a particular issue that had arisen to trouble the Thessalonian Church. The problem was caused by the spreading of a false teaching that the Day of the Lord (Tribulation) was already present (v2,3a), no doubt a panic reaction to increasing persecution. In responding to this issue, Paul began by highlighting and appealing to the established truth of the Rapture (v1). This can only be because he knew that this truth was the key to disproving this deceptive doctrine. Since the issue was whether or not the Church was in the Day of the Lord, it follows that this truth related to the Rapture must be to do with the relationship of the Rapture with the Day of the Lord. Since Paul is asserting that the Church was not in the Day of the Lord, the relevant truth to which he was appealing must be that the Church must be raptured before the Day of the Lord, and so since the Rapture had not yet happened, they could not possibly be in the Day of the Lord. We have seen that this is exactly the truth that Paul established both in 1Thessalonians and in 2Thessalonians 1. In fact, to be more precise, it is the truth that the Rapture will initiate the Day of the Lord. We will see that Paul goes on to restate this truth in 2Thessalonians 2:3, 6-8a, confirming that the

Thessalonians were not in the Day of the Lord, or about to suffer under the antichrist, because the Rapture must happen first (2:1).

So now we can see the perfect harmony and flow of Paul's teaching. Having described Christ's Coming to glorify His Church in the Rapture and initiate the Tribulation (1:6-10), he then applies this truth (2:1) to refute the false teaching that the Church was presently in the Tribulation (v2), because it was obvious the Rapture had not yet taken place. He then confirms this by declaring that the Day of the Lord will only begin and the man of sin be revealed, once the Church has departed (v3), for the Church is restraining the manifestation of antichrist, so that he will only be revealed after the Church is taken out of his way (v6-8). Thus, the context confirms our interpretation of 2Thessalonians 1:6-10. It not only agrees with the preceding context of 1 Thessalonians, but also with what immediately follows in 2Thessalonians 2. With this interpretation, we can see clearly how the 2 chapters are closely connected, and how 1:6-10 sheds extra clarity and light on 2:1-8. The fact 2Thessalonians 1:6-10 teaches Dual Imminence (the truth of the Rapture initiating the Tribulation), brings it into harmony with 1Thessalonians 1:10 and 4:15 - 5:10 and 2Thessalonians 2:1-8 (which all teach the same truth). Thus, we see the perfect consistency of Paul's prophetic teaching throughout his 2 letters to the Thessalonians.

In conclusion, 2Thessalonians 1:6-10 is speaking about the Coming of Christ, when He reveals Himself to His Church in the Rapture, and immediately initiates the Tribulation on earth. This all happens in one day (v10). There are opposing descriptions of what happens to the just and the unjust at this time, emphasised by an alternating pattern, where v6 is expanded by v8-9, and v7 is expanded by v10. (This provides a confirmation that the Tribulation (v6) is also a time of Divine Judgment = Vengeance - v8). Although there is some resonance of these verses with the 2nd Coming (as the climax of the Day of the Lord), understanding Dual Imminence (the Day of the Lord starts with the Rapture, a truth that is embedded throughout the New Testament prophetic passages) helps us to see there is a far greater resonance with the Rapture, followed immediately by the judgments of the Day of the Lord.

2Thessalonians 2

2Thessalonians 2 provides further confirmation that the Rapture initiates the Tribulation. Having described the judgments of the Tribulation initiated by the Lord's Coming in the Rapture in 2Thessalonians 1:6-12, Paul continues his discussion of these end-time events in chapter 2. At this point transitions to applying what he has already established to refute a false teaching that was troubling the Church at that time, namely that the Day of the Lord, the

Tribulation, the time of antichrist's dominion, had already come: **"Now, brethren, concerning the Coming of our Lord Jesus Christ and our gathering together to Him** (the Rapture)**, we ask you, not to be soon shaken in mind or troubled, either by spirit or by word or by letter, as if from us, as though the DAY of the LORD** (the Tribulation, see 1Thessalonians 5:2-3) **had come"** (v1-2). Paul's response to this was: **"Let no man deceive you by any means: for that DAY** (the Day of the Lord) **shall not come unless the falling away** (*apostasia* = departure) **comes first, and the man of sin** (the antichrist) **is revealed, the son of perdition** (destruction)**"** (v3).

In 2Thessalonians 2:1-3, Paul is refuting the false doctrine, that was beginning to spread, which said that the Day of the Lord (Tribulation) had already begun, so that they were now living in that time (v2). The best explanation for why they were taking this doctrine seriously is based on the increasingly intense persecution that they had been experiencing (1:4-7). They knew from Christ's teaching that the Tribulation would be marked by terrible persecution of the saints on an unprecedented scale, coming to its head with the time of antichrist's dominion (Matthew 24:9-12, 15-21), which Paul would have taught them (he went on to describe antichrist's activity in the Tribulation in v3-8, mentioning that he had already taught them these things in v5). Moreover, Paul had taught them that this was the Day of the Lord, a time of Divine Wrath (1:10, 5:2,9, reaffirmed in 2Thessalonians 1:6-8). So, in the face of their severe persecutions, some overreacted and assumed that things were so bad that the Tribulation must have already begun (people make exactly the same mistake today, when they claim one of the Seals, Trumpets or Bowls has taken place). This was then reinforced by people getting overexcited and giving false prophecies out of their own heart, as well as others claiming that Paul taught this false doctrine, even to the point of writing a forged letter in his name teaching it. Naturally, many of the Thessalonians were troubled by this teaching, that they were in the Day of the Lord, because they knew that this was a time of Divine Wrath, as well as great persecution, and they had been taught by Paul, that they were not appointed unto Wrath (1Thessalonians 5:9), and would be rescued from it by the Rapture (1:10), before the Tribulation.

2Thessalonians 2:1-3 is a difficult passage and its correct interpretation depends on an accurate understanding of a few specific words, complicated somewhat by bad translations. Firstly, some translations say 'the Day of Christ' rather than 'the Day of the Lord' in v2, however the best manuscript evidence points to 'the Day of the Lord' as being correct, as this is reflected by the majority of translations. This is important, as we have previously established the meaning of 'the Day of the Lord' as being the Tribulation. Many assume 'the Day of the

Lord' here refers to the day of His 2nd Coming (which Post-Tribbers identify with v1). However, this is impossible. If the false teaching was that Christ had already come in power and glory and raptured His Church, Paul would not have had to give any arguments to refute it, because this event had manifestly not taken place yet. Indeed, the Thessalonians would not have been troubled by such a teaching that was so obviously wrong, for they surely knew Christ hadn't yet returned in power and glory. In order to avoid this inconsistency, some translations of v2 say: **"as though the DAY of the LORD was AT HAND."** However, this is simply wrong. The verb is in the perfect tense, signifying completed action in the past with existing results, meaning it "has come and is here." Thus, the false teaching was that the Day of the Lord had already come and was present. Thus, the phrase does not denote imminence, but actual presence. This is an established grammatical fact, and the only reason for translating it otherwise was the need to make sense of the verse, which makes no sense, if the Day of the Lord is assumed to mean the 2nd Coming. Thus, the translation: **"as though the Day of the Lord had come"** is much better than: **"as though the Day of the Lord was at hand"**, which is just wrong. However, even this does not carry the full meaning of the perfect tense. A more accurate translation would be: **"as though the Day of the Lord had come and is now present"** or even just: **"as though the Day of the Lord is now present."** You might be thinking, what difference does it make? Surely: **"as though the Day of the Lord had come"** carries much the same meaning as: **"as though the Day of the Lord is now present."** This translation 'is present' which captures the meaning of the perfect tense of this verb is confirmed by its usage elsewhere (Romans 8:38; 1Corinthians 3:22, 7:26; Galatians 1:4; Hebrews 9:9). As far as v2 is concerned it does not make much difference, but the correct translation and understanding of v3 depends on getting v2 right.

1Thessalonians 2:2: **"…as though the Day of the Lord had come. v3 Let no one deceive you by any means; for *that DAY will not come* unless (1) the falling away (*apostasia*) comes first, and (2) the man of sin is revealed."** Clearly Paul is determined to prove that they were not in the Day of the Lord, and he points to 2 events that have not happened to make his point. However, the text does not explicitly say whether these events come before the Day of the Lord or immediately after it begins, because the Greek sentence is not complete, for the words in italics in v3 are not there in the original Greek. Paul expects us to supply the missing phrase from the previous verse, which is what all translators do (it is normal not to repeat a verb, if it is the same verb as before, for example, we can say: "I go to the shops, then home" rather than: "I go to the shops, then I go home."). Now most translators add: *"that Day will not come"* based on their translation of verse 2: *"as though the Day of the Lord had come."* This gives the verb a future sense, which changes Paul's meaning. In making his correction, Paul is not so much focusing on the future, but addressing the present situation. He is establishing the current non-presence of the Day of the Lord, so that therefore they could not be in that Day. However, if we translate verse 2 correctly, and then supply the missing phrase in v3, according to the correct version of v2, we get this result: **"...as though the Day of the Lord is now present. Let no one deceive you by any means; for *that DAY is not present* unless (1) the falling away** *(apostasia)* **comes first, and (2) the man of sin is revealed."**

The reason why it is important to get this right is that we need to correctly discern the order of events in v3. Are the *apostasia* and the revelation man of sin within the Day of the Lord, or must they come before it, or perhaps the *apostasia* comes before the Day of the Lord, but the man of sin is revealed within the Day of the Lord? If v3 reads: **"for *that DAY will not come* unless (1) the falling away** *(apostasia)* **comes first, and (2) the man of sin is revealed"**, then all of the above are possible. In particular, many use this translation as a basis for saying that the *apostasia* and the revelation of the man of sin must both take place before the Day of the Lord, which contradicts the imminence of the Day of the Lord. This interpretation does not necessarily follow, as a parallel sentence demonstrates: "for the hour of lecture will not come, unless the bell rings first, and the teacher begins to speak." In this case, the bell initiates the lecture, and the teacher speaking is part of the lecture. Thus, in this case, both events are within the hour, not events that come before it. Thus, this translation of v3 leaves the question of the order of events as unknowable, which was surely not Paul's intention.

However, translating v3 correctly, removes this ambiguity: **"for *that DAY is not present* unless (1) the falling away** *(apostasia)* **comes first, and (2) the man of sin is revealed."** Now the plain meaning is that both events are within the Day of the Lord, and they indicate its arrival, with the *apostasia* happening right at its start. Our parallel sentence would be: "for the hour of lecture is not present, unless the bell rings first, and the teacher begins to speak."

Another issue to settle relates to the word 'first' *(proton)* in v3. Some take it to mean that one or both of these events must happen before the Day of the Lord begins. But we have shown this to be incorrect. Therefore, this 'first' tells us about the order of events within the Day of the Lord, that the *apostasia* precedes the revelation of the man of sin. This is confirmed by its position in the sentence. If Paul intended to say that both these events come before the Day of the Lord, he could have made himself clearer by placing 'first' before these 2 events.

A final confirmation to our conclusion is that we have grammatically parallel constructions elsewhere in the New Testament (John 7:51, Matthew 12:29, Mark 3:27), where (1) the main clause has a present tense verb, followed by (2) an 'unless' clause with two events separated by an 'and', and (3) the word 'first' connected to the first event. In each case, the 'first' does not indicate that the events precede the time of the main clause. Rather, it indicates the order of the 2 events within the time when the main clause is being fulfilled. A literal translation of John 7:51 is: **"Our Law does not judge the person unless (1) it first hears from him and (2) knows what he is doing, does it?"** (NASB). The verb translated 'judge' is in the present tense, signifying the judicial process, not the final verdict. The judicial process is not carried out until (1) the court has heard from the defendant, and (2) has gained knowledge of his actions. These 2 things do not precede the judicial process; they are part of it. The word 'first' indicates the order of events within the judicial process - that the court must first hear what the man has to say before it can come to a knowledge of what he has been doing. We see the same pattern in Mark 3:27: **"No one can enter a strong man's house and plunder his goods, unless (1) he first binds the strong man, and then (2) he will plunder his house."** Again, the word 'first' clearly does not indicate that these 2 events must happen before he can enter the strong man's house. Instead, it signifies the necessary order of events once he has entered the house.

To summarise, 2Thessalonians 2:3 can be paraphrased as: "the DAY of the LORD is not present, unless first in sequence within that Day the *apostasia* comes as its initial event, followed immediately by the revealing of the man of sin." Thus, it tells us that the Day of the Lord is not already underway unless 2 events happen; first, the *apostasia*, and then the revelation of the man of sin. Both these events take place WITHIN the Day of the Lord, not before it, which preserves imminence. Thus, these verses cannot be used to disprove the imminence of the Day of the Lord. This in turn frees Paul from the accusation that he is contradicting what he previously said in 1Thessalonians 5:2, that: **"the DAY of the LORD will come as a THIEF in the night"** (that is, without advance notice, without any warning signs).

So, the issue Paul was addressing in 2Thessalonians 2:1-3 was the false belief that the Day of the Lord had begun (v2). The event to which he appealed to refute it was the RAPTURE of the Church (v1), which he had previously affirmed would happen BEFORE the Day of the Lord, in fact, it was the event that initiated the Day of the Lord (1Thessalonians 1:10, 4:15 - 5:9, 2 Thessalonians 1:6-10), for **"the DAY of the LORD comes (begins) as a THIEF in the night"** (1Thessalonians 5:2). That is, the Day of the Lord is initiated by Christ's Coming as a thief (the Rapture). Therefore, his argument is clear – since the Rapture has not yet happened, it follows the Day of the Lord cannot possibly be present. It simply remained for him to make this point explicitly to complete his proof, which is exactly what he does in v3: **"Let no man deceive you by any means: for that DAY** (of the Lord) **is not present, unless the falling away** (*apostasia*) **comes first, and** (then) **the man of sin** (antichrist) **is revealed, the son of destruction."**

To show that this is the case, it is necessary to understand the correct meaning of the word *apostasia* in v3. Unfortunately, most translations miss the point of what Paul was saying, and translate it as 'falling away'. However, the basic meaning of this word is 'departure' – either a physical or spiritual departure (a departure or falling away from the faith). Since this word is often (but not always) used for spiritual or religious departures, many translations assume it is a spiritual departure in this case (rather than letting us decide for ourselves from the context), and so translate it as 'falling away.' In Part 2, I proved that *apostasia* does not always refer to a spiritual departure, as many assume. Sometimes, in other places where *apostasia* is used, it is obvious from the context that describes it a spiritual departure, and in that case, it would be valid to render it as 'falling away.' However, that is not true in this case, so it should be translated 'departure' (as in the older English translations), thus leaving it open for the reader to discern the nature of the departure. In v3, Paul does not specify what this departure is; he simply calls it 'the *apostasia*' that is, '<u>the</u> departure', which means he was referring to a specific, well-known departure, and that he assumed the nature of this departure would be obvious from the context. So, we have to look in the preceding verses to see what departure Paul was talking about, and it is right there in v1, where he announced the key event central to the discussion: **"Now, brethren, concerning the Coming of our Lord Jesus Christ and our gathering together to Him."** So, he is talking about the Rapture, the Departure of the Church from the earth! This is confirmed by the fact there is no mention of a departure from the faith. So, the right interpretation of v3 is: *"Let no man deceive you by any means: for the Day of the Lord is not present, unless the Departure of the Church (the Rapture) comes first (see v1), and then the man of sin is revealed."* In other words, he is explicitly saying that the Tribulation will not start until the Rapture comes first, and then immediately after that the antichrist will be revealed, who is destined for destruction. Therefore, since the Rapture had obviously not taken place yet, the Tribulation was not present, and so, they were not to worry that they were in the Tribulation, nor was it the time yet for antichrist to be revealed. Thus, in v1, Paul stated the key event – the Rapture (v1), that was the basis for demolishing the false teaching described in v2 - that the Day of the Lord was already present. Then in v3, He affirmed his teaching that the Day of the Lord will only become present when the Rapture happens, so since the Rapture had clearly not happened yet, the Day of the Lord could not possibly be present. In this way, Paul proved that this was a false teaching.

If the correct translation of v3 is: **"that DAY** (of the Lord) **is not present, unless** (1) **the DEPARTURE** (of the Church) **comes first, and** (2) **the man of sin is revealed"**, then it also follows that the Rapture is the initiating event of the Day of the Lord. It is not sometime before the Day of the Lord, but it is within the Day of the Lord, at its very beginning. This confirms the very truth that we have seen emphasised in the teaching of Jesus and in 1Thessalonians 1:10, 5:2 and 2Thessalonians 1:6-10 – the truth that we have put under the heading of Dual Imminence.

So far, I have focused on the fact that the Day of the Lord will only be present once the Rapture has taken place, but Paul also asserts that the Day of the Lord will only be present when the antichrist is revealed. Taken together with his statement that the Rapture must happen first, and then the revelation of antichrist, we must conclude that the revelation of antichrist must take place immediately after the Rapture, even on the same day (rather than just soon after). In this way, both events will be signposts of being in the Day of the Lord. Paul is pointing to 2 events that had not yet happened to establish the fact that they were not yet in the Day of the Lord.

In 2Thessalonians 2:4-8, Paul confirms the conclusion he established in v1-3, where he described the Day of the Lord as being initiated by (1) the Rapture, followed immediately afterwards by (2) the initial revelation (rise) of the antichrist on the world-scene. These 2 events characterise the start of the Day of the Lord, by which one can know that it is present, the disappearance of the believers and the initial manifestation of antichrist, being the first visible signs to those on the earth that the Day of the Lord has begun (v3). In v4-8, Paul fortifies us in this truth by developing our understanding in two areas – first, the relationship of antichrist to the Day of the Lord, and second, the reason why the revelation of the antichrist is so closely connected to the Rapture. We will see that the harmony of what Paul says in v4-8 with v1-3 gives a strong confirmation of our interpretation of v3, that the Rapture initiates the Tribulation.

First, in v3-8, Paul gives an overview of the relationship between the time of antichrist's prominence and the Day of the Lord, pointing out that the time of antichrist's activity on the world-stage corresponds exactly with the time of the Day of the Lord. He described the Tribulation in terms of (1) antichrist's initial revelation at its beginning, (2) his ascendency to world-dominance, and (3) his fall at its end. First, (1) there is his initial revelation or rise to power at the start of the Tribulation (v3,6,8), then (2) his self-exaltation in the middle of the 70th Week, when he takes over the Temple and claims to be God: **"who opposes and exalts himself above every so-called god or object of worship, so that he takes his seat in the Temple of God, displaying himself as being God"** (v4). At this time, He desecrates God's Temple erecting the Abomination of Desolation – an idol-image of himself (the image of the beast). At this time, he rises to world-power supported by the false prophet and speaking satanically inspired words, supported by supernatural signs and wonders, resulting in multitudes being deceived by him, as the world as a whole follows him and worships him (this is when he becomes world dictator). He introduces the mark of the beast and demands that the world worship him. This results in a massive persecution of the saints, because they refuse to take his mark of ownership, as this would require them to disown their Lord God (Jesus). Those who rejected the truth of the Gospel in the Church Age and the first half of the Tribulation will be open to this strong delusion and will take the mark of the beast as the outward sign of their absolute loyalty and surrender to the antichrist in worship, resulting in their eternal condemnation (Daniel 7:21,25, 12:7, 9:27, Matthew 24:15-21, Revelation 11-14, 2Thessalonians 2:9-12). Then finally, (3) Paul describes his final destruction by Christ at the end of the Tribulation: **"whom the Lord will consume with the breath of His mouth and destroy with the brightness of His Coming"** (v8). Thus, the whole Tribulation, from its beginning to its end, can be seen as the time of antichrist, from his revelation to destruction. In teaching these things, Paul said he was just reminding them of what he had already told them (v5). Later, Revelation confirmed the very same facts, with the Tribulation starting with the initial rise of antichrist (6:1-2), followed by his activity in the middle of the 70th Week, when he takes over the Temple and becomes world-dictator, commanding the peoples to worship him as God, and persecuting the saints throughout the world (Revelation 11-13), before being destroyed by Christ at the end of the Tribulation (Revelation 19).

Thus, the Day of the Lord can be seen in 2 complementary ways. First, it is a time of God's wrath upon the whole world, and second, simultaneously, it is a time when evil is allowed to come to its fullness, especially as personified in antichrist. These 2 aspects are represented by the 2 main terms for this period of time, the Day of the Lord and the Tribulation. These 2 aspects are closely connected, because as evil increases, it becomes increasingly ripe for judgment, and so in the Day of the Lord, evil reaches a point where God responds to it by pouring out His wrath. Man's rebellion against God continually increases throughout the Tribulation, which in turn calls forth increasingly severe judgments from God, leading up to His total destruction of all the powers of evil and all evil-doers at His 2nd Coming. 2Thessalonians 2:3-12 tracks this increase in evil and corresponding increase in Divine Judgment, by viewing it through the rise and fall of the antichrist, from the very start of the Tribulation to its final end, and this simultaneous increase in evil and Divine wrath is described in much more detail in Revelation, as we will show later. In particular, after showing the raptured Church in Revelation 4-5, it describes the judgments by Christ, right at the start of the Tribulation, starting with the breaking of the 1st Seal, releasing the rider on the white horse (the antichrist) going forth to conquer the world (Revelation 6:1-2). This corresponds to the initial revelation (rise) of the man of sin in 2Thessalonians 2:3,6,8. Later, he achieves world-power (v4, Revelation 11-13), and evil comes to a head his one world-system (in the Great Tribulation), resulting in the 7th Trumpet and 7 Bowls. His evil comes to a head at Armageddon, when he tries to annihilate God's elect nation (Israel), resulting in the destruction of his world-system (Babylon) in Revelation 18, and his own final destruction at the 2nd Coming in Revelation 19. Thus, the time of the Tribulation is exactly the same as the time of antichrist.

Secondly, in 2Thessalonians 2:6-8a, Paul sheds extra light on why the 2 key events in v3 at the start of the Day of the Lord (the Rapture and initial revelation of antichrist) are so closely connected: **"you know what restrains him** (the man of sin) **now, so that in his time he will be revealed. For the mystery of lawlessness is already at work; only he who now restrains will do so, until he is taken out of the way** ('removed from the midst'). **Then that lawless one will be revealed."** Notice that the revealing of antichrist (v3) is mentioned twice more in v6,8, where we are told he will be revealed at a time determined by God. God has a RESTRAINING POWER in place, which prevents his revelation, and only when it is removed, will he be revealed. Paul expected the readers to know the identity of the Restrainer. Indeed, it's clear both from the context and the New Testament as a whole, that it can only be the Church, empowered by the Holy Spirit. Those who seek to avoid this obvious conclusion (because it confirms a Pre-Tribulation Rapture), offer a number of speculative alternatives, none of which have any basis in the text itself. But, if we look in the context, it is clear that the Church and its removal is the very subject under discussion (v1), and this is confirmed by the mention of the Departure of the Church in v3. Moreover, the nature of the Church is that it consists of those who are in Christ, the Body of Christ, which means by its nature, it is set in opposition to the antichrist. Moreover, from its first mention, Christ authorized the Church to stand against the powers of evil (Matthew 16:18-19). Moreover, the spirit of antichrist is the denial of Christ and His Gospel (1John 2:18,22, 4:3, 2John 1:7), and so it is the Church, through carrying the Presence of Christ, and releasing His Presence through our prayers and our proclamation of Christ and His Gospel, which restrains the spirit of antichrist at this time, because the Spirit of Christ in us opposes the spirit of antichrist. The Restrainer is described in a 2-fold way, as a WHAT in v6 and a HE in v7, signifying a 2-fold identity. This confirms it is the Church, empowered by the Holy Spirit, which restrains the antichrist. When the Church is removed from the earth in the Rapture, the Spirit is still present on earth, but His restraining ministry through the Church is removed, allowing the antichrist to be manifested. Therefore, the taking out of the way of that which restrains the antichrist is the Departure of the Church (v3), when we are gathered together to Him at His Coming (v1).

Thus v6-8a says that the true Church is presently restraining the antichrist, preventing him from being revealed, and this state of affairs will continue until it is removed in the Rapture, and then he will be revealed. When the Church is taken out of the way, then evil can come to its fullness, especially in the person of the antichrist, to which God will respond by increasingly pouring out His wrath on the world system in the Day of the Lord. (God allows evil to come to its fullness, in order to complete His judgment on evil). Thus v6-8a explain why the 2 events in v3 (the Departure of the Church and the revelation of the antichrist) are so closely connected, and why the Departure must happen first, followed immediately by the revelation of antichrist. It is like an archer, who has attached the arrow and pulled the bow back fully, ready to fire the arrow. But someone stronger is restraining his hand, so he cannot release the arrow. Then at a certain time, when that restraint is removed, the arrow will be immediately released, without delay. Likewise, Paul paints the picture, that as soon as the restraint of the Church is removed, the antichrist will be released into world-scene. This explains the close connection between the Rapture and the initial revelation of antichrist, which was revealed in v3, in particular, why the antichrist's manifestation happens immediately after the Rapture. Thus, in v6-8a, by focusing on the relationship between the Rapture and the revelation of antichrist, Paul confirms his assertion in v3 that the Departure of the Church, when the one restraining the antichrist is taken out of the way, is the initiating event of the Day of the Lord, since the Tribulation corresponds exactly with the time of antichrist, the time characterised by his rise at its start, his rule and his destruction at its end. Thus v6-8a explains, clarifies, confirms and agrees perfectly with the thought of v3, that the Day of the Lord starts with the Rapture, followed immediately by the revelation of the antichrist. In this way, we can see with this interpretation, that the whole passage (v1-8) harmonises together perfectly, with the Rapture being the key central event, just as v1 clearly states. In v3, he says the Rapture initiates the Tribulation, the time of antichrist's revelation. Then in v6-8a, he says the same thing again in other words. From this we can also see that

Paul used the word for 'departure' for the Rapture in v3, to make it easier for us to see that he is talking about the same event in v7, when he talked about 'the taking away' of the Church.

Thus, the central truth that unifies the whole passage is that the Day of the Lord begins with the Rapture. In this chapter, we are discovering that this truth, along with the imminence of His Coming, is at the heart of many of the major prophetic passages in the New Testament. The combination of these 2 truths tells us that the Coming of the Lord is imminent, and that when He comes, He will (1) receive His Church in the Rapture, and at the same time (2) initiate the Day of the Lord on earth. In other words, both the Rapture and the Day of the Lord are imminent events (Dual Imminence), and the fact that we often see the prophetic Scriptures witnessing to Dual Imminence provides further evidence, which confirms the correctness of this central truth.

To summarise, the Thessalonians had heard a false teaching that the Day of the Lord had already begun, and so was present, and therefore they had entered into the time of the antichrist. In response, Paul assured them that the Day of the Lord, with its associated rise and activity and dominion of the antichrist, would not be present until first the Church departed (was removed) from the earth in the Rapture, and only then would the antichrist be revealed (v1-3). In order to establish and reinforce this key truth, he then explained why antichrist can only be revealed after the Church is removed in the Rapture (v6-8), the reason being that the Church is restraining the manifestation of antichrist, implying also that as soon as it is removed, antichrist will start to be revealed. (The close connection between v1-3 and v6-8 is seen in the fact that they discuss the relationship between the same 2 events - the removal of the Church and the revelation of the antichrist). This then also explains why the Day of the Lord starts with the Rapture (**"the Day of the Lord comes as a thief in the night"** – 1Thessalonians 5:2), because the Rapture itself is the initiating judgment of the Day of the Lord, when God starts to removes His hand of restraint on evil. It also explains why his claim in 2Thessalonians 2:3 is true, that the start of the Day of the Lord on earth is marked by the Rapture followed immediately by the manifestation of antichrist. Therefore, this claim in v3, supported by v6-8, provided 2 reasons why the Day of the Lord was not yet present: (1) the Rapture had not happened yet, and (2) the antichrist had not yet been revealed. Thus, this whole passage explains the connection between the Rapture, the Start of the Day of the Lord, and the initial revelation of antichrist. The Rapture is the initiating event of the Day of the Lord (1Thessalonians 5:2, 2Thessalonians 2:2-3, 6-8), which is immediately followed by the revelation of antichrist. The Rapture must happen first, resulting in the revealing of the antichrist (v1-3), for he cannot be revealed until the Restrainer (the Church empowered by the Spirit) is taken out of the way, and then he will be revealed (v6-8a). Thus, the start of the Tribulation is marked by the Rapture followed immediately by the revealing of antichrist, as he arises on the world-stage. This agrees with the Book of Revelation, which describes the Rapture (4:1), and the raptured Church in Heaven, represented by the 24 elders (Revelation 4-5), followed soon after by Christ breaking the 1st Seal, resulting in the rider on the white horse (the antichrist) going forth to conquer (Revelation 6:1-2).

Chapter 6: Dual Imminence
in the Teaching of James, Peter, and John

In the last chapter, we saw how the apostle Paul consistently taught Dual Imminence. In this chapter, we will see how this same truth was also revealed by the other apostles, James, Peter and John, concluding our demonstration of the unity and harmony of the whole teaching of the New Testament in this area, which shows that the prophetic teachings of all the apostles were built on the foundation of the prophetic teaching of our Lord Jesus Christ Himself.

The Apostle JAMES

James 5:1-8 warns about a coming time of judgment on the ungodly, especially the wealthy, who have used their position and power to oppress the poor: **"Come now, you rich, weep and howl for your miseries that are coming upon you! Your riches are corrupted, and your garments are moth-eaten. Your gold and silver are corroded, and their corrosion will be a witness against you and will eat your flesh like fire. You have heaped up treasure in the LAST DAYS. Indeed, the wages of the laborers who mowed your fields, which you kept back by fraud, cry out; and the CRIES of the reapers** (for God to intervene and judge on their behalf) **have reached the ears of the LORD of SABAOTH** (the Lord of Hosts or Armies)**.**" **You have lived on the earth in pleasure and luxury; you have fattened your hearts** (for judgment) **as in a DAY of SLAUGHTER. You have condemned, you have murdered the just** (righteous)**; he does not resist you."** **Therefore, be PATIENT, brethren, until the COMING of the LORD. See how the Farmer** (Christ) **WAITS for the precious fruit of the earth, WAITING PATIENTLY for it until it receives the early and latter rain** (of the Holy Spirit)**. You also be PATIENT. Establish your hearts** (on the promise of His Coming)**, for the COMING of the LORD is AT HAND. Do not grumble against one another, BRETHREN, lest you be judged. Behold, the JUDGE is STANDING at the DOOR!"**

Although the wicked face judgment and punishment when they die (Hebrews 9:27, Luke 16:19-28), this is not the judgment that James is primarily warning about here. The reference to "the last days" (v3) point to the eschatological judgments coming on the world at the end of the Church Age. The fact that the cries of the oppressed have reached the ears of the Lord of Armies (v4), not only means that He has heard their prayer, but that He is ready to move in judgment, by coming with His angelic armies to judge the wicked. This describes the Day of the Lord, which is likened to a Day of Slaughter (v5). Thus, this does not describe the everlasting punishment of the wicked after death, but the Day of the Lord, in which multitudes will be killed in a short time. This is made plain in v7a, which says that this judgment of the wicked will take place at the COMING of the LORD. Then James assures them that this COMING of the LORD is AT HAND, that is it is imminent (it could happen at any time). Then in v9, James confirms that the Lord is coming as the JUDGE, and further emphasises the imminence of His Coming, by picturing Him as standing at the door, about to enter into the courtroom to render judgment. The timing of this Coming of the Lord is described as the end of the Church Age, when He has determined that the full harvest (the precious fruit of the earth), has been brought forth from the sowing of the Gospel Seed in the Church Age (v7b), and is therefore ready for reaping, by the Rapture (Romans 11:25). Meanwhile, Christ is waiting patiently for the full harvest of souls to be brought forth, before He returns to gather them all to Heaven. This agrees with 2Peter 3:9, which explains the apparent delay in His Coming as His longsuffering in granting to all those who are to be saved in the Church Age, the time and opportunity to come to repentance.

In this passage, James applies the truth of the Lord's COMING to 2 groups of people: (1) the WICKED, warning them of the judgment that Christ will bring upon them when He returns, and (2) the suffering BRETHREN, in the family of God, encouraging them that the Coming of the Lord to deliver them and bring judgment on their oppressors is at hand. Therefore, this passage describes the dual aspect of the same COMING of the Lord at the end of the Church Age: (1) He is COMING as the JUDGE, to release His judgment upon the unrighteous (v1-9), and also at the same time (2) He is COMING for the righteous, to rescue them from their oppression and suffering. In view of this, the righteous are told to patiently wait for His Coming to deliver them: **"be PATIENT, BRETHREN, until the COMING of the LORD... See how the farmer** (Christ) **WAITS for the precious fruit of the earth, WAITING PATIENTLY for it until it receives the early and latter rain. You also be PATIENT. Establish your hearts, for the COMING of the LORD is AT HAND. Do not grumble against one another, BRETHREN, lest you be JUDGED** (called to account at the Judgment Seat of Christ). **Behold, the JUDGE is STANDING at the DOOR!"** (v7-9). The key to developing patience, while enduring suffering and oppression, is to establish our hearts in His promises of His imminent return to rescue us, for: **"the COMING of the LORD is AT HAND."** One sign of a lack of patience under oppression is when we "grumble against one another", blaming those who are close to us for our troubles. The antidote to this is to focus on the imminent Coming of the Lord, who is not just coming to initiate the judgments of the Day of the Lord upon the world, but who is also coming to judge all believers at the Judgment Seat of Christ. However, this is not a judgment for condemnation, but to determine eternal rewards. Nevertheless, it is a serious matter and those who spend their time pointing the finger rather than encouraging others and serving the Lord, will suffer loss of reward. James conjures up an amusing picture of some, who are about to be judged for their faithfulness to Christ, getting impatient as they wait for His Return, so they get into the Judge's Seat and start passing out judgments on their brethren. Meanwhile, the Judge is standing at the door, about to enter the Courtroom. You can easily imagine the reaction of a judge, if he enters his courtroom and catches someone sitting on His seat – they will surely face a stricter judgment, as Jesus said: **"Judge not, lest you be judged"** (Matthew 7:1).

The dramatic force of James' appeal to both the lost and the saved on the basis of the Coming of the Lord is heightened by his emphasis on IMMINENCE: **"the COMING of the LORD is AT HAND... Behold, the JUDGE is STANDING at the DOOR!"** (v8,9). The picture he paints is that Christ is ready to return at any moment; His hand is on the door handle. (The DOOR imagery derives from the teaching of Jesus in Mark 13:33-37 and Luke 12:35-38). Christ For the lost, this means they better repent quickly, before it is too late. For the brethren, it strengthens the encouragement to be patient and not lose hope, because their deliverance by Christ is imminent. He is telling them: *"be patient, hold on, stay faithful because Jesus is coming at any moment to rescue you."* Notice, James is speaking about the imminent Coming of the Lord, which means He is not describing His 2nd Coming, which is not imminent, but rather is heralded by all the events of the Tribulation. Thus, he is telling believers to focus their hope on Christ's imminent Coming in the Rapture. It follows that the judgments that He initiates at this same Coming must be the judgments of the Day of the Lord. In other words, when He comes to rescue His Church in the Rapture, He is also coming to initiate the Day of the Lord on the earth. Moreover, this Coming of Christ is imminent, which means both the Rapture of the Church and the Day of the Lord are imminent. Thus, James teaches the doctrine of Dual Imminence, that is, the Tribulation will start at the same time as the Rapture, and that both events are imminent.

In summary, James teaches that Christ's COMING is IMMINENT, when He will both (1) JUDGE the unbelieving world, by initiating the DAY of the LORD, and (2) RESCUE His own in the RAPTURE, and then judge them at His Judgment Seat for their faithfulness to Him. Thus, we see that James teaches the very same doctrine of Dual Imminence that is at the heart of all the prophetic teaching of the New Testament, starting with the teaching of Jesus, then also the apostle Paul, and as we shall shortly see, both the apostles Peter and John also.

The Apostle PETER

The Apostle Peter's end-time teaching builds upon and develops Jesus' teaching, especially in relation to what He taught about the days of Noah and the Flood. He takes up Jesus' analogy of Noah's Flood, and uses it, as Jesus did, to describe the coming time of God's WRATH on the whole unbelieving world, which includes the TRIBULATION (the DAY of the LORD).

1Peter 3:20-21

1Peter 3:20-21: **"When once the Divine longsuffering waited in the days of Noah, while the ARK was being prepared, IN WHICH** (Ark) **a few, that is, 8 souls, were SAVED through water. There is also an ANTITYPE to this** (salvation of believers, through being in the ARK), **which now SAVES US—BAPTISM** (into CHRIST, our ARK of SALVATION), **not** (by providing) **the removal of the filth of the flesh** (by a physical bath), **but** (by providing) **the answer of a good conscience toward God, through the resurrection of Jesus Christ."**

Some translations interpret the BAPTISM in v21, as the ANTITYPE of the WATER in v20, but that can't be right, because the WATER in the days of Noah was the instrument of JUDGMENT (v20), whereas the ANTITYPE is the instrument providing our SALVATION. What v20 describes is the salvation of believers from the wrath of God, through being in the Ark, which is a type of Christ, God's provision for their salvation. Just as the Ark bore the judgement of God, so that those, who by faith entered into the Ark, under its protective covering, were saved, so Christ on the Cross, bore the wrath of God upon Himself, so that those who trust in Him, come under the protective covering of His Blood, and are saved from God's wrath. Verse 21 is saying that the corresponding antitype to this salvation of Noah's family is our SALVATION, which we received when we were spiritually BAPTISED into CHRIST (our ARK of SALVATION), at the moment we trusted in Christ. This is not talking about our physical BAPTISM in WATER, but our spiritual BAPTISM into CHRIST by the Holy Spirit, at the moment of our salvation: **"BY one SPIRIT, we were all BAPTISED into one BODY** (of CHRIST), **whether Jews or Greeks, whether slaves or free, and have all been made to drink into one Spirit** (the New Birth)" (1Corinthians 12:13). Our BAPTISM into CHRIST, which SAVES us, by bringing us under His covering (atonement), happens when we put our trust in Christ. It is because we are IN CHRIST, that we are SAVED from God's JUDGMENT, just as it was because the 8 souls were in Noah's Ark, that they were saved from God's judgment. It is interesting that in the immediate context (v16), Peter uses the expression 'IN CHRIST.' (Baptism in water is an outward ritual signifying and testifying to our Baptism into Christ).

Now IN CHRIST, we are born again through the RESURRECTION of Christ (1Peter 1:3), who was fully accepted by God on our behalf. In Christ, we stand before God in Christ's righteousness, with all our sins having been forgiven (Ephesians 1:7). Therefore, through our union with Christ, we have been given a GOOD CONSCIENCE before God, for there is no condemnation for those who are in Christ (Romans 8:1), Thus, Noah's salvation in the Ark from the wrath of God is a picture of our salvation in Christ from God's wrath, which took place when we trusted in Christ, which includes our deliverance from God's everlasting wrath in Hell.

However, there is also a second application of this typology, which must have also been in Peter's mind, as we will see confirmed by other passages in his letters, where he uses Noah's worldwide Flood as a picture of the future Divine Judgment of the Day of the Lord, when God's wrath will be poured out on the whole world. The typology of 1Peter 3:20-21 has both a physical application as well as a spiritual one, for just as God provided a physical salvation from judgment through the Ark, for all the believers in the days of Noah, so likewise God will provide a physical salvation through Christ for all believers (rescue through the Rapture) from the Day of the Lord.   Just as our spirits have been saved by the impartation of Christ's resurrection power to them (v21, Ephesians 2:4-10), when they were baptised into Christ, our Ark of Salvation, so likewise, our bodies will be saved, by the impartation of Christ's resurrection power to them at the Rapture, when our Adamic bodies are put into Christ (1Corinthinas 15:47-57), and thereby we will rescued from physically going through the Tribulation-Flood. We would expect this to be in Peter's mind, because, as we have seen, Jesus used Noah's Flood as a picture of the Day of the Lord (Tribulation), and Noah's escape from Judgment in the Ark as a picture of the Rapture, and Peter built his teaching on the foundation of the words of Jesus, in obedience to Matthew 28:20.

Therefore, the typology of 1Peter 3:20-21 of the SALVATION of Noah from Divine WRATH, is not just a picture of (1) the SALVATION of believers from HELL, but also of (2) their SALVATION from the DAY of the LORD by the Rapture. It makes sense that Peter was thinking of our physical salvation in the Rapture, and deliverance from the Day of the Lord, as well as our spiritual salvation in the New Birth and deliverance from Hell (our physical salvation being a manifestation and outworking of our spiritual salvation), because JESUS used Noah's Flood as a picture of the Tribulation, and Noah's escape from judgment in the Ark as a picture of the Rapture. This is confirmed by what we will see in 2Peter, that just like JESUS before him, Peter uses Noah's world-wide FLOOD as a picture of the future judgment of the DAY of the LORD, when God's WRATH will be poured out upon the whole world. So, this teaches that we are not just delivered from the

WRATH of HELL, but also from the WRATH of the DAY of the LORD. Thus, this typology of tells us that just as God provided a physical salvation from the worldwide judgment of the Flood for all believers, by them being relocated into the Ark in the days of Noah, so God will also provide a physical rescue from the worldwide wrath of the Day of the Lord for all believers, by their physical Rapture into the Presence of Christ.

As confirmation of the fact that Peter built his prophetic teaching on the teaching of Jesus, in both 2Peter 2 and 2Peter 3, he used the very same analogy that Jesus used (Luke 17:26-27, Matthew 24:37-41), namely Noah's FLOOD is a type of God's coming wrath upon the whole world in the Tribulation, with God providing a rescue for believers before pouring out His wrath.

2 Peter 3:3-13

In 2Peter 3:3-10, Peter follows the teaching of Jesus in Matthew 24:37-39, in using Noah's world-wide FLOOD as a picture of the imminent future judgment of the DAY of the LORD, initiated by the imminent COMING of Christ, when God's WRATH will be suddenly poured out upon the whole world. Jesus compared what would happen at His COMING to the worldwide FLOOD, that suddenly fell without any warning signs. Peter makes the very same comparison.

2Peter 3:3-6: **"Knowing this first: that scoffers will come in the Last Days** (the Church Age)**, walking according to their own lusts, and saying: "Where is the PROMISE of His COMING? For since the fathers fell asleep, all things continue** (as normal), **as they were from the beginning of Creation." For this they wilfully forget: that by the Word of God the heavens were of old, and the earth standing out of water and in the water, by which the world that then existed PERISHED, being FLOODED with WATER."** Peter talks about the promise of His COMING, which the scoffers reject. Peter's response is to point to Noah's FLOOD, saying they wilfully ignore the truth (message) of the worldwide FLOOD, that when God warns of coming world-wide judgment, He means what He says. It is clear from this passage that Christ's COMING will be connected to a judgment upon the whole world, corresponding to the FLOOD, that His Coming will initiate a worldwide judgment, which can only be the Day of the Lord: **"the DAY of the LORD WILL COME as a thief in the night"** (v10).

Moreover, he is saying that in the Church Age, even up to the moment it ends, unbelievers will scoff at the warning of Christ's COMING to judge the world, pointing to the fact that life is going on just as it always has done (v3-4). In this, Peter is reaffirming the teaching of Jesus that normal life will be going on in the time leading up to Christ's COMING, just as it was in the time leading up to the FLOOD: **"As the days of Noah were, so also will the COMING of the Son of Man**

be. For as in the DAYS BEFORE the FLOOD, they were eating and drinking, marrying and giving in marriage, until the DAY that Noah entered the Ark, and did not know until the FLOOD came and took them all away, so also will the COMING of the Son of Man be" (Matthew 24:37-39). We have also seen that Paul made the very same point: **"The DAY of the LORD so COMES as a THIEF in the night. For when they** (in the world) **say: "PEACE and SAFETY!", then SUDDEN DESTRUCTION** (of the Day of the Lord) **comes upon them, as labour pains upon a pregnant woman. And they shall not escape** (it will be a world-wide judgment)**"** (1Thessalonians 5:2-3).

This tells us 2 things about the COMING of the Lord in view in these verses: (1) it is IMMINENT, and (2) it is not the 2nd Coming of Christ at the end of the Tribulation, which is not imminent, because all the events of the Tribulation must precede it, and which is by no means characterised by people living their normal lives, and saying "peace and safety" (Matthew 24:21-22, Revelation 6-18). This does NOT describe life just before the 2nd Coming, near the end of the Tribulation, but rather what people will be saying in the Church Age, before the imminent COMING of the Lord (as a thief) in the Rapture, when He will initiate the judgments of the Day of the Lord (Tribulation).

This implies that when Peter is talking about the promise of Christ's COMING (v4), he is not talking about His signposted 2nd Coming (as is commonly assumed), but His imminent COMING in the Rapture. Then in v5-6, he points to the fact that once before, God suddenly interrupted history by releasing a world-wide JUDGMENT (the Flood), implying that He will do so again in fulfilment of the promise of His COMING (v4). In other words, at Christ's COMING, He will immediately initiate a world-wide judgment (the DAY of the LORD), which is exactly what he confirms a few verses later: **"the DAY of the LORD will COME as a THIEF in the night"** (v10). Thus, Peter uses the worldwide FLOOD as a type of the DAY of the LORD, and teaches through this analogy that Christ will initiate the DAY of the LORD at His COMING.

Now we can see that Peter is essentially restating the teaching of Jesus in Matthew 24:37-39. (1) The days BEFORE His COMING in the Rapture will be like the days of Noah before the Flood, when people in the world will be living normal lives, totally unaware of the worldwide judgment that was about to take place (imminence). (2) Just as the world-wide FLOOD suddenly fell upon all the people in the days of Noah, so the worldwide DAY of the LORD will suddenly fall upon the whole world at His imminent COMING: **"As the days of Noah were, so also will the COMING of the Son of Man be... they did not know until the FLOOD came and took them all away, so also will the COMING of the Son of Man be"**

(Matthew 24:37-39). Thus, Jesus taught that He will initiate a worldwide judgment, corresponding to the FLOOD, at His imminent COMING. It is clear that He was using the worldwide FLOOD as a type of the DAY of the LORD, which He will initiate at His imminent COMING.

It's also clear that Paul gave the same teaching in 1Thessalonians 5:2-3, but instead of comparing the DAY of the LORD to the Flood, he compared it to a time of worldwide LABOUR PAINS, which will suddenly come upon the world, bringing great destruction. He says that the DAY of the LORD will be initiated by the imminent COMING of the LORD as a THIEF (to bring loss and judgment to the house of the earth, and to remove His Church from it, and then to leave the house to return to His own house, Heaven (Matthew 24:43, Luke 12:39, John 14:1-3).

Thus, Peter is reminding us of Jesus' teaching that in the time before His COMING (v4) to initiate the DAY of the LORD (v10), it will be like the days of Noah, when life was going on as normal before the FLOOD, and Noah was warning them of coming judgment (but they scoffed at him), and then the FLOOD suddenly fell (Luke 17:26-27, Matthew 24:37-39). He says it's going to happen the same way again. Normal life will be going on, with many in the world scoffing, when warned about the coming judgment of the DAY of the LORD (Tribulation), and then then suddenly the Tribulation-Flood will fall. This worldwide judgment of the Day of the Lord, corresponding to the Flood (v6), is imminent and will come suddenly upon the world, having been initiated by His COMING (v4, Matthew 24:37,39), for: **"the DAY of the LORD will come as a THIEF in the night"** (v10). Thus, Peter agrees with Jesus and Paul, that Christ's COMING is IMMINENT, and that when He COMES, He will initiate the DAY of the LORD. They all connect this imminent COMING with the removal of the Church in the RAPTURE (Matthew 24:36-44, 1Thessalonians 1:10, 4:14-5:10, 2Thessalonians 2:1-8, 2Peter 3:3-10, 2:5-9). It follows both the RAPTURE and the DAY of the LORD are imminent (Dual Imminence).

In the next verses, Peter develops his answer to the scoffers. Having declared that Christ will judge the world at His Coming, which is a temporal judgment, he then also warns them about His eternal judgment of the ungodly at the end of time, after the destruction of this universe. 2Peter 3:7: **"But the heavens and the earth which are now preserved by the same word, are reserved for fire until the Day of Judgment and perdition of ungodly men."** This verse corresponds exactly with Revelation 20:11-15.

Peter then explains the apparent delay in the fulfilment of God's Promise to COME and JUDGE the world: **"But, beloved, do not forget this one thing, that with the Lord ONE DAY is as 1000 years, and 1000 years as ONE DAY. The Lord**

is not slack concerning His Promise (the Promise of His COMING – see v3), **as some count slackness, but is longsuffering toward us, not willing that any should perish** (by being judged), **but that all should come to repentance** (and so be saved)" (2 Peter 3:8-9). He is not slow or late in fulfilling His Promise. He is not delaying unnecessarily, but rather He will be right on time according to His Timetable, governed by the principle of ONE DAY = 1000 years (v8). Moreover, He is motivated by His longsuffering love for us, which causes Him to give men time to repent. Therefore, He is withholding His judgment, so that as many as possible might be saved, so that the full harvest of the Church Age might be gathered to glory in the Rapture (Romans 11:25). In making these points, he is not only warning the godless to repent before it is too late, but also encouraging the 'beloved' to not lose heart in the meantime, but to remain patient and faithful, even if it means suffering, working together with God so that all the elect might be saved, remembering that if He tarries it is because of His same longsuffering toward others, that brought us to salvation.

Peter concludes His argument by declaring: **"BUT the DAY of the LORD** (the Tribulation) **WILL COME** (start) **as a THIEF in the night"** (2Peter 3:10, Paul made the same statement in 1Thessalonians 5:2). Having described the longsuffering of God, which is why He has withheld this coming judgment thus far, he then uses a 'BUT' to declare that despite His longsuffering, He will not delay forever, for He WILL judge the world. He describes this time of judgement as 'the DAY of the LORD.' It is clear that he must be referring to the same judgment that he described at the start of this passage, and is its main subject (v3-6). In other words, the DAY of the LORD is a worldwide judgment, corresponding to the FLOOD, that will be initiated by Christ's COMING, for He relates this coming JUDGMENT to the Lord's COMING (v4). Thus, he compares the FLOOD (v6) with the DAY of the LORD (v10). As we have seen, 'the Day of the Lord' is used consistently by Scripture to describe the Tribulation. So, Peter is using the Flood as a type of the Tribulation, just as Jesus did (Matthew 24:37-39). He is saying that His COMING (v4,9) will initiate the DAY of the LORD on earth (v10). Moreover, just as the worldwide FLOOD fell suddenly, without any warning signs, taking the world by surprise, so likewise the DAY of the LORD will come suddenly 'as a THIEF' upon the whole world and overtake it, without any warning signs. Therefore, the coming of the DAY of the LORD is imminent. Moreover, since the DAY of the LORD (v10) is initiated by the COMING of CHRIST (v4), and since he compares the coming of the DAY of the LORD to the COMING of a THIEF, it is clear that He is describing the imminent COMING of CHRIST as a THIEF to initiate the DAY of the LORD on earth.

The use of the image of Christ COMING as a THIEF does not just communicate imminence, but also it the fact that He is coming to the earth to remove something (the precious things in the house), which is the essential defining characteristic of a thief. Thus, His Coming as a THIEF also speaks of His Coming to remove His precious people from the world in the Rapture. Since He is only taking what belongs to Him, He is not actually a thief, but the effect of His Coming to those who remain will be as if a thief had come. Moreover, in removing that which is valuable, the coming of a thief necessarily has a negative effect in the house (it results in loss). In the case of Christ's Coming as a thief, this speaks of His Coming as being also an act of judgment upon the world, the initial judgment of the Day of the Lord. In other words, when Christ suddenly COMES as a THIEF, He will at the same time, (1) take His own from the world in the RAPTURE, and (2) initiate the DAY of the LORD on the earth. Thus, the Rapture and the Start of the Tribulation are simultaneous, for the act of receiving His Church to Himself, is in itself the initiating act of the Tribulation, as it removes a major restraint on evil – 2Thessalonians 2:6-8. Thus, Peter teaches that the Rapture and the Start of the Tribulation are simultaneous and imminent. This is precisely the doctrine of DUAL IMMINENCE. The reason why both the Coming of the Lord in the Rapture and the Coming of the Day of the Lord (in judgment) are described as imminent, is that they are simultaneous.

Another reason why the choice of the word 'THIEF' is a perfect choice in describing Christ's Coming in the Rapture, is to contrast it with the word 'ROBBER' (see John 10:1,8). The difference between a thief and a robber is that unlike a robber, a thief removes stuff from a house, but without using direct force or violence against the inhabitants. This perfectly describes the Rapture, because although it is an act of judgment on the world, bringing loss, it is an indirect judgment, rather than Christ judging the world by a direct application of His power (force), as He does in the Trumpet and Bowl Judgments of the Tribulation, and especially at His 2nd Coming. Thus, the picture of a THIEF fits Christ's Coming in the Rapture, but not His Coming at the end of the Tribulation, when He forcefully takes over the world, not only because (1) it communicates imminence, but also because (2) it accurately describes the nature of the Rapture, as an indirect judgment on the world, through the taking away of His Church, in contrast to His direct judgment of the world at the 2nd Coming, when He releases His power against all evil-doers, and kills them. Thus, in 2Peter 3-10, Peter must be describing the imminent Coming of Christ before the Tribulation, to rapture His Church and initiate the Day of the Lord, not His sign-posted Coming at the end of the Tribulation to forcefully establish His Kingdom on the earth.

Now we can see the perfect agreement of this prophetic teaching of Peter with the teaching of Jesus in <u>Matthew 24:36-44</u>. Peter uses the very same language in the same sequence as Jesus did to describe His imminent COMING to remove His own and to initiate the Day of the Lord, first (1) by comparing it to what happened in the days of Noah, when the believers were removed from the scene of judgment by entering the Ark, followed immediately by the worldwide FLOOD (v36-39), and then (2) by comparing it to the sudden COMING of a THIEF (v42-44, also Luke 12:39-40). It is clear that Peter and Jesus are talking about the same events, and that therefore Peter is consciously expounding the teaching of Jesus here.

Peter was also fully aware of Paul's writings, which he regarded as Scripture (2Peter 3:15-16), so when he wrote: **"the DAY of the LORD will come as a THIEF in the night"** (2Peter 3:10), he knew Paul had made the same statement (1Thessalonians 5:2-3), and so he was surely describing the same event as Paul. Since we know Paul was describing the TRIBULATION, initiated by the Coming of Christ in the RAPTURE, it follows that the time of worldwide Divine Judgment, that will come upon the earth at Christ's COMING (2Peter 3:4), which he compared to Noah's FLOOD (v6), and which he called 'the DAY of the LORD' (v10), must be the TRIBULATION, which will come suddenly (as a thief), just like the FLOOD (Matthew 24:37-39). Peter's teaching in 2Peter 3 must be in agreement with Paul's teaching in 1Thessalonians 5, although Paul describes the TRIBULATION by using the image of BIRTH PAINS (v2,3), whereas Peter uses the image of the FLOOD (2Peter 3:4-6). Both Peter and Paul got these images from Jesus Himself, whose teaching they were faithfully expounding. Therefore, consistency demands that Jesus Himself taught His imminent Coming to rescue His own, immediately before the Tribulation, which He compared both to worldwide BIRTH PAINS (Matthew 24:7,8), and to the worldwide FLOOD (Matthew 24:37-39), and indeed we have seen that Jesus did exactly that in Matthew 24:36-44. Therefore, Jesus, Paul and Peter all taught Dual Imminence.

Peter completes His description of God's coming judgments, by looking at the bigger picture, taking in the whole Day of the Lord, which does not just include the Tribulation (the dark part of the Day), but also the 2nd Coming, the Great and Awesome Day of the Lord (Sunrise – Malachi 4:2, Hosea 6:3), and the Millennum (the light part of the day), which then ends with the destruction of this universe: **"But the DAY of the LORD will come** (start) **as a thief in the night, in which** (at its END, after the Tribulation and the Millennium) **the heavens will pass away with a great noise, and the elements will melt with fervent heat; both the earth and the works that are in it will be burned up"** (2Peter 3:10, see Revelation 20:11). This fiery destruction of the universe is a reference back to v7, which says it will be immediately followed by the final and eternal judgment of the ungodly (Revelation 20:11-15).

This total destruction of the universe, along with all of man's works of the flesh, should inspire us to holy living, as we look forward to the DAY of GOD (the Eternal State), which is not the same as the Day of the Lord), when there will be a NEW HEAVEN and EARTH, a place of perfection, where His people will live forever in a state of perfect righteousness: **"Therefore, since all these things will be dissolved, what manner of persons ought you to be in holy conduct and godliness, looking for and hastening** (towards) **the coming of the DAY of GOD, because of which the heavens will be dissolved, being on fire, and the elements will melt with fervent heat? Nevertheless we, according to His promise, look for NEW HEAVENS and a NEW EARTH in which righteousness dwells"** (v11-13, Revelation 21:1).

2 Peter 2:5-9

In 2Peter 2, Peter also links the FLOOD to the future judgment of the DAY of the LORD, just as Jesus did in Matthew 24:36-39 and Luke 17:26-27. Jesus used this typology to not only teach that at His imminent Coming, He would release a judgment upon the whole world, but also that He would provide an escape from this judgment for believers BEFORE this judgment is released, just as He did in the days of Noah. The believers escaped into the Ark; they were not in the Flood. They experienced a pre-Flood rescue. In Luke 17:28-30, Jesus used the example of what happened in the days of Lot to make the same point. Lot was not in the fire and sulphur, and then rescued out of it, but was rescued before the judgment. Thus, the deliverance of Noah and Lot, which Jesus used as a template for what would happen at His Coming, can only illustrate the Rapture of the Church before the Day of the Lord – the Pre-Tribulation Rapture.

In 2Peter 2:5-9, he uses the very same 2 examples Jesus used in Luke 17 of NOAH's pre-FLOOD rescue in the Ark (v26-27), and LOT's pre-FIRE rescue from Sodom (v28-30), when God removed the righteous from the scene of judgment, just before pouring out His wrath on the earth, to emphasise this very same point that Jesus made, that God will provide a deliverance (rescue) for the righteous from God's wrath, before the Day of the Lord judgments are released.

The whole passage is focused on making 2 points: (1) that there is a coming Day of the Lord, when God will pour out His wrath upon the whole ungodly world, but that (2) He will personally provide a rescue for His believers, just before that wrath is released. The key verse that summarises his conclusion derived from the examples of Noah and Lot is 2Peter 2:9: **"the Lord knows how to DELIVER the GODLY out of temptations** (*ek peirasmou* – better translated as 'from Tribulation' – a reference to the Pre-Tribulation Rapture), **and to KEEP the UNJUST under PUNISHMENT** (the Day of the Lord), **for the Day of** (final) **Judgment."**

2Peter 2:5-9: **"For (1) if God did not spare the ancient world, but SAVED NOAH, one of 8 people, a preacher of righteousness, bringing in the FLOOD on the world of the ungodly; and (2) turning the cities of SODOM and Gomorrah into ashes, condemned them to destruction, making them an EXAMPLE to those who AFTERWARD would live ungodly; and DELIVERED righteous LOT** (before the judgment was poured out), **who was oppressed by the filthy conduct of the wicked, (for that righteous man, dwelling among them, tormented his righteous soul from day to day by seeing and hearing their lawless deeds)— then** (based on the examples of NOAH and LOT) **the Lord knows how to (1) DELIVER** (rescue) **the GODLY out of temptations** *(ek peirasmou*, from Tribulation or Trial), **and (2) to keep the unjust under PUNISHMENT, for the Day of Judgment."**

In this passage, Peter is using God's actions in the times of Noah and Lot as EXAMPLES of what He will do in the future. In each case, God rescues the righteous before pouring out His wrath on the ungodly. The key thought is that as in the days of Noah and Lot, God will judge the unrighteous, and being just, He knows how to separate the righteous from the unrighteous before He releases His judgments. Peter is saying that as God delivered Noah and Lot from His wrath, by removing them from the scene of judgment before it began, so He will deliver the righteous from the coming Day of the Lord.

Now this might not be immediately obvious, since in v9 he uses the word *peirasmos* (wrongly translated as 'temptations') to describe this coming time of judgment. For a start the word is in the singular, not the plural, and the context indicates that a better translation would be TRIBULATION, TRIAL or TEST (the key issue about temptations is that they are a test of our faith in God and loyalty to God). This is a key word used to describe the Tribulation, since it is a time of trial and test for all who live on the face of the earth, as in Revelation 3:10: **"I will KEEP you from** *(ek)* **the HOUR of TRIAL** (testing – *peirasmou*), **which shall come upon the whole world, to TEST** *(peirazo)* **those who dwell on the earth."** So, in Revelation 3:10, *peirasmos* describes the TRIBULATION, just as it does in 2 Peter 2:9, and both verses promise that God will deliver His people from this special time of trial. The Tribulation will be the final time of test for all those still alive to see if they will turn to God and trust in Christ, or reject God and give their loyalty to antichrist. Now, if v9 was read in isolation, we might assume *peirasmos* refers to the general trials and temptations of life in the Church Age, which God helps us overcome. However, the context makes it clear that the time of trial (*peirasmos*) of v9, that he is talking about, from which the godly will be delivered, does not refer to the normal trials that we all face, but rather to a special future time of TRIAL (the TRIBULATION), which is also a time of Divine JUDGMENT in history, which he compares to Noah's world-wide FLOOD and the destruction of Sodom by FIRE (in v5-8). This agrees with the overall context of Peter's message, because we have seen in 2Peter 3, that Peter clearly uses the worldwide FLOOD as a type of the coming DAY of the LORD, using the Flood to explain what Christ will do at His Coming - judge the wicked world, but first rescue the righteous. If that is the way he is thinking about the Flood in 2Peter 3:3-10, it implies that the same is true in 2Peter 2, where he again appeals the Flood (v5) as a type of a future time of TRIBULATION and PUNISHMENT (Divine Judgment), from which the godly will be delivered, just as they were in the days of Noah (v9).

The main thought is that just as God SAVED Noah (v5) and DELIVERED Lot (v7), before releasing His wrath, so God knows how DELIVER the godly from the coming Time of God's Wrath upon the unjust (v9). Since the 2 previous judgments, used as examples, were physical, on the stage of earth's history, it follows that the future judgment Peter has in mind is also physical, and on the stage of earth's history – the eschatological Day of the Lord. He uses *peirasmos* (test) to describe a future judgment in history (the Tribulation), that will come on men while they are still living on the earth (as in the days of Noah and Lot), to distinguish it from the final eternal judgment, which will come after man's time of testing (this life) is over. The TEST for those in the TRIBULATION is: Will they repent and turn to God, or harden their hearts and confirm their rejection of God?

Thus, since the context for Peter's conclusion (in v9) is the DELIVERANCE of Noah and Lot from special Divine JUDGMENTS in history, this is a promise to us of our DELIVERANCE by the RAPTURE from the world-wide JUDGMENT of the TRIBULATION – a special time of TRIAL (*peirasmos*) for all who dwell on earth. The fact that the specific TRIAL in v9 is the future DAY of the LORD, a time of Divine Judgment, is confirmed by the second description of this time in v9, as being a PUNISHMENT: **"The Lord knows how (1) to DELIVER the GODLY out of TRIAL** (the DAY of the LORD)**, and (2) to KEEP the unjust under PUNISHMENT, for the Day of Judgment."** Peter is contrasting what will happen to (1) the GODLY and to (2) the UNJUST at this time – the GODLY will be DELIVERED from the TRIAL, but the unjust will be KEPT (held) under PUNISHMENT. Thus, this TRIAL is a time of PUNISHMENT upon the UNGODLY, which is why the godly are delivered from it (for in Christ, under His Blood, we are delivered from all condemnation). As God delivered Noah and Lot from judgment, by removing them from the scene of judgment before it began (v5-8), so He will (1) DELIVER the righteous from the coming Day of the Lord by removing them from the unrighteous, BEFORE (2) immediately releasing His JUDGMENTS on the unbelieving world in the Day of the Lord - a Time of Trial for all those who remain on the face of the earth (v9). This agrees perfectly with Jesus' teaching in Luke 17:26-30, where He used the same examples of Noah and Lot as pictures of the future deliverance of believers from the Tribulation by the Rapture, saying: *"as it was in the days of Noah and Lot, so will it be at My Coming."*

Peter is clearly describing and contrasting what happens to the saved and unsaved at the SAME TIME – the dual aspect of the same event, for the godly are delivered from the judgment, while the unjust are forced to endure it. This is confirmed by the 2 examples of Noah and Lot, which Peter uses to illustrate and confirm the point he makes in v9, for the PUNISHMENT fell on the unjust immediately after the RESCUE of both Noah and Lot (on the same day). Thus, this not only confirms the Pre-Tribulation Rapture, but the fact that the Rapture initiates the Tribulation. Moreover, just as these past judgments of the Flood and Sodom fell suddenly, without warning, on an unbelieving, unsuspecting world, so Peter implies God's coming time of judgment, the Day of the Lord, will come suddenly upon the earth, like a thief (imminence).

But thank God, just as God rescued Noah and Lot, just before releasing His wrath, so God also has an imminent rescue for the righteous in the Rapture, before He releases His Day of the Lord wrath upon the world, for: **"the Lord knows how (1) to DELIVER** (rescue) **the godly out of TRIAL** (the Tribulation)**, and (2) to keep the unjust under PUNISHMENT** (the Day of the Lord)**, for the Day of** (final) **Judgment** (at the end of time)" (v9). Thus 2Peter 2:5-9 also teaches the doctrine of Dual Imminence. As there was Dual Imminence of the simultaneous rescues and judgments in the days of Noah and Lot (v5-8), it follows there will be Dual Imminence of the (1) Rapture and (2) Tribulation (v9). (Later, we will see how well this verse agrees with Revelation 3:10-11). God will bring about this rescue by lifting the godly above the realm of judgement (as he did with Noah), and by removing them from the scene of judgment (as He did with Lot).

This future judgment will ultimately result in the death of all the wicked on the earth, so that only believers will enter the Millennial Kingdom. However, those who go through the Tribulation will have a chance to repent and turn to God, but for those who die in their sins, God will continue to keep them under punishment, by removing them from the earth into Hades, a fiery place of punishment for their souls, where they will be kept under guard, until the final Day of Judgment at the Great White Throne, after which they will be cast body and soul into the Lake of Fire, their everlasting abode and place of punishment (Revelation 20:11-15).

The prophetic passages in 2Peter 2 and 3 should be read together, as having a common theme that God's time of Judgment (the Day of the Lord) will fall suddenly on the unbelieving world like a THIEF (imminence), but at the SAME TIME, He will also provide an imminent RESCUE for His own, as with Noah and Lot, for: **"the Lord knows how to (1) DELIVER the GODLY out of TRIAL** (the Tribulation)**, and to (2) KEEP the UNJUST under PUNISHMENT** (the Day of the Lord)**"** (2Peter 2:9). This is the truth of DUAL IMMINENCE.

*The Apostle JOHN

The major part of John's Book of Revelation is a detailed description of the Day of the Lord leading up to its climax at the 2nd Coming (Revelation 4-19). Revelation 1:1,3: **"The Revelation of Jesus Christ, which God gave Him to show His servants—THINGS** (the Day of the Lord — Revelation 4-19) **which must SHORTLY take place** (meaning they could start at any time). **Blessed is he who reads and those who hear the words of this PROPHECY** (of the Day of the Lord)**, and keep those things which are written in it; for the TIME is NEAR** (its time of fulfilment is imminent)**."** In other words, the events of the Day of the Lord could break upon the world at any time. Thus, Revelation starts with a declaration of the IMMINENCE of the DAY of the LORD, which brings a sense of urgency to its readers.

Likewise, Revelation ends with a clear declaration of IMMINENCE, but this time it is a proclamation from the lips of Jesus of the IMMINENCE of His COMING to rescue and reward His Church. He gives this message great emphasis by repeating it 3-times, and by the fact these are the last words of Jesus in the Bible: **"Behold, I am COMING QUICKLY!... Behold, I am COMING QUICKLY, and My reward is with Me, to give to every one according to his work... Surely, I am COMING QUICKLY"** (Revelation 22:7,12,20).

Thus, Revelation starts and ends with imminence: (1) of the Day of the Lord and (2) of the Rapture of the Church, which together mean Dual Imminence. Both events are imminent, because when Christ returns for His Church, He will also initiate the Day of the Lord on earth.

In Revelation 1:19, Jesus tells John: **"Write the things which (1) you have seen** (the vision of Christ in Revelation 1)**, and (2) the things which are** (the present Church Age in Revelation 2-3)**, and (3) the THINGS which will TAKE PLACE AFTER THIS** (after the Church Age — Revelation 4-22)**."** The fact that the transition from the Church Age to what happens after the Church Age takes place at the end of Revelation 3 is confirmed by Revelation 4:1: **"After these things** (the description of the Church Age in Revelation 2-3) **I looked, and behold, a door standing open in Heaven. And the first voice which I heard was like a trumpet**

speaking with me, saying: "Come up here, and I will show you THINGS which must TAKE PLACE AFTER THIS." Therefore, Revelation 4-22 describes what will happen after the CHURCH AGE: (1) The Tribulation (Revelation 4-18), (2) the 2nd Coming (Revelation 19), (3) the Millennium (Revelation 20), and (4) the Eternal State (Revelation 21-22).

Since the Church Age ends with the Rapture, it follows that in the sequence of events in Revelation, the Rapture takes place at Revelation 4:1. This is confirmed by the fact that John experiences a personal rapture to Heaven in this verse, and that he then sees the whole Church in Heaven, as represented by the 24 enthroned and crowned elders (Revelation 4-5), who represent the whole redeemed Church in Christ from every nation, as their song in Revelation 5:8-10 demonstrates. The fact that these 24 leaders of the Church have been resurrected or raptured, and enthroned in Heaven in their glorified bodies at this point, means the whole Church must also be in Heaven at this point, having been resurrected or raptured and glorified, because the whole Church is resurrected and raptured at the same time, and stands before the Judgment Seat of Christ at the same time, and is glorified at the same time. The presence of the Church in Heaven at this time is also signified by the: **"7 lamps of fire burning before the throne"** (4:5), which correspond to the earlier description of the Church (1:12-13,20). Therefore, Revelation testifies to the Rapture of the Church before the Tribulation starts.

We have seen that the Rapture itself is the initiating judgment of the Day of the Lord, which is confirmed by the fact that when Jesus returns in the Rapture, He is no longer sitting at God's right hand, which indicates that it is judgment time, when He will start to put His enemies under His feet, according to Psalm 110:1. The simultaneity of the Rapture and Start of the Day of the Lord is also confirmed by the fact that immediately after John's Rapture and a time of worship in Heaven (Revelation 4-5), Christ in Heaven breaks open in quick succession the first 6 Seals, which release the Birth Pain Judgments on earth. In other words, the Tribulation judgments are released on earth only a short time after the Rapture, certainly on the same day.

Christ's Letter to the 7 Churches in Revelation 2-3

In Christ's messages to His 7 Churches, He pointed to His future Coming to both rescue the Church and initiate the Tribulation, to motivate them, (1) warning those who were not yet saved to repent because His Coming to judge the world was imminent, and (2) encouraging those who were saved to stay faithful, even in the face of persecution, because His Coming to rescue them was imminent. Thus, we will see Dual Imminence in the 7 letters to the 7 Churches.

Although, these 7 letters are written to 7 specific Churches in AD 95, each letter ends with Christ saying: **"He who has an ear, let him hear what the Spirit says to** (all) **the Churches."** In other words, as with all the New Testament letters, these 7 letters were designed to be Christ's message to His whole Church. 7 is the number of spiritual perfection and so the 7 Churches represent the whole Church, and so, Christ's words are applicable to the whole Church, and should not be dismissed as being of purely local application. These letters have special importance in that they constitute Christ's final word to His Church, so we would expect them to point to His Coming.

*To the Church at Pergamos, Jesus said: **"Repent, or else I will COME to you QUICKLY** (His imminent Coming) **and will fight against THEM** (He is coming to judge those who hold the false doctrines of Balaam and the Nicolaitans, which endorse and encourage worldliness and sexual immorality – see v14-15) **with the sword of My mouth"** (Revelation 2:16). Note, the TIMING of His Coming does not depend on whether they repent or not, but rather His actions toward them when He comes are conditioned by their response to Him, for He will bless the faithful and judge the faithless. This also applies in Revelation 2:22 and 3:3.

*To the Church at Thyatira, Jesus said: **"Indeed** (1) **I will cast HER** (Jezebel – the false, sexually immoral Church – see v20-21) **into a sickbed, and those who commit adultery with HER into GREAT TRIBULATION, unless they repent of their deeds. I will KILL her children** (followers) **with DEATH… And** (2) **I will GIVE to each one of YOU according to your WORKS"** (2:22-23). Here Jesus gives a two-fold message concerning what He will do at His Coming with (1) the unrepentant sinners and (2) the true believers within the Church. He will deal with them both at the same time, but in very different ways. (1) He warns the immoral followers of Jezebel that He will judge them by casting them into the Tribulation, and they will then suffer a two-fold death (physical and eternal) if they do not repent. (2) He tells the believers that He will reward them for their good works at His Judgment Seat, which happens immediately after the Rapture. Again, we see the simultaneity of the Rapture and the Start of the Tribulation.

The Jesus continued His message to the true believers in the Church by giving a more detailed description of the rewards He will give them at His Judgment Seat, confirming that He will do this when HE COMES, and encouraging them to live in the light of His imminent Coming, by continuing to HOLD FAST to the truth, in the face of the pressures coming from Jezebel and her children to compromise: **"Now to YOU I say, and to the rest in Thyatira, as many as do not have this** (false) **doctrine… I will put on you no other burden. But HOLD FAST what you have** (the truth of God's Word) **UNTIL I COME. And he who overcomes,**

**and keeps My works until the end, to him I will give power over the nations...
as I also have received from My Father; and I will give him the MORNING STAR"**
(2:24-28). The rewards for the faithful include great share in Christ's authority
and glory (we saw in Part 2 that the promise of the Morning Star refers to the
release of Christ's glory within us at the Pre-Tribulation Rapture – see 1Peter 1:19,
Revelation 22:16). Christ said their urgent need was to HOLD FAST in the face of
evil, and the incentive He gave them to stay faithful was the hope of His
IMMINENT COMING to rescue and reward them: **"HOLD FAST ... UNTIL I COME."**
He tells them to live continually in the expectancy that He could come for them
at any time. Since His Coming to reward His own is imminent (v23b-28), so also
the Tribulation (v22-23a).

*The Church at Sardis had a reputation of being alive, because of its
spiritual heritage, but was now largely dead, with unregenerate people, without
the Spirit, being in the majority (v1,4), which is why Jesus introduced Himself as
the One, who has the fullness of the Spirit to give them (v1). He calls the Church
as a whole to **"be WATCHFUL** (gregoreo)**"** (v2), which means spiritually alive and
awake (in fellowship with God), and in prophetic passages it carries the additional
sense of being alert and ready for (living in the light of) the Lord's imminent
Return. We have seen that the origin and primary use of this word comes from
the teaching of Jesus. Watchfulness is a scriptural hallmark of true believers. Only
by being watchful can the Church fulfil its purpose, and accomplish what God has
called it to do (v2). Then in the next verse, Jesus explains how the Church can be
revived: **"Remember therefore how you have received and heard; hold fast and
REPENT"** (v3a). The problem was that they had let go of the Gospel. He told them
(1) to remember the message that they had heard and received, on which the
Church was founded and which had brought it into existence, (2) to hold fast to
the Gospel, and (3) repent from their dead works, and put their trust in Christ
alone for salvation. Then He warned them of what would happen if they ignored
this command: **"Therefore, if you will not WATCH** (gregoreo)**, I will COME upon
you** (in judgment) **as a THIEF, and you will not know what hour I will COME upon
you** (in judgment)**"** (3:3). Those who do not respond to the Gospel and repent,
will remain in the sleep of spiritual death, and so will not be watchful. These will
experience Christ's Coming as a THIEF, that is, they will suffer loss (judgment) at
His Coming.

This would have especially resonated with the Sardis Church, as Sardis
was built on an elevated cliff and so they felt invulnerable and secure, and so
were not alert and watchful. Twice in their history, they were taken by surprise
by a surprise attack by an enemy, who scaled the cliff at night, and coming like a
thief, took their valuables and destroyed their city. Jesus is warning them that if

they do not repent, they will experience His Coming in this way, and they will find themselves, in the Day of the Lord, facing loss and destruction.

Thus, Revelation 3:3 is a warning to the unsaved nominal Christians of Sardis, that He will suddenly, without warning, come upon them in judgment like a thief. Therefore, Christ's Coming to bring them into judgment is imminent. This judgment is the Day of the Lord (1Thessalonians 5:2,4, 2Peter 3:10). This is Christ's message to all nominal believers in all the Churches): **"He who has an ear, let him hear what the Spirit says to the Churches"** (v6). The emphasis on imminence is not only in the use of the image of a THIEF, but also the affirmation that they will not know the time of His Coming – it will happen suddenly, without warning, taking them by surprise. Further emphasis on imminence is communicated by the word 'WATCH' *(gregoreo)*, which Scripture always uses in connection with an imminent event.

The 'coming as a thief' terminology originates in the teaching of Jesus (Matthew 24:43; Luke 12:39), and was also used by Paul (1Thessalonians 5:2,4), Peter (2Peter 3:10) and John (Revelation 3:3, 16:15). Consistency of interpretation requires these uses of the THIEF analogy to be references to the same event the imminent Coming of Christ before the Tribulation, not the signposted Coming of Christ at the end of the Tribulation. Some of these Scriptures speak of CHRIST coming as a THIEF (Matthew 24:43; Luke 12:39, Revelation 3:3, 16:15), while others speak of the DAY of the LORD coming as a THIEF (1Thessalonians 5:2,4, 2Peter 3:10). These 2 descriptions can should be harmonised, and this is easily done. Since CHRIST is 'the THIEF', in His COMING as a THIEF, He must initiate the DAY of the LORD. In this way, the DAY of the LORD also comes as a THIEF. This explains why all the references to Christ's Coming as a THIEF (including Revelation 3:3) are primarily warnings to the unsaved of the imminent judgment coming upon them, namely the DAY of the LORD, initiated by the Lord at His imminent Coming. However, the picture of the coming of a thief also includes an encouraging revelation of what will simultaneously happen to the saved at His Coming, for by definition a thief comes to take the precious things from the house. Therefore, when Christ comes as a thief to initiate the Day of the Lord, He will also remove His precious people from the earth in the Rapture. Therefore, again we see the truth of Dual Imminence.

The parallelism between Revelation 3:3 and the other references to the coming of a thief is reinforced by the combination of the use of both THIEF and WATCH in relation to Christ's Coming - we see this in Matthew 24:42-44, Luke 12:39-40, 1Thessalonians 5:2,4,6,10 and Revelation 3:3, 16:15. Moreover the revelation that no one will know the hour of His Coming (3:3) is also stated in

Matthew 24:42-44 and Luke 12:39-40. Moreover, these statements in Revelation are from the lips of Jesus, just as they are in the Gospels. Therefore, it is clear that the teaching to be WATCHFUL in the light of Christ's imminent Coming as a THIEF, originates from Jesus Himself (there is no parallel use of this language in the Old Testament or in Jewish literature before Christ), and that the apostles, in being faithful to His teaching, used His terminology to describe the same event to which Christ was referring, namely the imminent Coming of Christ to receive His Church to Himself, and to initiate the Day of the Lord on earth.

In Revelation 3, Jesus then distinguishes between the just and the unjust in terms of their clothing. The just wear undefiled garments (v4a), having made them white in the blood of Christ (7:14), and they will be rewarded at Christ's Coming with robes of glory (v4b-5). But the unjust are characterised by garments defiled by unrepentant sin, and so they come under judgment.

A parallel verse to <u>Revelation 3:3-4</u> is <u>Revelation 16:15:</u> **"Behold, I am COMING like a THIEF! (1) BLESSED is the one who stays awake** (WATCHES – *gregoreo*) **and keeps his CLOTHES** (those clothed in Christ's righteousness will be blessed in the Rapture), **so that** (2) **he will not be caught NAKED** (in an unrighteous state) **and his shameful** (fallen) **condition be seen** (manifested to all, because he will have to go through the judgments of the Tribulation)."

We see the same combination of the THIEF, and WATCHING and CLOTHING. Again, Jesus declares that His Coming is imminent, for it will be sudden and unannounced like a THIEF. The fact He could come at any time is emphasised by the need to be constantly WATCHFUL for (living in the light of) His Coming. This imminent Coming of Christ has a 2-fold result, of (1) BLESSING for the righteous, who are clothed in Christ's righteousness, and (2) JUDGMENT for the unrighteous, who are manifested as unclothed (naked) as far as righteousness is concerned (see also 3:18). The righteous are also described as being WATCHFUL, which is a function of their fellowship with God, which is a matter of degree. Thus, all the righteous will be blessed at His Coming, but the more they are walking with Him and watching for Him, the more blessing (eternal rewards) they will receive. Thus, His Coming as a THIEF is imminent for both believers and unbelievers. In His Coming He will (1) bring BLESSING to watching believers, who are prepared for Him, and to (2) initiate JUDGMENT upon the godless world. The BLESSING for believers is the Rapture and eternal rewards that they will receive at His Judgment Seat after the Rapture. The Judgment is the Day of the Lord. Thus, at His imminent Coming as a thief, He will (1) RAPTURE His Church, and at the same time (2) initiate the Day of the Lord upon the lost, by which He is giving them a final opportunity to repent. This is DUAL IMMINENCE.

*To the Church at Laodicea, Jesus said: **"So then, because you are lukewarm, and neither cold nor hot, I will** (literally: 'I am about to') **vomit you out of My mouth"** (3:16). This describes an imminent judgment on a Church that consists entirely of the unregenerate, according to the description in v17-18, which is why Christ is on the outside seeking entry (v20). This will be ultimately fulfilled by Christ rejecting the apostate Church, which remains on earth after the Rapture. He will immediately disown it, and it will come under His judgment in the Tribulation (it will become part of the harlot of Revelation 17, see also Matthew 24:47-51).

*To the Church at Philadelphia, Jesus said: **"Because you have kept My command to persevere, I also will KEEP you from THE HOUR of TRIAL** (the Tribulation), **which shall** (literally: 'is about to') **come upon the WHOLE WORLD, to test those who dwell on the earth** ('earth-dwellers'). **Behold, I am COMING QUICKLY! Hold fast what you have, that no one may take your crown"** (Revelation 3:10-11).

This passage gives strong evidence for the Pre-Tribulation Rapture and Dual Imminence. 'The Hour of Trial, that will come upon the whole world' surely relates to the future Tribulation. First of all, the Tribulation will be a time of worldwide judgment and tribulation (trouble). Also, these verses have not yet been literally fulfilled, so they await a future fulfilment. Moreover, the context of these verses, indeed the subject of most of the remaining chapters of the book (6-19), is the Tribulation, which indeed is a special Time of Trial for all who dwell on the earth, and so Revelation itself tells us what this Hour of Trial is, and describes it in great detail. Moreover, in using the definite article, Jesus is describing a specific unique time period that He expects His readers to know about, which is indeed the case, as far as the Day of the Lord is concerned, being revealed by the Old Testament Prophets, Jesus Himself in the Gospels, and His Apostles. Also, the people being tested during this Hour of Trial are described as 'earth-dwellers' (those who love this world, in contrast to believers, whose main citizenship is in Heaven). It is interesting the Bible only uses this term to describe unbelievers in the Tribulation (Revelation 6:10, 8:13, 11:10, 12:12, 13:8,12,14, 14:6, 17:2,8), confirming that the Hour of Trial is the Tribulation.

Jesus says this Hour of Trial (the Tribulation) is IMMINENT, for He literally says: **"The HOUR of TRIAL, which is ABOUT TO COME upon the whole world."** This is an Hour that is getting closer every moment, and could begin at any moment. Therefore, this says that the Start of the Tribulation (the Day of the Lord) is imminent.

Christ's promise in these verses is not limited to the first century Church of Philadelphia, but is for the whole Church, as Jesus said a few verses later: **"He who has an ear, let him hear what the Spirit says to** (all) **the Churches"** (v13). Moreover, the same promise is also made elsewhere to the Church as a whole (1Thessalonians 1:10, 5:9). Christ's promise to all believers of the Church Age is: **"I also will KEEP you from** (ek – 'out of') **the HOUR of TRIAL."** This says that they will not just be kept from the Trial, but from the Hour of Trial (from the very time period itself).   This can only mean they will not go through any part of the Tribulation – they will be delivered from the whole Day of the Lord. If He had just said: "I will keep you from the Trial", then one possible interpretation could be that they will go through the Tribulation, but God will protect them from harm during this time. However, since He promises to keep them from 'the Hour of Trial', this interpretation is impossible. The promise is not to be kept from the trial of the time, but from the time of the trial. In any case, considering the great persecutions and martyrdoms that the Tribulation saints will suffer (Daniel 7:21, Revelation 6:9-11, 7:9-17, 13:7,15, 16:6, 17:6, 18:24), it is clear that believers in the Tribulation will not protected from harm during this Time of Trial, so this cannot be the correct interpretation.

Since this Time of Trial comes upon the whole world, to test all who dwell on the earth, the only way for the true Church to be kept from this whole time-period, and not experience this Trial and testing, is to be removed from the earth before this time-period begins. The removal of all believers before this Hour of Trial is confirmed by the stated purpose of this time-period, which is **"to test those who dwell on the earth** ('earth-dwellers')**."** As we have seen, this phrase 'earth dwellers' refers only to unbelievers, signifying that this Time of Trial is ordained only for those who are unbelievers at the end of the Church Age. Thus, at the start of this Time of Trial there will be no believers, although many will come to Christ during the Tribulation. The test that God initiates in the Tribulation for all who dwell on the earth will be whether or not they will repent, turn to God and believe the Gospel in the face of the escalating Divine Judgments and fulfilments of Bible Prophecy (14:6-7). This test will be men's last chance and in a short time it will force everyone off the fence, so that they will have to choose to either worship Christ (God) or the antichrist (Satan). Thus, by the end of this Hour of Trial, this process of testing will separate all men into 2 groups, and multitudes will indeed be saved in the Tribulation, many of whom will be martyred (Revelation 7, 13:7,10, 14:12, 16:6, 17:6, 18:24, 20:4). It is not necessary for the Church-Age believers to endure this Time of Testing, because they have already received Christ and proved the genuineness of their faith, through all the tests of life, which is exactly the reason Jesus gave for their exemption from this Hour of

Trial: **"Because you have kept My command to persevere** (in faith through testing)**, I also will keep you from the Hour of Trial."** So, although we are not exempted from tests and trials, we are exempted from the Trial, coming on the whole earth to test the unbelieving earth-dwellers. Christ promises us that He will not put us into the period that will have the purpose of testing a very different group of people.

So, Jesus Himself promises that He will keep His true Church from this Hour of Trial, by removing them from the earth before it starts. Surely, He must be referring to the Rapture of the Church at the His Coming, when He will take her to Heaven with Him (John 14:1-3). In this case, since the Hour of Trial is imminent, it follows that the Rapture must also be imminent, as well as simultaneous with the Hour of Trial, otherwise the Tribulation would not be imminent. This implication of v10 that Christ will remove His Church from the earth in the Rapture at His imminent Coming before the Tribulation is confirmed by what He says next: **"Behold, I am COMING QUICKLY! Hold fast what you have, that no one may take your crown"** (v11). His coming quickly is a classic statement of imminence. This must be talking about His imminent Coming to rescue His Church in the Rapture, which is confirmed by what He says next when He makes a practical application based on this revelation: **"hold fast what you have, that no one may take your CROWN."** He is pointing to the rewards (crowns) that believers will receive at this imminent Coming. Since He could come at any time, it is urgent that we hold fast and stay faithful to Christ and what He has called us to do, so that we will receive a crown of glory from Him at His Coming. Therefore, this must be His Coming in the Rapture, for immediately after the Rapture, believers will receive their eternal rewards (Revelation 22:12, 1Corinthians 4:5, 2 Timothy 4:8, Luke 14:14, Matthew 16:27). Therefore, Christ is urging us to live in the light of His imminent Coming, when He will rescue us from the Tribulation (which could come suddenly upon the world at any moment), and reward us at His Judgment Seat.

Therefore, Revelation 3:10-11 is a clear revelation of DUAL IMMINENCE, for (1) the HOUR of TRIAL is IMMINENT, for it is about to come upon the whole world, and (2) Jesus' COMING to rescue (keep) us from the Tribulation, by means of the Rapture is IMMINENT, for He is COMING QUICKLY. The only way both statements can be true is if His Coming to deliver His Church from the Tribulation coincides with His Coming to initiate the Tribulation. Thus, He is COMING QUICKLY (v11) to (1) rescue His Church in the Rapture from the Hour of Trial (v10), and at the same time (2) enforce this Time of Trial upon the whole godless world. So, both (1) the coming *(erchomai)* of Jesus for His Church (v11), and the coming (erchomai) of the Hour of Trial upon the world (v10), are imminent, for Jesus is also coming as its Judge.

Thus, we see that the truth of Dual Imminence is also integral to John's prophetic teaching. In some passages, Christ speaks of the imminence of His Coming to rescue, deliver and bless His people, bringing relief from their suffering through the Rapture, and in other passages He warns the unsaved in the Church about the imminence of His Coming to bring judgment on them. His Coming is consistently described as imminent, whether for deliverance or for judgment. The only way this can happen is for the deliverance in the Rapture and the judgment (the Start of the Tribulation) to occur simultaneously. Since relief for the believer through the Rapture and judgment for the unbeliever through the Tribulation are concurrent events, imminence is correctly used to describe both occurrences. Moreover, some passages combine both ideas, confirming the truth that when He comes, He will both (1) rescue the Church in the Rapture, and at the same time, (2) initiate the Day of the Lord (Tribulation) on the earth, so that both of these events (one for the saved and one for the unsaved) are simultaneous and imminent.

So, we have seen abundant evidence from Christ's teaching in the Gospels and in the Book of Revelation, and from the teaching of the apostles, Paul, James, and Peter, the truth of Dual Imminence. If this truth is so strongly emphasised in the Bible, it is surely of great importance!

Jesus is coming soon, so wake up before it is too late and make sure you are ready for Him. Receive Him as your Lord and Saviour, and live your life accordingly, loving Him in humble gratitude, waiting expectantly for His imminent Return at any moment. Make sure that you will not one of those who will be overtaken by the terrible events of the Day of the Lord.

Chapter 7: The Rapture, the Tribulation, and the 70th Week

In this chapter, I aim to establish the relationship between the Rapture, the Tribulation, and Daniel's 70th Week. The fact I make a distinction between the latter two may be a surprise, as it is normal for prophecy teachers to identify the Tribulation with the 70th Week. I myself have experienced how ingrained this assumption can be in one's thinking, making it hard to question it. But once I did, I found it opened up the solution to a number of problems. Obviously the 70th Week is closely connected to the Tribulation, but they are not necessarily identical, and there is no scriptural basis for making them identical. In fact, to equate the Tribulation with the 70th Week is an over-simplification.

First, let me explain the problem that arises if the Tribulation is exactly the same as the 70th Week, that is, if they start on the same day (they obviously both end on the same day – the Return of Christ).   In that case, the Tribulation will start with the antichrist making a covenant with Israel (Daniel 9:27).   But if the Tribulation starts immediately after the Rapture, then the antichrist covenant must take place immediately after the Rapture, but this contradicts imminence - one of the key scriptural attributes of the Rapture – that is, it could happen at any time.   Clearly, if the rapture must happen at the same time as the antichrist-covenant, it could not happen today or any time very soon, contradicting imminence. The usual solution to this is to say that the Tribulation or 70th Week does not begin immediately after the Rapture, but that there is an unknown time-interval (months or even many years) after the Rapture before the Tribulation begins with the antichrist covenant.   This also can be used to explain why prophesied events like the Rebirth of Israel do not contradict imminence. Even though this has to happen before the antichrist covenant, it did not have to happen before the Rapture, for it could have happened in the time between the Rapture and the Tribulation.   However, I was not satisfied with this explanation, because it ignored the scriptural evidence that says the Tribulation begins on the same day as the Rapture, which I set forth in this chapter.

The only other way to protect imminence is to question the assumption that the Tribulation is identical to the 70th Week, that is, that it starts with the antichrist covenant. Upon reflection, I realized there is no scriptural basis for the assumption, and when I abandoned it, I found that all the scriptures, especially Revelation, harmonize much better. In this new way of thinking, the Tribulation starts on the same day as the Rapture, but there is an unknown period of time (months or years) before the 70th Week starts with the antichrist-covenant. This then begins the final 7 years of the Tribulation, which ends with Christ's Return.

Thus, the Tribulation will be a bit longer than 7 years, and the 70th Week will be the last 7 years of the Tribulation. This protects imminence in the same way as the previous explanation, because there is an unknown time-interval between the Rapture and the 70th Week, so the Rapture can happen at any time, and fulfilled prophecies like Israel's Rebirth could have happened in that interval. Moreover, there are no unfulfilled prophecies (like Ezekiel 38 and the rebuilding of the Temple) that have to happen before the Rapture, because they can happen in the Tribulation, either in its initial time-period before the 70th Week, or during the 70th Week itself.

The advantages of this way of thinking are: (1) It is true to the scriptures that teach the Tribulation starts on the same day as the Rapture, and (2) it fits perfectly with the sequence of events in Revelation, which is what we will consider next.

Immediately after the Rapture, we see the Church in Heaven represented by the 24 elders (Revelation 4). There immediately follows a scene where the Lamb takes the Scroll with 7 Seals from God the Father, accompanied by great rejoicings (Revelation 5). Then the Lamb breaks the first 6 Seals with little delay (Revelation 6), which initiate the judgments of the Tribulation (the birth pains). Thus, all these events (the Rapture and the Start of the Tribulation) happen on the same day. The judgments of the Tribulation begin immediately with the 1st Seal in Revelation 6:1-2, which releases the antichrist beginning his rise to power on the world-stage (the rider on a white horse going forth to conquer), which agrees with the teaching of 2 Thessalonians 2 that says that the antichrist will only be revealed after the Restrainer (the Church, indwelt by the Holy Spirit) is removed in the Rapture. The first way he will be revealed is his rapid rise to power at the start of the Tribulation. This is different to the covenant he makes with Israel, which initiates the 70th Week. In fact, his rise to power has to happen at least a few months before he can be in position to make this covenant, because it requires him to have sufficient power, and be able to gain the confidence of Israel, so they put their trust in him. Thus, the Tribulation starts right after the Rapture, but there's a gap of at least a few months between the start of the Tribulation (antichrist's initial rise to power) and the start of the 70th Week (antichrist's covenant with Israel).

Moreover, this harmonizes with the sequence of the early events of the Tribulation as described in Revelation. We have seen that there is an initial period of time between the Start of the Tribulation and the antichrist covenant, which starts the 70th Week. Similarly in Revelation there is an initial period of time between the Start of the Tribulation when the 1st Seal is broken (6:1-2), and later when the 7th Seal is broken (8:1-2), which is described in Revelation 7. Its purpose is the preparation, anointing and sealing of 144,000 Jewish evangelists (who spearhead evangelism in the Tribulation), for as soon as they are sealed, the 7th Seal is broken. The obvious solution into which everything fits perfectly is that these are the SAME periods of time. Thus, it is **the deceptive covenant of death that Israel makes with antichrist in unbelief** (Daniel 9:27), **which calls forth the breaking of the 7th Seal, and its direct Trumpet Judgments.** The antichrist-covenant is the only event early in the Tribulation that could correspond to the 7th Seal.

This synchronism of the antichrist-covenant and 7th Seal is confirmed when we consider that the time-period between the start of the Tribulation (1st Seal) and the 7th Seal is the time during which God's new Representative (Israel, specifically the 144,000) is prepared. During this time neither the Church Clock nor the Israel Clock are running, since God has no Representative on earth. Therefore, it is unreckoned time. The Israel Clock starts running again with the Start of the 70th Week (the antichrist covenant), which is when Israel's final 7-year Countdown starts for her to receive her Messiah and His Kingdom. This must also be when God has a functioning Representative (witness) on earth, that is, when the 144,000 have been sealed and start their ministry, which is when the 7th Seal is broken (Revelation 7:1 - 8:2). Therefore, the Start of the 70th Week with the antichrist covenant (on earth) must synchronise with the 7th Seal (in Heaven). Thus the 7th Seal can be seen as Heaven's response to this evil covenant. Thus, the initial time-period of the Tribulation, before the 70th Week begins, is the time from the breaking of the first Seal on the day of the Rapture (6:1-2), to the breaking of the 7th Seal (8:1-2). Thus, it is the time-period covered by Revelation 7, describing the preparation and sealing of the 144,000, before the 7th Seal is opened, which releases the Trumpets.

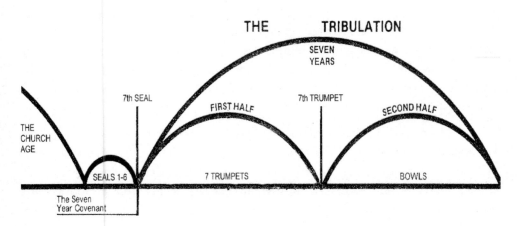

This Synchronism of the 7th Seal with the Start of Daniel's 70th Week is also confirmed when we look at the ministry of the 2 witnesses in Revelation 11, for they minister in the Temple for 1260 days, as a vital part of the Temple Ministry. This must be during the first half of the 70th Week. Thus, they start their ministry at the Start of the 70th Week, which is also required by the fact that they are God's prime representatives, so the start of their ministry should coincide with the restarting of Israel's Clock.

Revelation 11:10 says that when the antichrist kills them at Mid-Tribulation: **"those who dwell on the earth will rejoice over them, make merry, and send gifts to one another, because these 2 prophets tormented (all) those who dwell on the earth."** Why should these 2 prophets be blamed for troubling and tormenting everyone on the face of the earth? The only explanation is that they announced and called down the Judgments of the first half of the Tribulation, especially the first 6 Trumpets (the 7th Trumpet is blown after their death and resurrection). With the TV cameras upon them they will announce each Trumpet Judgment to the world and then soon after that Trumpet will be blown in Heaven, and its Judgment will be released upon the earth. Thus, the ministry of the 2 witnesses corresponds to the time of the first 6 Trumpets, and so the start of their ministry at the start of the 70th Week should synchronise with the 1st Trumpet, which is blown when the 7th Seal is opened (8:1-7).

We can now reconstruct the sequence of events on this dramatic day. Immediately after the antichrist covenant is made (which initiates the 70th Week), these 2 witnesses will suddenly appear on the Temple Mount and announce God's response to that evil covenant - the breaking of the 7th Seal and the release of the first Trumpet Judgment, which will fall soon after on that same day – a most dramatic way to launch their ministry and get the attention of the world! They will be clothed in sackcloth, preaching Christ for 3.5 years, warning of coming judgments, and calling Israel and the nations to repent. On the same day, as we've seen, the 144,000 also start their ministry of preaching the Gospel. Thus, with the 2 Jewish witnesses (Moses and Elijah) and the 144,000 Jewish evangelists functioning as God's anointed representatives, Israel's Clock restarts and begins the final 7-year Countdown (Daniel's 70th Week). Thus, all these events take place on the same day: On earth, antichrist makes a covenant with Israel, and the 2 witnesses and 144,000 start their ministry, starting the 70th Week (Daniel 9:27). Also in Heaven, the 7th Seal is opened and the 1st Trumpet is blown (Revelation 8:1,2).

Thus, we have established that the 70th Week is not identical to the Tribulation, but is the last 7 years of the Tribulation. The 70th Week starts on earth at least a few months after the Rapture and Start of the Tribulation (1st Seal), and its timing coincides with the 7th Seal and 1st Trumpet in Heaven (Revelation 8:1-7).

The manifestation of the antichrist (2 Thessalonians 2:3-9), by which he will be identified, is in 4 Stages, each of which marks crucial turning points of the Tribulation.

(1) His initial rise to power at the 1st Seal, at the start of the Tribulation.
(2) His making a covenant with Israel, at the 7th Seal, at the start of the 70th Week.
(3) His Abomination of Desolation desecrating the Temple, at the 7th Trumpet, half-way through the 70th Week. At this point, he also manifests supernatural power from satan, proclaims himself to be God, demanding the worship of the whole world, and brings in the mark of the beast, and his identifying number will be 666.
(4) At the end of the Tribulation, He will gather the armies of the world to Israel, for Armageddon, where he will be destroyed by Christ at His Return.

The Tribulation starts on the same day as the Rapture

It remains to show the time of Divine Judgment known as the Tribulation or Day of the Lord begins immediately after the Rapture. We will see this (1) in the teaching of Jesus in the Olivet Discourse (Matthew 24), and (2) the teaching of Paul in 1 Thessalonians 5 and (3) the teaching of John in Revelation 4-6.

*1. The Teaching of Jesus. Jesus taught that the Day of the Lord began immediately after the Rapture in the Olivet Discourse in Matthew 24.

The 3 Questions in verse 3 define the whole structure of His talk: **"Tell us, (Question 1) when will these things** (the destruction of the Temple) **be?** (Jesus' answer to this is in Luke 21). **And** (Question 2) **what will be the Sign of Your Coming** (the 2nd Coming), **and** (Question 3) **what will be the Sign of the End** (Consummation) **of the Age** (the Tribulation)?"

Jesus answered Question 2 in verses 6-35, and then Question 3 in verses 36–44. He indicated that He was moving onto a new topic (the answer to Question 3) in verse 36, by the use of 'peri de', since that is the standard purpose for using this phrase. Therefore, He started His answer to Question 3, which asked about the signs leading up to the start of the Tribulation by saying: **"BUT** ('peri de') **of THAT DAY and hour no one knows"** (v36). By not specifying which DAY He was talking about, He was assuming we would know it from the context, and therefore 'that DAY' must refer to the Start of the End of the Age or

Tribulation, because He was answering Question 3, which is about when the End of the Age begins.   Although He said no one can know the day when the Tribulation will start (in other words, it's a sign-less, imminent event), He then went immediately on to associate this Day with the COMING of the Son of Man in the Rapture in Matthew 24:36-37: **"But of THAT DAY and hour** (when the Tribulation starts) **no one knows, not even the angels of Heaven, but My Father only. But as the days of Noah were, so also will the COMING of the Son of Man be."**   In other words, the Coming of the Son of Man in the Rapture will immediately initiate the Tribulation, and therefore both the Coming of the Lord and the start of the time of world-wide Judgment (the Day of the Lord or Tribulation) are imminent.   This is just one example of what is known as Dual Imminence – that in Scripture both the Coming of Christ for the Church and the Coming of God's wrath on the earth are imminent, which implies that they must both happen at the same time, which is the exact point we are establishing in this Section (see Chapters 4-6 for more on Dual Imminence).

The fact the world-wide judgment of the Tribulation starts on the very same day as the Coming of the Lord (in the Rapture) finds further confirmation in Matthew 24:36-39: **"But of that day and hour** (of the Rapture and the Start of the Tribulation) *no one knows...* **But as the days of Noah were, so also will the COMING of the Son of Man be. For as in the days before the Flood, they were eating and drinking, marrying and giving in marriage, UNTIL the DAY that Noah entered the Ark, and did not know until the FLOOD** (world-wide judgment) **CAME and took them all away, so also will the Coming of the Son of Man be."**

Here Jesus teaches that His Coming (in the Rapture, before the Tribulation) will be 'as in the Days of Noah' (before the Flood).

*1. It is IMMINENT – it can happen any time, with no warning signs.

*2. As in the days of Noah, there will be a time of worldwide judgment: The FLOOD is a type of the DAY of the Lord, the TRIBULATION.

*3. As in the days of Noah before the Flood suddenly fell, life will be going on as normal before the Coming of Christ in the Rapture triggering the world-wide judgment of the Tribulation to suddenly fall upon the world. This is in total contrast to the days before the 2nd Coming of Christ, when the 7 Bowls are poured out leading up to the Battle of Armageddon, and when all flesh on earth is about to die, according to Jesus in Matthew 24:22.

*4. As in the days of Noah, the last event before worldwide judgment falls will be the disappearance of all believers into Christ, our Ark of Salvation. Immediately after Noah and his family (the believers) entered the Ark, the global

Flood fell. Likewise, immediately after the believers disappear into Christ, when He comes for them in the Rapture, the Tribulation Flood will fall upon the whole earth.

*5. As in the days of Noah, the very day the believers are removed from the earth (in the Rapture), the Flood of Judgment (Tribulation) will fall, as Jesus said in   Thus Jesus is saying that just like the Flood fell on the same day the believers were removed to safety, so the Tribulation Flood will fall on the same day that believers are removed from the earth in the Rapture. Thus, just as the world-wide Flood fell on the very SAME DAY that the believers disappeared into the safety of the Ark, so the Tribulation Flood will fall upon the whole world on the SAME DAY that the believers will be taken into the safety of Christ, our Ark of Salvation, when He comes for us in the Rapture.

The fact that Jesus is talking about His Coming in the Rapture to take the believers to a place of safety with Him before the Tribulation-Flood is released upon the earth is confirmed by what He said next in v40-42: **"Then 2 men will be in the field: one will be taken and the other left. 2 women will be grinding at the mill: one will be taken and the other left. Watch therefore, for you do not know what hour YOUR Lord is COMING."** This tells us that this Coming of the Lord is His Coming for us, to take us to be with Him, whereas those who don't belong to Him will be left behind to go through the Tribulation. Notice He is talking about OUR Lord COMING for us, to take us to be with Him. It is His Coming for His Church in the Rapture that's imminent – v42 is an imminence verse, just like v36. The imminence is further reinforced by v 44: **"Be ready, for the Son of Man is COMING at an hour you do not expect."** In other words, not only do we not know when Christ is coming for us, but we also do not know when He is not coming! Thus, as far as we're concerned, He could come at any time – it's God's secret.

In Luke 17:26-30, Jesus made the same point from the example of Lot: **"As it was in the days of Noah, so it will be also in the days of the Son of Man: They ate, they drank, they married wives, they were given in marriage, until THE DAY that Noah entered the Ark, and the Flood came and destroyed them all. Likewise, as it was also in the days of Lot: They ate, they drank, they bought, they sold, they planted, they built; but on the DAY that Lot went out of Sodom it rained fire and brimstone from Heaven and destroyed them all. Even so will it be in the DAY when the Son of Man is revealed."**

In both cases of Noah and Lot the main point is made that before Judgment fell God removed the believers first so that they would not come under the judgment, and that it was on the very same day that they were removed, that

God released the Judgment. The example of Noah also teaches that just as the Flood was a worldwide judgment, so likewise the Tribulation. The example of Lot makes it clear that the believers will be removed from very scene of the judgment (rather than preserved through it). This is also taught by the Noah example, because the Ark raised Noah above the waters, rather than God helping him survive in a cave on the earth, but the Lot example is clearer on this point.

Lot's removal from Sodom by the Lord and His angels, who came personally to extract him, before the Lord released His Judgment later that same day, is a picture of the Rapture when the Lord and His angels will come to take us out of this world, before He initiates the world-wide judgments of the Tribulation later that same day. Luke 17:30 then confirms that this DAY when the believers are taken out of the world and the Tribulation Judgments are released, is also the DAY of the Coming of the Lord when He will be revealed: **"Even so will it be in the DAY when the Son of Man is REVEALED"** (Luke 17:30). Thus, the Lord Himself will come and reveal Himself to the believers, and remove them from the world, before He starts to pours out His Day of the Lord Judgments on that same day.

The reason the Judgment falls on the same day as the removal of the believers, is that they are the only reason why Judgment was withheld. When Abraham interceded for Lot, he stood on the principle that it would not be righteous for God to judge the righteous along with the wicked. Genesis 18:25: **"Far be it from You to do such a thing as this, to slay the righteous with the wicked, so that the righteous should be as the wicked; far be it from You! Shall not the Judge of all the earth do what is right?"** Although God answered in a different way than Abraham expected, he was successful in his intercession, for God honoured that principle, by removing Lot first before sending Judgment. Once the believers were removed, there was no longer any reason to delay Judgment any longer, which is why it was on the same day. Likewise, as soon as the righteous in Christ are removed in the Rapture, there is no reason for God to delay releasing the Tribulation Judgments, which He does by breaking open the first 6 Seals.

Thus, the Rapture is the key event that initiates the Tribulation. This agrees with Psalm 110:1: **"The LORD said to my Lord: "SIT at My right hand, UNTIL I make Your enemies Your footstool."** Thus, Christ will be SEATED UNTIL the time He is released by the Father to move in Judgment and put His enemies under His feet. He will STAND up from His throne when it is time for Him to return in the Rapture. This means His Return in the Rapture is also when He starts to judge His enemies, confirming the Tribulation starts on the Day of the Rapture.

Next Jesus compared His Coming in the Rapture to the coming of a THIEF. Matthew 24:42-44: **"Watch therefore, for *you do not know what hour your Lord is coming.* But know this, that if the master of the house had known what hour the THIEF would come, he would have watched and not allowed his house to be broken into. Therefore, you also be ready, for *the Son of Man is coming at an hour you do not expect."*** The analogy of a thief confirms that He will come suddenly without warning (imminence) to take the precious things (the believers) from the house (the earth), while it is still in darkness, rather than coming to take over the house and flood it with His light as He will do in His 2nd Coming. Of course, He is not actually a thief, because He is only taking what belongs to Him (those He has purchased with His Blood, who've received Him as their Lord and Saviour), but to the world it will appear as if a Thief had come, as it wakes up to find a billion believers have suddenly disappeared. For us His Coming is not the coming of a Thief, but of our Bridegroom coming for His Bride (John 14:1-3).

*2. The Teaching of Paul in 1 Thessalonians 5 essentially expounds on Jesus' teaching in Matthew 24, using the same imagery - for example, the 'Thief' and 'Birth Pains.' **Paul confirms that the Day of the Lord or Tribulation starts immediately after the Rapture.** Jesus had compared His Coming in the Rapture as a THIEF (Matthew 24:43), coming suddenly to take the precious things (believers) from the earth.   That's why Paul said in 1Thessalonians 5:2-4: **"You yourselves know perfectly that the DAY of the LORD** (the Tribulation) **so comes** (starts) **as a THIEF in the night** (the Coming of Christ in the Rapture – Matthew 24:43). **For when they** (in the world) **say: "Peace and safety!"** (normal life is going on, 'as in the days of Noah' – see Matthew 24:38), **then sudden destruction** (the Tribulation) **comes upon THEM** (the unbelieving world, but not on us, who are raptured), **as LABOUR PAINS upon a pregnant woman** (Jesus described the start of the Tribulation as the sudden onset of labour pains - Matthew 24:7-8). **And THEY** (the world) **shall not escape. But YOU, BRETHREN, are not in** (the kingdom of) **darkness, so that this DAY** (the Tribulation) **should overtake you as a THIEF** (the world will experience the Rapture as if a Thief had come removing all the believers, but the believers will experience the Rapture as a Bride being taken by her Bridegroom)."**

Paul confirms here that Christ's Coming in the Rapture (as a Thief) immediately initiates the Day of the Lord (Tribulation). He says: **"the DAY of the LORD so comes** (starts) **as a THIEF in the night."** The coming of the Thief will immediately initiate the sudden onset of Labour Pains (the first 6 Seals).   This is confirmed by 2 Peter 3:10: **"the DAY of the LORD will come like a THIEF."** Thus this confirms the Tribulation will start on the Day of the Rapture.

*3. This is also confirmed by what John reveals in Revelation.

In Revelation 1:19 he was told: **"(1) Write the things which you have seen** (this is the vision of Christ in chapter 1), **and** (2) **the things which are now** (that is the revelation of the course of the Church Age in chapters 2 and 3), **and** (3) **the things which will take place after this** (that is, after the Church Age)." The transition to: **"the things, which will take place AFTER THIS"** takes place in 4:1, when John is called (raptured) up to Heaven, and told: **"Come up here, and I will show you things which must take place AFTER THIS."** So, the events that he sees in Heaven in Revelation 4-6 will take place immediately after the Church Age, that is, immediately after the Rapture. He sees the whole Church now glorified in Heaven represented by the 24 elders, singing of how they have been redeemed by the Blood of the Lamb from every nation (Revelation 4-5). Directly after that he sees Christ take the Scroll with 7 Seals and breaks the first 6 Seals, releasing the Birth Pain Judgments upon the earth that initiate the Tribulation (Revelation 6). Again, this confirms that the Day of the Lord starts on the very same day that the Church Age closes with the Rapture. The first Seal immediately releases the antichrist onto centre stage agreeing perfectly with 2 Thessalonians 2, which says the Church is now restraining the antichrist and will do so until it is taken out of the way in the Rapture, and then the antichrist will be immediately revealed – this is the event that marks the start of the Tribulation on earth.

2 Thessalonians 2:1-4: **"Now, brethren, concerning the coming of our Lord Jesus Christ and our gathering together to Him** (this tells us that the subject under discussion is the Rapture) **we ask you, not to be soon shaken in mind or troubled, either by spirit or by word or by letter, as if from us, as though the Day of the Lord** (Tribulation) **had** (already) **come. Let no one deceive you by any means; for that Day** (the Tribulation) **will not come unless the DEPARTURE** (Rapture of the Church) **comes first, and** (then) **the man of sin is revealed, the son of perdition."** Thus, immediately after the Rapture the Day of the Lord (Tribulation) begins with the revelation of the antichrist – the Rider on the White Horse in Revelation 6:1.

This is confirmed and explained in v6-7: **"And now you know what is restraining** (the antichrist), **that he may be revealed in his own time. For the mystery of lawlessness is already at work; only He who now restrains will do so UNTIL He is taken out of the way** (at the Rapture), **and then the lawless one will be revealed."** Thus, presently the Holy Spirit through the Church is restraining the manifestation of antichrist, and will do so UNTIL the Church is taken out of the way at the Rapture, and then antichrist will be revealed immediately after that, and this marks the Start of the Tribulation on earth according to Revelation 6:1.

SUMMARY

So, the Tribulation starts on the Day of the Rapture. We have seen that there will then be an initial period of at least a few months before the 7th Seal is opened, which contains the 7 Trumpet Judgments. During this time God is saving and preparing the 144,000, who will spearhead the evangelism in the Tribulation. When they are sealed and ready to start their ministry, then the 7th Seal is opened in Heaven and the 1st angel blows his Trumpet. We saw this happens at the same time as Israel binds herself to the antichrist by covenant, initiating the start of the final 7 years (Daniel's 70th Week). This is also when the 2 witnesses start their powerful ministry for 1260 days based at the Temple. Thus their ministry covers 3.5 years (the first half of the 70th Week). During this time, they will preach to the whole of Israel, as they come to their new Temple, declaring that Jesus Christ is their true Messiah, who has already died for them as the Lamb of God. Also, they will preach the Gospel to the world through the TV cameras, and call the world to repent, warning them of the upcoming judgments. In fact, they will announce each of the first 6 Trumpet Judgments in advance, which is why the world blames them for tormenting all who dwell on the earth (Revelation 11:10).

So, we have this order of events (from Matthew 24, 1Thessalonians 5 and Daniel 9:27).
(1) The Rapture of the Church (which is imminent).
(2) The Day of the Lord (Tribulation) begins on the same day.
(3) The initial period of the Tribulation (maybe a few months, during which time antichrist is released and begins his rapid rise to power).
(4) Daniel's 70th Week begins with antichrist's covenant with Israel. This marks the start of the final 7 years to the Second Coming.

This order of events agrees perfectly with what we have found in the Book of Revelation.
(1) The Rapture of the Church to Heaven (Revelation 4)
(2) The Judgments of the Tribulation are immediately initiated from Heaven as Christ opens the first 6 Seals (Revelation 5-6).
(3) The first Seal releases the rider on the white horse, the antichrist, who rapidly rises to power during these first few months.
(4) At some point he will have sufficient power and be able to gain the confidence of Israel sufficiently that they put their trust in him and make a covenant with him, which initiates the 70th Week.

So, Jesus, Paul and John teach the Day of the Lord (Tribulation) Judgments begin on the same day as the Rapture. Thus the 70th Week, which starts with Israel's covenant with antichrist and describes the last 7 years before the 2nd Coming, cannot be identical with the Tribulation, for if the Rapture and start of the Tribulation was on the same day as the antichrist covenant, that would contradict the imminence of the Rapture. The only solution is to reject the assumption that the 70th Week is identical with the Tribulation as false. Instead, we should say the 70th Week is the last 7 years of the Tribulation. Thus, there is a period of time between the Rapture (and start of the Tribulation) and the start of the 70th Week (which is initiated by the antichrist covenant).

We can summarize the logic as follows:
(1) The Tribulation starts on the same day as the Rapture.
(2) The Rapture and Start of the Tribulation is imminent.
(3) The antichrist-covenant, which starts the 70th Week, is not imminent.
(4) Therefore, the Start of the Tribulation is not the same as the start of the 70th Week. Therefore, the Tribulation is not identical to the 70th Week.
(5) Therefore, the Rapture must take place BEFORE the start of the 70th Week, because Israel's Clock and her final 7 years cannot start running again until after the Church is removed. Moreover, the only alternative that the Rapture and start of Tribulation take place after the start of 70th Week destroys imminence and results in much contradiction.

In conclusion, the Tribulation starts on the same day as the Rapture of the Church, with the opening of the first 6 Seals (Revelation 6). There follows an unknown time-period until the antichrist covenant, on the same day as the 7th Seal (8:1-2), which marks the Start of Daniel's 70th Week, and the ministries of the 2 witnesses and the 144,000. Thus the 70th Week consists of the last 7 years of the Tribulation, which is brought to a close by the Lord's Return in power and glory. Thus, the Tribulation consists of 2 parts: (1) an initial period of unknown duration, followed by (2) the 7 years of the rerun 70th Week.

Additional Information

Derek Walker is the Pastor of OXFORD BIBLE CHURCH
which meets Sundays at 11 am and 6pm
at Cheney School Hall, Cheney Lane, Headington, Oxford, United Kingdom.

See www.oxfordbiblechurch.co.uk for a map and more info about the Church.

Other Books by Derek Walker include:
A Chronological Commentary on the Book of Revelation   Joshua's Jericho
How to receive your Healing   Keys to Long-Life
A Panorama of Prophecy   Revelations at Caesarea Philippi
Daniel's 70 Weeks   Gospel of John   Growing Up Spiritually

A number of CD Series and DVDs are also available,
including DVDs of our TV programmes.

Go to our online shop at: www.oxfordbiblechurch.co.uk to see the full range of
Derek Walker teaching products which are available (Books, CDs and DVDs).   All of
Derek's books are also available on Amazon in print and kindle form.

Also, at www.oxfordbiblechurch.co.uk you will find many free teaching materials by
Derek, including written Bible Studies, Books, Audio messages (from our Sunday
Services). In addition, you can find a large number of Derek's videos at his YouTube
Channel: www.youtube.com/DerekWalkerOBC

You can also find many teachings by Derek Walker, on the Oxford Bible Church YouTube
Channel: www.youtube.com/OxfordBibleChurchOBC This Channel contains all the
videos of his teachings at Oxford Bible Church (both from the Sunday Morning Services,
and the Wednesday Evening Bible Studies, which go through the Books of the Bible).
You are also most welcome to join us on Sundays at 11am and Wednesdays at 7.30pm
(UK time) on the OBC YouTube Channel for our live-streamed Church Services.

For more information about Oxford Bible Church or to order BOOKS, CDs or DVDs
contact: OBC Church Office, Cotswold House,
363 Banbury Road, Oxford, OX2 7PL, UK.
Tel: (0)1865-515086. obc.church@yahoo.co.uk

Printed in Great Britain
by Amazon

37593419R00089